W9-BFV-479

38
BASIC SPEECH EXPERIENCES

Ninth Revised Edition

by
Clark S. Carlile, *Professor Emeritus,*
Idaho State University
and
Dana V. Hensley
Wichita Collegiate School

Consulting Editor
Ruth Kay, *Wayne State University*

CLARK PUBLISHING

PO Box 19240
Topeka, KS 66619-0240
In US: 1-800-845-1916

Fax & Phone:
913-862-0218

Acknowledgments

Many individuals helped us make this 9th edition a reality. Ann Ozegovic designed the book and prepared the manuscript for press. Brenda Houk and Carrie Springer at Kaw Area Technical School assisted in the manuscript preparation. Howard Youngberg, Don Mathers, Steve Maxwell, and Sharon Hester at Jostens Printers provided invaluable assistance to help us produce a high quality book. Jack Kay, Pam McComas, and Karla Leeper helped locate new speeches. John B. Naughtin Graphic Design, Ingrid Grinbergs Lien, and Jack Ozegovic assisted with the cover design.

FOREWORD TO THE NINTH REVISED EDITION

In this ninth revised edition we have updated bibliographies, activities and assignments and included numerous new sample speeches by new authors. Previous model speeches have been retained. New suggested speech topics have been added and other minor changes have been made to make the text relevant for today's speech student. We have also changed the book's format. Student's outlines and assignment sheets along with other instructional materials are now contained in a separate teacher's manual. All forms in the manual may be duplicated. The revision remains committed to the original concept of providing speech teachers and students with self-contained, basic speech experiences.

THIS BOOK WAS WRITTEN FOR STUDENTS AND TEACHERS who want to learn and teach public speaking by the simple process of *giving speeches*.

To those teachers who are plagued by the everlasting question of "What shall I assign my students for their next speeches?" this text provides thirty-eight completely worked-out projects. These speech projects are of the kind a student will be asked to continue in real life situations when students are no longer enrolled in a speech course. They are practical because they meet the needs of students who will be tomorrow's business and social leaders. The teacher may assign any one of the speaking experiences and know that the student will have all the information needed *in the assignment* in order to prepare and present a dedication speech, a eulogy, a sales talk, an after dinner speech, a panel, a debate, a speech to inform, or any one of dozens of others.

The text is adaptable and flexible. Any sequence of assignments or modifications a teacher desires may be scheduled. Any basic speech text may be used as a supplement. The teacher's manual contains a complete bibliography of speech textbooks.

Students' jobs are made easy because they know from each assignment what they must do to fulfill adequately the purpose of a specific speech. They know because the assignment specifies clearly what they must do. The requirements, such as time limits, outlining, organizing, and research materials, are not easy. They are not intended to be easy. They are basic to all good speech making. While some students may complain that it takes too much effort to time a speech properly, to make a complete sentence outline, to read two or more sources, and to rehearse aloud, these same students will quickly discover that as a result of such preparation they can present excellent speeches. They will also see their grades and self-confidence improve.

A speech course, well taught, and earnestly applied by the student, does more than train a person for public speaking. With this training comes the feeling of self-adequacy and high self-esteem that can last a lifetime.

CLARK S. CARLILE
Professor Emeritus, Idaho State University

DANA V. HENSLEY
Wichita Collegiate School

iii

TABLE OF CONTENTS

PROLOGUE

CHAPTERS

THE BASICS OF PUBLIC SPEAKING

HOW TO PREPARE A GOOD SPEECH

The first law of good speaking is adequate preparation. Preparing a good speech is like preparing to run a four-forty yard dash in a track meet. Each requires many trial runs before the event actually starts. To attempt a speech without preparation is just as foolhardy as to attempt a quarter-mile run without practice. The well-trained and conditioned racer makes it look easy, just as does the well-prepared speaker. To an uninformed person, both the speaker and the racer may appear to be performing effortlessly and impromptu, yet in most cases nothing could be further from the truth. Only many hours of intense preparation make it possible for the good speaker and the good athlete to display great ability. If there is doubt about this point in anyone's mind, then *ask the person who makes speeches or who runs races.*

There are several initial requisites which should be considered at this time in order to explain adequate speech preparation. They are:

I. CHOOSE AND DEVELOP YOUR TOPIC CAREFULLY

A. *Be sure you can find sufficient material on your subject*, otherwise your speech may be too short, devoid of quantity as well as quality.

B. *Be sure the subject you plan to discuss is appropriate to you, your audience and the occasion.* Any subject not adjusted to these three factors simply is inadequate. If you are in doubt, consult your instructor.

C. *Be certain that your subject can be adequately discussed in the time allotted* for your speech. Preliminary investigation, narrowing the subject, and a few "trial runs" will clear up doubts about this phase of preparation.

D. Since it takes time for ideas to grow and develop, *weigh carefully the time you allow yourself for preparation*, otherwise your speech may not be past the rough draft stage when you present it, and frankly an audience dislikes seeing a practice run when it comes to see a finished product.

E. The importance of selecting a suitable subject need not be stressed since it is so obvious; however, *you should decide whether your topic is too technical, trivial, trite or broad.* If it falls into any one of these categories, then it must be altered accordingly or a new topic chosen.

F. The *title of your speech should be provocative, brief, relative to your subject, and interesting.* It is one of the first things your audience will read about in the papers or hear before you speak. A good title can add immeasurably to the initial interest in your speech.

II. THINK OF YOUR AUDIENCE

A. To best adapt material to an audience, understand the people in it. It is your obligation to find out what kind of people will likely come to hear you. How old will they be? What will their occupations be? What is their social standing? Their education? Their religion? Their prejudices and beliefs? Their wealth? *What do they want from you?* Since you are taking the time of ten or fifteen persons, perhaps several hundred, you will be wise to give them a speech which is *worth their time.* You can do this if you analyze your audience. This isn't something to be done on a moment's notice. Rather it will require a definite investigation from you, but it will be well worth the effort, provided your remarks are adapted.

III. MASTER THE MECHANICS OF SPEECH PREPARATION

Now that you have considered your subject and analyzed your audience, you are ready to begin the mechanical preparation of your speech. Here are the steps to follow:

A. *Decide on the purpose of your speech,* that is, what do you want to accomplish with your speech? What reaction do you want from the people who hear you? Do you want them to understand an idea better? To become stirred up and aroused about something? To perform an act, such as to vote for or against a candidate or contribute to a fund or join an organization? In your own mind it is absolutely essential that you know definitely what you want your listeners to do as a result of your speech. If you don't have this point settled, then you really don't know why you are giving your speech or why you organized it the way you did or why you are telling your audience "thus and so." In reality you don't know what you want and nobody else does. You cannot expect your audience to get anything from your speech if you yourself don't know what you want them to get. One of the most pronounced causes of poor speaking lies in the elementary act that the speaker has nothing in mind to accomplish with the speech. This need not happen if you decide on a purpose and direct all efforts toward achieving it.

B. Your next step is to *gather material for your speech.* Consult the next section entitled "Where To Go To Find Sources and Materials." Having located various materials, take comprehensive notes on what you decide to use. Be sure to indicate sources exactly and completely. This includes the specific names of the magazines or books the material was taken from, titles of articles, authors' full names, dates of publication, and chapters or pages where the material was found. If a source is a person, identify the source completely by title, position, occupation, etc. The data, telling exactly where you got your material, will prove most beneficial when someone later asks you where you found your material. The validity of your remarks will be no greater than the sources you use.

C. Your third step is to *organize the material* in an orderly and logical sequence. This means that all examples, analogies, facts, quotations, and other evidence which you use to support main ideas must be in their proper place where they will do the most good. The best way to achieve organization that is progressive and unified is to prepare a complete sentence outline of your speech. For a fuller understanding of a complete sentence outline, study the example in "Making An Outline of Your Speech." A complete sentence outline will assist in formulating and crystallizing complete thoughts prior to presenting the speech. Without this procedure you will discover it is exceedingly difficult to prepare and present a quality speech.

D. Step number four is *wording the speech.* Here you must decide what words you will use when you expand your complete sentence outline into a full speech. To get in mind the words you want to use, employ the methods best suited to you; however, two recommended methods follow.

One method for wording your speech is to rehearse aloud from your complete sentence outline or other outline until you have attained a definite mastery of the words you plan to use. It is wise to memorize the introduction and conclusion although you should not memorize the rest of your speech word for word. You should, of course, memorize the sequence of your main points irrespective of how you practice. The number of times needed for *oral rehearsal* will depend solely on you, but probably it will be at least four to six times and quite possibly even more, regardless of what method you use. In any case, if you plan to use notes while speaking, be sure to use the final copy of your speaking notes during your last few rehearsals. *Consider tape recording* your first or second practice to determine what changes in wording are necessary for clarity of ideas.

A second method for wording your speech is to write it out in full, then read your manuscript aloud several times to master the general ideas and the necessary details. After doing this, construct a set of very brief notes containing only the main ideas of your speech and *rehearse aloud* from them until you master the general wording and the order of the main points. Do not rehearse by mumbling in a monotone or by "thinking about" your wording.

One of the best ways to rehearse a speech is to stand before a mirror so that you may observe your posture and other body language. Some students object to using a mirror saying that it bothers them to observe themselves. This is a flimsy excuse since those same students know they must speak before their classmates who will be forced, through courtesy, to observe them while they stumble through actions, gestures and various postures which they themselves couldn't bear to see reflected in a mirror. A few "trial runs" before a mirror will vastly improve most speeches and speakers. A video tape is unexcelled in giving feedback.

E. Step number five involves the *development of a positive mental attitude about and the entire speaking situation.* You will be wise to expect nervousness and stage fright during the first few speeches. You should realize quite clearly that although stage fright will largely disappear after a reasonably short while, nervousness just before speaking probably will not. You should look upon it as a form of energy that will keep your speaking on a more vigorous plane than would otherwise be possible were you entirely devoid of nervous feelings. Your attitude should tell you that *you will gain self-confidence and poise* as you make more speeches, but do not expect a miracle. Your mental attitude should be one in which you recognize your own weaknesses, but you are not morbidly disturbed because you aren't a great success on the first attempt. You should be willing to seek advice from the instructor, to make honest efforts toward a more adequate preparation of speeches since this is the greatest guarantee for good speaking, and gradually as you progress you should take pride in your own personal improvement and feelings of self-confidence. Every beginning speaker should look forward to a feeling of adequacy and personal satisfaction, for if you do and if you possess a healthy mental attitude, you are sure to attain these goals – and a good speech.

WHERE TO GO TO FIND SOURCES AND MATERIALS

One of the biggest problems confronting students in speech courses is that of finding materials on subjects which interest them. Actually this problem is easy to solve if the student is willing to "look around a bit" to find sources of information and to read what is found. In preparing a speech, students should not say they cannot find enough material unless they have actually checked all of the possible sources.

The question which occurs most often concerning source materials is: "Where do I go to find these materials?" Aside from one's personal experience and interviews with business people, teachers, parents, and friends, there is one great source, the greatest and most valuable of all, namely, the library. Here a person can find just about anything desired, provided a willingness to look for it. It may well be admitted that whatever a person is hunting for will not be "growing on trees." It will be in books, magazines, newspapers, and pamphlets – often filed away on unfrequented shelves in the library, but it will be there. To find these forgotten sources or others, there is one sure method – ask the librarian to help locate materials for the speech. In most cases, a librarian will provide more materials in ten minutes than the student can digest in several hours.

Besides going to the librarian for assistance, there are many sources which an individual can check out. A person should learn what these sources are and how to use them in order to find speech materials quickly. A representative group of these research tools is listed below:

1. THE CARD CATALOGUE: check here for title and/or author of materials kept in the library.

2. ENCYCLOPEDIAS:
    A. General:
        (1) Britannica: general information.
        (2) Encyclopedia Americana: general information.
        (3) Collier's Encyclopedia: general information.

    B. Special:
        (1) International Encyclopedia of the Social Sciences: relates to social sciences.
        (2) Afro-American Encyclopedia: history, great personalities, literature, art, music, dance, athletic accomplishments of Black people from ancient to modern times.
        (3) The Encyclopedia of Education: concerns the history and philosophy of education.
        (4) The Encyclopedia of Religion: contains articles concerning all the religions of the world.

(5) Mythology of All Races: just what the title implies.

(6) Encyclopedia of Asian History: information about Asian countries and their history

(7) McGraw Hill Encyclopedia of Science and Technology: information on all branches of sciences, agriculture, and technology.

(8) Grzimek's Animal Life Encyclopedia: volumes on lower animals, insects, fishes, mammals, and birds.

3. YEARBOOKS:

A. Americana Annual: a source of current events.

B. Britannica Book of the Year: a record of events from 1937 to date.

C. World Almanac and Book of Facts, from 1868-: crammed full of information, largely statistical on hundreds of subjects.

D. Stateman's Yearbook: statistical and historical information of the states of the world.

E. The Costeau Almanac: an inventory of life on our water planet.

4. HANDBOOKS:

A. Chronology of World History: a history of the world in chronological outline.

B. Political Handbook of the World: concerns party programs, world leaders, and the press.

C. The Westpoint Military History Series: military history from ancient to modern times.

5. INDEXES:

A. Poole's's Index to Periodical Literature: covers years up to 1906; useful for finding old material on hundreds of topics.

B. Reader's Guide to Periodical Literature: covers years since 1900; lists sources of information in practically every field.

C. New York Times Index: lists information which is to be found in copies of the *New York Times*.

6. BIOGRAPHICAL DICTIONARIES:

A. Newsmakers: published three times per year with information about politicians, business leaders, movies, television, and rock music stars in headlines today.

B. Dictionary of American Biography: an encyclopedia of American biography of deceased persons. Kept up to date with supplements.

C. Who's Who: principally English biographies and a few internationally famous names.

D. Who's Who in America: brief biographies of notable living persons of the United States.

E. National Cyclopedia of American Biography: the most complete list of famous Americans living and dead available in any one source.

F. Encyclopedia of World Biography.

G. Current Biography: short biographies of people in the news.

H. Contemporary Authors: current writers of fiction, non-fiction, poetry, journalism, drama, motion pictures, and television.

7. SPECIAL DICTIONARIES:

A. Partridge. A Dictionary of Slang and Unconventional English.

B. Mawson, Dictionary of Foreign Terms.

8. QUOTATIONS FROM LITERATURE:

A. Stevenson. The Home Book of Quotations: approximately 50,000; arranged alphabetically by subject.

B. The Oxford Dictionary of Quotations.

C. Bartlett's Familiar Quotations: traces quotations to their sources in ancient and modern literature.

9. GOVERNMENT PUBLICATIONS:

These materials cover almost unlimited fields. Ask the librarian about them.

10. COMPUTERS:

Many libraries now have computer networks that will assist in accessing material you may need. Your librarian should be able to help you. There are also many sources of information that can be accessed through a home computer if you have a telephone modem. Refer to the instructions that came with your equipment for access information.

11. THERE ARE MANY OTHER SOURCES available on the above subjects and subjects not included here. Ask the librarian for assistance in locating them.

PREPARING SPEAKER'S NOTES

There are two ways to prepare your speech notes. You can put a few words on a card or sheet of paper, or you can prepare a sentence outline.

Below is a sample copy of notes a speaker might use in presenting a five to six minute speech on body language. Each word stands for an idea, each word is large enough to be easily seen at a glance, and the actual size of the note card is about equal to that of a post card. Speaking notes should serve *only as a guide*, not as a crutch. The actual speech should be in the mind of the speaker, not in a mass of notes.

Hold your card of notes by the lower right hand corner between your thumb and forefinger.

BODY LANGUAGE

1. MOVEMENTS TALK
2. EVERYONE USES
3. HELPFUL
4. CAN IMPROVE
5. BORN WITH

On the next page is a sample of a complete sentence outline. If you will study it carefully, you will note that every statement is a complete sentence. There are no incomplete sentences. There are no compound sentences. The outline is logically organized and divided into three parts: the introduction, body, and conclusion.

There are numerous ways to develop an outline and numerous sections into which it can be divided. The method followed by any one person is a matter of choice. If your instructor prefers a particular method of outlining, find out what it is. The important point to remember when constructing an outline (which is the skeleton of a speech) is that it must *make sense – logical sense*, which is easily followed. It takes time and effort to construct a complete sentence outline; yet the time and energy one spends in building a good outline will pay big dividends in improved speaking.

At the top of your outline include the following information:

Type of speech:_____(Informative)_____

Name: _____(Your Name)_____

Purpose of this speech: (What do you want your audience to learn, to think, to believe, to feel, or do because of this speech? e.g. I want my audience to have a better understanding of body language).

Title: BODY LANGUAGE

Introduction:

I. Your physical movements talk for you.
> A. They tell secrets about you.
> B. They tell what kind of person you are.
> C. I will discuss the behavior we call body language.

Body:

I. Everyone uses movements with spoken words.
> A. They are part of natural behavior.
>> 1. People are unaware of their movements.
>>> a. Posture reflects inner thoughts.
>>> b. Eyes, hands and feet talk eloquently.

II. Body language can be helpful.
> A. It can make a person attractive.
>> 1. Movements can reflect honesty.
>> 2. Appearance can bring favorable responses.
>> 3. Behavior patterns can make friends.
> B. Employers observe body language.
>> 1. They make judgments from what they see.
>> 2. They hire or reject an applicant by watching movements and posture.

III. Body language can be improved.
> A. A person can enhance personal appearance.
> B. Anyone can strive for better posture and walking habits.

Conclusion:

I. People are born with body language.
> A. It influences life.
>> 1. It speaks louder than words.

HOW TO BEGIN A SPEECH: THE INTRODUCTION

An introduction to a speech is what a coat is when you go outside in the winter – it is a necessity. Without it you might become ill. A speech without an introduction is ill. It has been said that every speaker has the audience's attention upon rising to speak and if attention is lost it is after the speaker begins to speak, hence the importance of the introduction becomes apparent.

There are several purposes speakers normally wish to achieve by means of their introductory remarks in order to be most effective. These purposes may be listed as follows:

I.   One purpose of the introduction may be to *gain attention, arouse the interest and excite the curiosity* of listeners. This may be effected in numerous ways.

A. The speaker may refer to the occasion and purpose of the meeting with a few brief remarks explaining and commenting on why the audience is gathered on this occasion. A speaker may refer to the audience's special interests and show how the subject is connected with these interests. In no way should a speaker apologize for a speech.

B. The speaker may *pay the audience a genuine compliment* relative to their hospitality, their interest in the subject to be discussed, or the outstanding leadership of the group sponsoring the speech. The sincerity of the speaker should be genuine since the audience's judgment of the speech will be strongly influenced by the opening phrases.

C. The speaker *may open by telling a story* (human interest, humorous, exciting, etc.) that catches interest and arouses curiosity. The story should be linked to the subject. If the story is not related to the subject, it should not be told.

D. The speaker m*ay refer to a recent incident with which the audience is acquainted.*
For example:
"Three persons were burned to death a week ago because a school building had improper fire escape exits."

This paves the way for the speaker's discourse, the need for a new school building.

E. The speaker *may use a quotation to open remarks* and set the stage for the introduction of ideas. The quotation should be relevant to the subject and be tied to it with a few brief explanations.

F. The speaker *may use a novel idea or a striking statement* to arouse curiosity and interest or to gain attention. This should not be overdone. If it is sensationalism, it will lose its punch because the remainder of the speech cannot be so shocking.

An example of an introduction to a speech on nuclear power is:

"It is hard to imagine fifty thousand persons destroyed in a few seconds–it is hard to imagine a ship driven around the world on a glass of water, or a rocket shot to the moon on a pound of metal, yet the day may not be far off when nuclear power will make these possibilities either horrible or helpful realities."

G. The speaker *may refer to a preceding speaker* in order to secure interest and attention; however, too much elaboration should not occur. For example,

"Ladies and Gentlemen: The preceding speaker, Mr. McIntosh, has given you a peculiarly striking and graphic picture of what we may expect within the next ten years in the development of nuclear power. I would like to expand his ideas further by telling you how this power may be harnessed so that it will wash your dishes and heat your houses."

H. The speaker *may put pertinent and challenging questions to the audien*ce to arouse their curiosity. "Did you know that. . . ? Do you want this to happen to you?" etc. These questions should have a bearing on the material which is to follow, otherwise they will be just so much noise.

I. Various combinations of the above suggestions may provide an effective introduction. The combinations which should be used will depend on the audience, occasion, speaker, speech and environment.

II.   A second purpose of the introduction may *be to prepare and open the minds of the audience for the thoughts which are to come.* This is particularly necessary if the audience is hostile. It may be accomplished by giving background and historical information so that the audience can and will understand the subject. This purpose may be further achieved if the speaker establishes a right to speak by recounting the research done on the subject, by naming prominent persons associated with the endeavor, and by modestly telling of certain honors, offices and awards received as a result of accomplishments in fields closely related to the topic.

III.   A speaker's third objective of an introduction may be to *indicate the direction and purpose of the speech and the end it will reach.* This may be achieved by stating generally the subject and by announcing and explaining the thesis of the talk. To give only a simple statement of the topic is not enough. It is uninteresting and in most cases dull. An appropriate and interesting exposition of any general statement of the subject should be made in reference to the topic. In other words, to announce only the title of a speech and to consider this an adequate introduction is a grave mistake. An example of a speech that forecasts is as follows:

"Ladies and Gentlemen: I have chosen to speak with you today on the subject of crime, which is costing our nation untold billions of dollars annually. It is my desire to explain to you the causes of crime as well some forms of prevention. It is only when crime is understood that people are enabled to combat it and decrease its scope."

There are a few points to remember when preparing and delivering an introduction. Dullness and triteness, undue length of opening remarks, false leads that are not followed up, suggestive or risque stories which are used only to fill time, or a mere announcement of the topic should all be avoided. Any apologies or remarks which might be construed to be apologies for the speech should definitely be omitted. There is nothing so invigorating, so appreciated, so likely to secure good will as an introduction which provides an original, fresh and sparkling meeting between the audience and the speaker and the subject. Work for it.

Generally speaking, an introduction is prepared last. This is practical because a speaker needs to have the *body of the talk outlined and the ideas developed* and ripe before determining how they should be introduced. The length of an introduction may vary considerably; however, it should not comprise more than one-fourth of the entire speech. It may comprise much less.

One more important aspect of the beginning of a speech is the speaker's behavior before taking the platform and after getting there. Speakers sitting on stage in full view of the audience should remain comfortably and calmly alert, yet politely seated. People are carefully appraising the speaker while they wait. When the speaker is introduced, he or she should rise easily without delay or noise and move to the appropriate place on the platform. After arriving there, the speaker should take a few seconds to deliberately survey the scene. Then after addressing the person presiding and anyone else who should be acknowledged, the speaker is ready to begin the introductory remarks.

HOW TO END A SPEECH: THE CONCLUSION

A day is never ended without a sunset of some kind. If the sunset is captivating, the entire day is often long remembered because of its impressive ending. A speech is much the same. It must have an ending, and to be most successful the ending should be impressive.

The conclusion brings together all the thoughts, emotions, discussions, arguments, and feelings which the speaker has tried to communicate to the audience. The closing words should make a powerful emotional impression on the listeners, since in most cases logic alone is insufficient to move an audience to act or believe as the speaker suggests. The conclusion is the last opportunity to emphasize the point of the speech. It should be a natural culmination of all that has been spoken. It should not contain weak, insipid remarks which are begun or ended just as the speaker starts a hesitant but very obvious journey away from the podium.

The conclusion should be, without exception, one of the most carefully prepared parts of a speech. Just when it should be prepared is largely a matter of opinion. Some authorities advise preparing it first because such a practice enables a speaker to point the talk toward a predetermined end. Other speakers suggest preparing the conclusion last because this procedure allows a person to draw their final words from the full draft of the speech. A third approach is to prepare it along with the introduction after the body is developed in order to coordinate both. Regardless of when a conclusion is prepared, there is one point on which all authorities agree, and it is that the conclusion must be carefully worded, carefully organized, carefully rehearsed and in most cases committed to memory or nearly so. The conclusion should be brief, generally not more than one-eighth to one-tenth of the entire speech, perhaps less, depending on the speech, the speaker, the audience, the occasion and the environment in which the speech is delivered. A conclusion should never bring in new material, since an action requires a discussion of the new material which in turn unnecessarily prolongs the speech. Also the introduction of new material brings about an undesirable anticlimax and frequently irritates an audience because a speaker runs past a perfect place to stop.

When a speaker moves into the conclusion, it should be obvious that it is the closing remarks. The speaker's intentions should be so clear that it is not necessary to say, "In conclusion..."

The importance of the delivery of a conclusion cannot be overemphasized. The total person – mind, body and soul – must be harmoniously at work. The eye contact should be direct, the gestures and actions appropriate, the posture alert, and the voice sincere, distinct and well articulated. The speaker's effort in delivering the conclusion may be likened to a foot racer who culminates an entire race in one great, last surge of power while lunging toward the tape – and victory.

Now that you have been told what should be contained within a conclusion, there remains one major question: "How do you actually go about attaining these ends, i.e., what methods should be used?" There are numerous ways to develop a conclusion. Some of the better known are listed as follows:

A. *Summary* is a method often utilized in closing a speech. It is sometimes expressed by restatement of the speech title, of the purpose, of some specific phrase that has been used several times in the speech, by an apt quotation, either prose or poetry, which adroitly says what the speaker wishes to be said, or by any other means which tends to bring the main point of the speech into final focus for the audience. An example of a very brief summary is contained in the following words which were once used by a speaker to summarize a speech against Russia's aggression in Czechoslovakia:

"Czechoslovakia will live again! The hordes of Russia, the Bears of Europe, the intrigue of Moscow shall not swallow up this mighty and prideful people. They shall rise up and fight their horrible aggressor. Yes, Czechoslovakia will live again!"

B. *Recapitulation* may be used in longer formal speeches when it is necessary to restate points in a one, two, three order. The danger of this method is that it may become monotonous and uninteresting. Short speeches do not require this type of conclusion, since the points are easily remembered. A short speech may close with the last main point if it is a strong point. Usually, however, more is needed to close a speech, even a short one.

"To be sure that we all understand my reasons for believing as I do, let me restate my main points. First, world federation is the only type of government which will save the world from destroying itself. Second, world federation is the only type of government which is acceptable to the several nations, and third, world federation is the most democratic type of world government yet conceived by man. It is for these reasons that I favor the establishment of a world government."

C. *A striking anecdote, an analogy, or a simile* may be employed as closing remarks, or any one of them or a suitable combination of them may be interwoven with the summary or recapitulation type of conclusion. One conclusion which utilized the analogy for a speech concerning our children in crisis is:

"Just as a wind snuffs out the light from a candle, the winds of turmoil and discontent in our cities are snuffing out the lives and potential light of too many innocent youth. It is time to act to save our children."

D. *An emotionalized or idealized statement of the thesis* may serve as a useful conclusion. If the topic were "Our country's future" a conclusion could be:

"I want the legacy of this generation of Americans to be one of viewing progress as a never-ending process. I want us to be able to show that we recognized those things that must remain unchanged, and we preserved them. And that we had the foresight to determine what needed to be altered, and we did it. Let us take our place among other generations of Americans who made decisions not just for today, but for tomorrow. And not just for themselves, but for all Americans."

E. There may be a *powerful restatement of the thesis.* If the subject were "Volunteerism Can Change a Life," the final words could be:

"Volunteerism, giving of your talents to improve someone else's condition, can change a life. In fact, it can change yours as well as the lives of those you help."

F. *A vivid illustration of the central idea* may fittingly conclude a speech. If it were on America's military might, the following words could be used:

"The famous words of John Paul Jones, who said he had not yet begun to fight, are emblazoned again across the world's horizon, for tonight American troops in Saudi Arabia were part of an international attack against an aggressor nation that will not go unnoticed!"

G. *A call for action* from the audience may clinch a speech. It must of course pertain to the ideas of the speaker. This is an excellent type of conclusion, particularly when the purpose has been to stimulate or to get action from the audience. If a speech were on "Building Good Government," a conclusion could be:

"Let us no longer sit here doing nothing while the professional politicians corrupt our government and squander our money. Let's go out one by one, by two's and three's or by the hundreds and vote for better, more representative government. Let's do it tomorrow – it's election day and our only hope!"

One final word of warning is this: When the speech is finished, the speaker should hold the floor for a second or two (this cannot be stressed enough), before leaving the podium. Display or frivolity of any kind on the part of the speaker after the speech may sharply alter many good impressions which were made while on the platform. A person should not let actions portray a self-assessment of the speech. The audience will decide this point.

COMMUNICATION – A FEW IDEAS ABOUT IT

Communication may not be what you think. So let's first agree on what it is. Basically whenever you do anything (intentionally or not) that people interpret, they receive a message from you. Most people think communication occurs only when someone speaks, yet you know how people gesture with their hands, nod their heads, move their legs or shoulders, smile or frown, raise eyebrows or wiggle their noses all while they talk. These physical movements which you see often tell more than what is said with the speaker's words. Actually we *express feelings and ideas* two ways simultaneously. One way is with words or verbal communication and another is with bodily movements or nonverbal communication. It is almost impossible to talk without accompanying nonverbals; thus, we often send out messages we do not intend to send because of nonverbals. An example would be an individual who claims with words to be unafraid but you know the person is scared to death by observing nonverbals. An embarrassed or frightened person often communicates feelings through actions.

The point is, communication occurs anytime someone else sees and/or hears you. What you communicate may be what you intended or it may not be. However, words are one of your most powerful communication devices.

As a small child learning to talk, every word you learned had a special meaning to you because of your association with it. The word "puppy" meant only your puppy because to you there was no other. And so it was with all your words. Each had your own special meaning and every time you spoke, your words referred to the meaning you gave them. This remained true as you grew from childhood and will remain true all your life. Your words now carry broader meanings because you have learned there are many kinds of puppies but you still attach your meaning to your words. The trouble in trying to convey (symbolize) your ideas to someone else is that for every word you speak listeners interpret it with their special meanings which are different from yours. When this happens they do not fully understand you. It means that you communicated something but not exactly what you intended.

The process of putting words together in phrases and sentences to represent feelings and ideas is called encoding. Listeners interpret your words by sorting out ideas they create in their minds, which is called decoding, somewhat like figuring out a message sent in secret code.

Still another way you communicate when talking is by how loud, how fast, how high or low your voice is. All reflect meanings about things *for which you have no specific words*. People hearing you usually can tell by your vocal variety whether you are happy, sad, tired or angry. A good example would be the way a friend greets you with, "Good morning." You know instantly something is bothering them because they communicated this feeling by their voice quality. Perhaps they muttered their words, possibly by a frown on their face or the way they walked, but they communicated this feeling whether they intended to or not. Because people don't have words to completely express all their thoughts and feelings they use vocal variety and thousands of muscular movements in addition to their words.

You also tell people all about yourself by your appearance. Your clothes, hair and personal hygiene tell who you are. Think about how you are describing yourself.

Since words have different meanings for the speaker and the listener the question arises, "How does one talk to be understood more precisely?" Perhaps the best way is to use accurate and specific words. For example do not say, "It was bright colored." Instead say, "It was red and orange." Instead of, "He was a big man," say, "He was six feet three inches tall and weighed 225 pounds." Omit words such as pretty, nice, beautiful, bad, good, great, very, most, much, fast, slow and similar terms with generalized meanings. In other words say specifically what you mean, use correct grammar, articulate clearly, and pronounce distinctly. And finally, say it in as few words as possible. Don't make a listener decode fifty words to get your message when you can say the same thing using twenty-five.

Now in a broader sense you hear much about business, social, political, economic, and educational communication. It's popular to say, "Mary didn't communicate," to explain misunderstandings; however, it would be more appropriate to say, "Mary wasn't specific," or "Mary wasn't definite," or "Mary wasn't accurate," or "Mary used technical language," or "Mary wasn't complete." You could say in many instances, "Mary didn't speak plainly," or "Mary wrote sloppily and misspelled words," or "Mary did not signal (communicate) her message when she was supposed to." (Too early or too late.)

On the other side it can be said that some people don't listen to understand but instead to argue and talk about their own thoughts. They don't read carefully, or they hear and read only a part of what is said and pretend they heard and read everything. Thus they only partially decode messages they receive and foolishly wonder why they don't understand.

We can summarize these remarks when we say communication can be improved by being definite, specific, accurate and complete in speaking and writing. When receiving messages we must listen, observe and read carefully and completely. It's that simple. Add to these communication principles, attentiveness, appropriate bodily movements and gestures, a clean and neat personal appearance and an earnest desire to understand or to be understood.

Here's an interesting device. Next time you argue with someone try to restate their point of view so they will say, "That's exactly what I mean." Have them restate your views likewise. Do this on every point of disagreement then each will know what the other is talking about. Continue your discussion only if you both can do this.

Chapter *1*

INTRODUCTORY SPEECH

Question: Does one ever overcome nervous tension before giving a speech?
Answer: Probably not entirely. Without some nervous tension you might end up with a lifeless speech.

Time limits: 1-2 minutes.
Speaking notes: See the end of the chapter.

PURPOSE OF YOUR FIRST SPEECH

This speech is your first to be presented in this course. Your first speech gives you a chance to stand before your classmates and to tell them something about yourself. You are not expected to give a long biographical account of your life. By answering the questions at the end of this assignment, you introduce yourself to your audience and you make your first speech. You will get the feel of standing on your feet and talking before a group of people. Since you must start somewhere, this experience will provide a good beginning.

HOW TO PREPARE FOR YOUR FIRST SPEECH

One reason for making this speech is to let the audience get acquainted with you. Another purpose of this experience is to give you an opportunity to learn what it is like to see many people sitting before you waiting to hear what you have to say. Some students get a thrill from it; others get a scare. Actually the scare is only a feeling that comes to a speaker because the adrenal glands are functioning more than they usually do. Because people dislike these feelings, they say they are scared. Instead of being scared of *speaking*, they are scared of a normal physical action taking place within themselves. They associate this feeling with speechmaking and, tying the two together, say, speaking "scares" them.

To be scared is normal. To be nervous is normal. To be tense is normal. You must experience these feelings; otherwise you would be as lifeless as an old shirt. These feelings are present in football players before and during a game. Great actors have them. Great speakers have them. Nervousness is the high octane gas which provides these persons with the drive to give life to their performances. They want a normal amount of it because they use it. You see, they *control* their nervousness (energy) and that is all you need to do. Do not try to *rid* yourself of nervousness entirely; you will gain control of this power. As you give more speeches throughout this course, you will discover your control growing stronger– and that is what you want.

Study the questions at the end of this assignment. Decide generally how you will answer them. It will help you to practice aloud several times by standing in front of a mirror while you speak. Do not memorize your answers words for word, since this would make your remarks sound like a recitation.

HOW TO PRESENT YOUR FIRST SPEECH

Look at the questions at the end of the assignment. On a note card jot down your answers in brief phrases. Take this with you when you speak.

When your name is called walk quietly to the front of the room. Do not do anything to call unnecessary attention to yourself. When you get there, stand politely on *both* feet. Keep your weight on both feet or on your slightly forward foot.

Let your hands hang loosely at your sides unless you care to bring the one holding your notes up in front of you. It is certainly permissible to place a hand on a table top, or a chair back, if you do not call attention to the act. Grasp your notes lightly between the thumb and index finger. Do not palm them, roll, crumple, twist or disfigure them in any way by continuous handling. When you refer to your notes, raise them high enough that you do not need to lower your head to glance at them.

If you feel like moving around a few paces, do so naturally, without shuffling or scraping your feet, or without continuous pacing. When you are not changing positions, stand still and keep your feet quiet.

When you begin your speech, talk with your normal voice just as you would if you were telling about yourself to a group of good friends. Good speaking is good conversation. Make an introductory statement for a beginning. Show some interest in your remarks. Be sure that everyone can hear you. Look your audience directly in the eyes; however, avoid a shifty, flitting type of gaze that never really stops anywhere. You may look at certain persons in different parts of the group, since you cannot very well look at everybody during the short time you are speaking.

When you are ready to close your remarks, conclude with a brief summarizing statement. Pause at least two seconds after your final words; then go easily and politely to your chair. Do not rush or hurry or crumple your notes into a wad and shove them in your pocket. Upon reaching your chair, avoid slouching down in it, sprawling out, heaving a big sigh and in general going through a pantomime which says in effect, "I'm glad that's over!" You may feel that way; however, this is one time that advertising does not pay. Sit comfortably in your chair and remember that you are still giving impressions of yourself. If you have done your best, no only will complain.

Answer the questions below on a note card or sheet of paper with a few brief words or phrases. Use the answers as the basis of your presentation.

1. My name is (what shall we call you?)
2. When and how did you spend your childhood? Explain.
3. Tell about your home town or neighborhood.
4. How do you spend your spare time?
5. Who is your favorite movie actor and actress? Why?
6. What is your favorite sport? Why?
7. Conclude with a summarizing statement about your school plans.

Chapter *2*

RECORDING A SPEECH

Question: Is speaking over the radio the same as speaking in person?
Answer: No. Radio speech depends on voice alone, is usually read, and has no body language for the listener to see.

Time limits: See your instructor for the exact time.
Speaking notes: Ten or fifteen words should be enough.

PURPOSE OF RECORDING A SPEECH

This assignment is proposed in order that you may hear and judge your own speaking. It calls for a speech that you will record and keep for yourself as a record of how you talked when this course started. At a later date near the end of the course you may wish to make another recording to compare with your first recording, thus noting progress.

EXPLANATION OF A RECORDED SPEECH

A recorded speech may be given for any kind of any occasion. It simply is a speech which is recorded and played back at will. The recording can be either audio, as in a cassette tape recorder, or video, for playback on a home video cassette recorder. In other words, it becomes a record in voice rather than a record in writing. These are its chief purposes: rebroadcasting from a radio or television station, private use, or classroom study. Its special feature is the time limit placed on the speaker. The time limits have to be observed within a matter of seconds. Any person who is not willing to adhere to the time limit pays for tape space they do not use because the speech is short. If they have too much speech and run out of time, they either make an awkward conclusion or are cut off in the middle of a sentence or summary.

Occasions for recording a speech occur any time a speech needs to be preserved for later use. Occasions may arise in the home, school, church, club, business, politics, government, theatre, radio station, TV station, and the like.

SUGGESTED TOPICS FOR RECORDING A SPEECH

If you are recording a speech during the first part of the school year with the thought in mind that you will make a later recording for purposes of comparison, it might be wise to use the first speech experience suggested in this book, the one in which you introduced yourself to the class. If you do not care to do this, check through the many possibilities listed under "Additional Topics" in Appendix A. Be sure your selection meets the time limit which you will be required to observe. Consult your instructor for further information.

If this is your first recording or you are inexperienced, do not try to be profound in your remarks. Rather, select a topic which will best represent you at your present stage of development as a speaker. On the other hand, if you merely wish to make a recording of a speech, your topic will have little to do with it.

H0W TO PREPARE A SPEECH FOR RECORDING

For this particular speech your purpose is to secure a record of your speaking ability. Decide if you will use audio or video. Decide according to the first lesson's assignment notes what you are going to say; then practice aloud until you have your thoughts well in mind, but not memorized. Know the general outline of your ideas. If you choose to speak on some other topic, simply prepare it as you would any speech by observing good speech preparation practices. In all cases observe your time limits within ten seconds if possible. Should you choose to read your speech (with your instructor's consent), organize it as you would any speech. Keep it right on the nose as to time. Do not plan on reading your speech if you will be videotaping.

HOW TO PRESENT A SPEECH FOR RECORDING

You should begin your speech by saying, "This is (Scott Jones) speaking on (date)." After your first sentence, go ahead with your talk. Speak in your natural voice as you normally would. Be careful not to vary the distance from the microphone by moving your head a great deal or your recording may be loud at first and then weak. Also avoid coughing, clearing your throat, sneezing, or shouting, into the "mike." Ask your instructor how close to stand to the microphone; however, ten inches is considered a good distance. While speaking, watch your progress so that you may be sure to finish before your time runs out. If you use notes, avoid rustling them near the microphone. Any sound they make will be picked up and exaggerated. When one piece of paper is finished, place it quietly behind or to the side of your other papers.

SPECIAL NOTES

When a group of recordings is concluded, the instructor may play them back to the class; then members of the class may discuss the individual speakers. Points to listen for are the whistled "s", nasality, harshness, resonance, pitch, force, articulation, pronunciation.

The instructor may keep the records on file until the end of the course when a final recording may be made for comparative purposes.

If a video tape machine is available it will afford an effective means for students to see and hear how they look and sound while speaking. Also it provides opportunity to those students wishing to use it for rehearsal. Wisely used, the video tape recorder can assist student speakers to become their own best teachers.

Chapter *3*

SPEECH OF PERSONAL EXPERIENCE

Question: How can you improve your pronunciation?
Answer: Keep a dictionary handy. Carry a small one
with you. Read aloud fifteen minutes daily making
sure of all pronunciations.

Time limits: 3-4 minutes.
Speaking notes: 10-word maximum limit.
Source of information: Use your own personal experience.
Outline of speech: Prepare a 50-100 word complete sentence outline to be handed to your instructor when you rise to speak. Your instructor may wish to write comments on it regarding your speech.

PURPOSE OF A SPEECH OF PERSONAL EXPERIENCE

You take a step forward in your speaking experience when you present a speech of personal experience. While this speech is essentially about yourself, it still requires definite preparation and interesting presentation. You should learn the importance of these two requirements early in your speech training. Aside from becoming acquainted with these aspects of speechmaking, you should feel increased confidence and poise as a result of this speech experience. Your ease before the group should improve noticeably. By giving your best to this speech you will achieve a creditable improvement and desirable personal satisfaction.

EXPLANATION OF A SPEECH OF PERSONAL EXPERIENCE

A speech of personal experience may be one of any four basic types: the speech may be given to (1) inform, (2) to stimulate or arouse, (3) to convince, or (4) to entertain. The specific purpose of your remarks will determine which of these types you plan to present. If you want to tell a funny or amusing personal experiences, you will plan to *entertain* your listeners. If you wish to tell about your stamp collection, your purpose will be to *inform* your listeners. It is advisable to confine your efforts to one of these two kinds of speeches.

This speech requires thorough preparation. You must know the order in which you plan to tell of your experiences. You also need to know how you will tell them, that is, the words you will use. *This does not mean you are to memorize your speech.*

Unlimited occasions for a speech of personal experience occur at all kinds of meetings – such as before school assemblies, clubs, business meetings, religious gatherings, and other groups. You have probably heard such a speech from a war veteran, a war correspondent, from a missionary, a newspaper reporter, a great athlete, or from persons such as yourself who tell what has happened to them. Topic suggestions for a speech of personal experience are given in the appendix at the end of this book.

HOW TO CHOOSE A TOPIC FOR A SPEECH OF PERSONAL EXPERIENCE

If you have had an exciting experience, select it for your speech. Whatever you decide to talk about should be vivid in your memory and quite clear. As you think about it you may feel prickly chills race up your spine, you may laugh, you may feel sad. But whatever it is, the experience should be personal.

Do not stall before making a choice of topic because you do not know anything interesting to talk about. This is an old, worn-out excuse. The topic that you choose may not be interesting in itself. It is your responsibility to plan to tell the personal experience in an interesting way. You can do this with a little effort. Choose a topic without delay, and then read the rest of this assignment to find out how to prepare and present a speech on the topic you have chosen.

HOW TO PREPARE A SPEECH OF PERSONAL EXPERIENCE

First, decide on your purpose for giving this speech. Do you want to inform your listeners? Do you want to entertain them? It will be wise to work toward one of these ends for this speech. Having decided this point, your next step is to find out how you go about informing or entertaining. You may do this by reading the chapters in this text dealing with these types of talks.

Now let us assume that you know generally what is expected of you when you give your speech. Let us assume, too, that you have your purpose constantly before you (to entertain or to inform). Now develop your speech in the following order:

I. Outline your speech in considerable detail. This means that you must set up the order of events you want to talk about.

A. Be sure your outline places these events in their most effective order throughout your talk. A little thought about arrangement will tell you how to place your ideas.

B. In arranging what you will talk about, include your own personal feelings and reactions, the activities of other persons or animals, and objects that made your experience thrilling, exciting, funny. This will add interest.

II. *Practice your speech aloud* before friends and in front of a mirror. Do this until you have memorized the *sequence* of events, *not the words*. You will quite naturally tend to memorize certain words and phrases and this is all right. But do not under any circumstances memorize the whole speech word for word. Every time you rehearse you will tell the same things, but never with exactly the same words. Each rehearsal will set the pattern of your speech more firmly in mind until after several practices (the number depends on the individual) you will be able to present your speech with full confidence and the knowledge that you know what you are going to say; that is, you know the events and feelings you are going to talk about and describe.

II. Make a final evaluation of your speech before marking it "ready for presentation." Ask yourself the following questions and be sure that your speech answers each question adequately:

A. Does your speech merely list a series of persons, places, things, and times without telling what happened to these persons and things? (You should vitalize these persons and things by describing what happened and by pointing out unusual or exciting incidents, such as: dangers, or humorous occurrences.) Avoid unnecessary details.

B. Is your speech about *you only*? If so, you can improve it by talking about the influences that were operating in your presence. For example, if you rescued a drowning person, do not be satisfied to say, "I jumped in and pulled him out." Tell what he was doing, describe his struggles, tell how deep the water was, how far he was from shore, recount your fears and other feelings as you pulled him toward shore, tell how the current almost took you under, demonstrate the way you held him by the hair. Emphasize such items as your fatigue and near exhaustion as you fought to stay afloat. Here is an example of a "thriller": "We were in swimming. I guess we'd been in about an hour. John got the cramps and yelled for help. I swam over and pulled him out. He almost took me under once, but I got him out and gave him artificial respiration. I learned that when I was a kid. Boy, I sure was scared."

(If this were your speech ask yourself: Was this an interesting story of an experience? Could it have been told with more vividness and description?)

C. Do you have a curiosity-arousing introduction, one that catches the attention? Check this point carefully.

D. Do you have a conclusion? A speech is never finished without one.

HOW TO PRESENT A SPEECH OF PERSONAL EXPERIENCE

Your attitude regarding yourself and your audience will exert a singular influence upon you and your listeners. You should have a sincere desire to entertain or inform. If it is information that you earnestly desire to give, then you must try to make your audience understand what you are telling. If it is entertainment you want to provide, then you must strive to give enjoyment by amusing the audience and causing smiles and perhaps some laughter. You should not feel that what you have to say is simply not interesting and never was, which is the attitude of some students. Consider for a moment the child who runs to you eagerly, grasps your hand, and excitedly tells you about a big dog two doors down the street. The story no doubt captivates your interest; yet there is nothing inherently interesting about a big dog you have seen many times. Why then are you interested? The answer lies largely in the extreme desire of the child to tell you something. *A child wants you to understand and is excited about the event,* and therein lies the basic secret of giving information to which people will listen attentively. You must have a desire to make your audience understand you or enjoy what you are saying.

As for your body language, demonstrate those points which you can. Let your arms and hands gesture whenever you need to physically add to what you are saying, otherwise your hands may hang comfortable at your sides, rest easily on a speaker's stand or chair back. Be calm about putting your hands anywhere. Change your stage position by moving laterally a few feet. This will cause attention to be drawn to your presentation.

Use your voice normally and conversationally. Talk earnestly and loudly enough to be heard by everyone present. If you are truly interested in your audience's understanding you, your vocal variety and force will take care of themselves very well.

If you use speaking notes, observe the the word maximum limit. Have these written in large handwriting so that they may be easily read. Use notecards at least three by five inches in size. Do not fiddle with the card or roll it into a tube. Hold the notes calmly between your thumb and forefinger in either hand. When referring to your notes, *raise them* to a level that permits you to glance at them without bowing your head. Do not try to hide them, nor act ashamed of using them. They are your map. Treat them as casually as you would a road map were you taking a trip.

THE EARTH TREMBLED
A Personal Experience Speech by Gail Anderson

"And Jesus uttered a loud cry, and breathed his last. And the curtain of the temple was torn in two, from top to bottom." Mark 15:37-38. For Christians, Good Friday holds a point in destiny unequaled since the dawning of all mankind. March 27, 1964, Good Friday alike, holds an eminent position in the stream of my life as the day of the Alaska earthquake.

I was thirteen at the time, living in Anchorage, Alaska. The fact was that a "Good Friday suppertime" sort of atmosphere was beginning to creep into the minds of each of the members of my family. We might even have been bored had it not been for the anticipation of the evening meal that was near completion.

The day was calm. My father was typically absorbed in the newspaper. "Kitchen-puttering" occupied my mother. My brother was both engaged and absorbed in some nonsensical whiling away of time. Snow was falling in a soft and gentle manner, combatting boredom with me. The subtle and peaceful cloaking it lent the earth, could only be viewed as ironic now, in the face of what was to come.

The snow was still falling when the hanging light fixtures began to swing and the rattle of furniture could be heard on the tile floor. At first, our reaction could only have been termed amusement. But our amusement soon became terror. As we stumbled down stairs and through doors, trying to avoid tumbling objects, we heard and felt the rumble of our earth mount. As the front door forcibly flung us into the mounds of snow in the front yard, the earth continued to roll and groan. And then sprawled on the sidewalk, the ground ceased to tease us with its laughing rumbles. Now it was cracking. Around me the snow was forming rifts as great expanses of the frozen earth were separating.

The noises somehow were strangely deafening. Hysterical cries of neighbors blended with the laughing of the earth and the creaking of the houses to produce a wicked sound system matched only the horror of its backdrop.

Our station wagon bounced like a rubber ball. Trees on high-crumbling mountains in the distance were waving like a wheat field in a breeze.

Finally the earth became dormant once again. Now it was still. And as the curtain of night shrouded our stricken Alaska, we were left to our contemplations. The hesitancy of the only partially existent radio gave our woes a universality. Only then did we realize the encompassing scope of this earthquake. Sitting in my rocking chair (attempting to camouflage any further shaking), I heard of this demon which had left me alive and glad with my saved family, and spared home, but had taken the lives and homes of so many others.

In Anchorage, homes, schools, and businesses lay in ruin, paradoxically powdered with snow. But the people were together, helping one another. The homes left standing were crowded, but a unity of cause made these conditions endurable.

Immediately work began to rebuild, to restore. Radio announcers neglected their families to keep the people informed, as televisions and newspapers were not to be lines of communication for some time. People were living without heat, water, mail service, and many other things. Essentials were the essence of a united survival.

I wish that I could have understood the agonizing pleas for survival, for salvation. But only now, as my mind becomes a victim of time, do I have any understanding of the emotional or intellectual influence a natural disaster exercises on life and the perception of it.

And so, as on the original Good Friday, man was to be a recipient of one of the most vividly educational experiences in a lifetime. As the tragedy of the crucifixion and resurrection of Jesus Christ, the tragedy of the earthquake was to bring man closer to God, more desirous of salvation, and more understanding of both his God and himself.

A MICROPHONE? HOW DO I WORK WITH A MICROPHONE?

1. Speak clearly and distinctly. Avoid slurring words. Articulate words and sounds.

2. Speak in a normal tone of voice. A microphone amplifies your voice, there is no need to be exceptionally louder.

3. Avoid speaking too rapidly. This may cause words and sounds to run together.

4. Practice with a microphone before giving a final performance.

5. Stay at a constant distance from the microphone. Place four fingers of one hand together and put your index finger lengthwise next to your lips. This is a rough estimate as to how far away you should be from the microphone.

Chapter **4**

THE PET PEEVE OR OPINION SPEECH

Question: Is it all right to ask questions when giving a speech?
Answer: Yes. Rhetorical questions are effective. These ques-
tions should be directed to the entire audience, however, no
answer is expected or required.

Time limits: None.
Speaking notes: Do as you like – you will probably be more effective without them.
Source of information: Yourself.
Outline of speech: None is required.

PURPOSE OF THE PET PEEVE OR OPINION SPEECH

Thus far in your speeches you have probably felt varying degrees of nervousness and tension. As a result you may have taken stage fearfully spoken in hushed and weak tones, used little or no bodily action, and scarcely any gestures. Perhaps you have not looked your audience in the eye (called eye contact) or you may have lacked sufficient enthusiasm. Such behavior on your part is probably caused by thinking of yourself and how you are doing.

One way to overcome tensions and nervousness is by talking of something about which you are intensely interested. This speech is designed to give you the feeling of real, live speaking in which you cast aside all inhibitions, fears, and thoughts of yourself. See what you can do with it.

EXPLANATION OF THE PET PEEVE OR OPINION SPEECH

Your talk should be about your pet peeve or your opinion about something. It should concern your innermost personal feelings on that peeve which causes you greater disturbance and anger or stronger feeling than anything else. It should make your blood boil just to think about it. It may be about something of recent occurrence or it may concern an event that happened some time ago. It must, however, be about an incident that is vivid in your memory. Probably it should be of recent date; otherwise, you may have cooled off too much to make a strong speech about it.

HOW TO CHOOSE A TOPIC FOR A PET PEEVE SPEECH

My pet peeve – or anything else that stirs you up. Think about the last time you were irritated about something and remember why. Check Appendix A for ideas.

HOW TO PREPARE A PET PEEVE OR OPINION SPEECH

No particular preparation is required. All that you need do is to decide what your most annoying and irritating pet peeve is. Once you make your choice of peeve or opinion, mull over the irritating idea and make up your mind that you are going to "blow off a lot of steam" to your audience. If you wish to rehearse before presentation, so much the better. However, for this specific assignment you are not asked to practice. All that you are asked to do is to make sure that you are "red hot" about a particular subject. *If you are,* your preparation is sufficient for this speech.

HOW TO PRESENT YOUR SPEECH

There is just one way to deliver a speech about a pet peeve or opinion. Put your whole body and soul into it. Mean every word. Use plenty of force framed in dynamic and colorful appropriate language. Let a slow fire that has been smoldering within you suddenly explode. Pour hot verbal oil on the blaze and let it roar and burn! In other words, let yourself go as never before. Be strong and do not be afraid to let the world know it. If your arms feel like waving, let them wave. If you feel like scowling in disgust – scowl. If you feel like shouting – shout. Whatever you do, just be sure you go all out. No doubt you will be surprised at your own ability – when you really "unload."

After your speech, the instructor and class will comment orally on your effectiveness. They should be able to tell you whether or not you really meant what you said. It will be helpful to you to find out how they reacted.

GREED AT THE TOP
A Pet Peeve Speech by Jack Ozegovic

One of the more annoying topics to surface and be discussed recently has been a study of the salaries and bonuses paid to CEOs of some of America's largest corporations and industries. This information has been highly controversial and, to many of us, infuriating.

The main thrust of these exposés has been a revelation of rampant greed among leaders of American business, according to their more vocal critics. Even William S. Buckley has joined the chorus of those who are outraged by the imbalance between executive salaries and that of other employees, not to mention the growing question on how these standards are set. What tasks do these people perform to justify salaries of one million and more, plus stock options and bonuses? Some of these executives have accepted raises and bonuses even when their companies were in financial trouble with stock dividends being stopped or raises to other employees being denied or employees being laid off. There definitely is a growing public outrage towards this arrogance and lust for power.

When the President went to Japan seeking fair trade practices, he made the monumental blunder of dragging the three top auto CEOs with him which infuriated management of Japanese auto makers. With salaries reputed to be as much as $3 million, they represented bloated gluttony to their Japanese counterparts whose salaries are one quarter of that or less. They could not understand how they could accept that much money when the growth of their companies was stagnant at best. They didn't see their skills as that outstanding.

This growing concern and criticism reminds me very much of the movie, "Roger and Me," which I believe was the one of the first germs of an exposé on corporate corruption in America. The once revered CEO is stripped of his mantle of respect and godliness and presented as a human with the same weaknesses as anyone else. I grew up only 40 miles from where "Roger and Me" was filmed. Roger Smith and General Motors dominated my home state. Their alleged mistakes and their haughtiness and disregard for the well being of their workforce is notorious. If there is to be a return of respect towards and cooperation with American business and industry, the excesses of corporate leadership must stop. The country is tired of this injustice. Part of the revival of American industry has to be a more modest and streamlined profile of its leaders.

Chapter *5*

BODY LANGUAGE – THE PANTOMIME

Question: What is posture?
Answer: It is the speaker's bodily
position in any upright or sitting position.

Time limits: 2-3 minutes.
Source of information: Yourself.
Outline of pantomime: Prepare a 50-100 word complete sentence outline of the pantomime you intend to present. Hand it to your instructor when you rise to take stage.

PURPOSE OF THE PANTOMIME

This experience, a pantomime, should assist you in acquiring a new freedom of bodily actions and gestures. Unhampered bodily action is highly important to effective speech. By producing a good pantomime you will emphasize all of the elements of speech except the spoken word itself. In so doing, you will bring into play the silent but yet extremely important factors that often speak what words cannot. Once you master these silent helpers you should find your speech improved. This pantomime is intended to help you to learn to use your body and gestures more freely with the result that in your next speech you will communicate with your entire body not just your voice.

EXPLANATION OF THE PANTOMIME

Pantomime is utilized as a part of drama, as an individual performance, and as a part of communicating. As you know, it involves only body language. It requires that you express ideas and thoughts, emotions and feelings by actions instead of sound (voice). The purpose of pantomime is to tell your audience with your actions what you normally would say with voice and action. If you have seen people give a stage performance called pantomime, you have seen it as one generally thinks of it. However, every time you observe someone telling someone else something without using vocal or written expression, you see pantomime. You might say that pantomime accompanies the spoken word, if we think of pantomime as actions. From this point of view, watch how your friends do pantomime while they talk. They beckon and wave and show by a thousand different motions what they are trying to tell another person. Sometimes they shrug their shoulders, kick their feet, frown, scowl, grin, smile, blink their eyes, wrinkle their foreheads, shake their heads from side to side or up and down. They use all these motions and many, many more.

Some people actually carry on conversation and never utter a sound. They are the hearing impaired who talk with a highly organized sign language. As for yourself, you probably have talked to many of your friends without speaking a word. Think of the times you have sent a sly wink across a room, have placed a finger to your lips as you pursed them to indicate silence, or have crooked your finger toward yourself and moved it rapidly to say in effect, "Come here." When you used these actions alone, they were pantomime. When you used them while you were speaking, they were a part of communication.

HOW TO CHOOSE AN ACT TO PANTOMIME

Any everyday experience can be translated into pantomime. Consider the following possibilities: riding the subway, playing a video game, driving a car, hailing a cab, trying to get someone's attention, arguing, trying to choose between two items in a store, pitching a baseball, watching a ball game, fishing, or making a sandwich. Be sure you have an interest in the subject you plan to pantomime. Select a topic that allows you to incorporate a variety of body movement and facial expressions. Do not put off making a choice until just before class time. If you do you will not have time to prepare an outline or practice, the lack of which will definitely weaken your performance.

HOW TO PREPARE A PANTOMIME

Follow the methods you would normally use in preparing a speech regarding topic, audience, occasion, and rehearsal. Your purpose for this pantomime will be to work out a series of meaningful actions that tell something. It will help you to list (outline) the scenes you intend to present; then break them down into smaller and more detailed scenes until you have a complete series of well-planned actions. Your next step is rehearsal. Practice as many times as necessary to completely master your act. Ask a friend to observe you and offer helpful suggestions. Use a video recorder, if available, to determine if your actions are large enough to be seen. It is well to note here that you should have little reason for not utilizing the proper time limits. Remember the pantomime should take the same length of time to perform as the action would take in real life.

HOW TO PRESENT A PANTOMIME

Before beginning your performance, make a thorough check to make certain that all the chairs or other properties you intend to use are in place. Any unusual use made of properties should be briefly explained to your audience. You may then announce your act or you may begin the performance at once and permit your audience to discover the act as it unfolds.

In presenting your pantomime, stay in character. Be watchful that you express fully what you desire to tell your audience. In most instances it is safe to "let yourself go" and not to worry about over-acting. Your bodily actions, facial expressions and other gestures, if freely employed, should ensure a successful portrayal. You should keep in mind that no one expects you to do a professional pantomime. The act is, in its final analysis, an experience that will help you to improve your speaking through better body language.

After concluding your performance, it will be helpful to you to remain at the front of the room while your classmates comment on your act. They will tell you whether or not you communicated your ideas effectively. They will give you suggestions for improvement.

Helpful hints:

1. Complete any activity you start. For example, if you are dressing for a party, do not forget to put your shoes on.

2. Observe the timing of your movements so they are natural.

3. At the conclusion of your act break character only after the last detail has been finished. Walk politely to the front of the stage and bow slightly to indicate that you have ended your pantomime.

HOW CAN YOU EFFECTIVELY USE VISUAL AIDS?

1. Choose visuals which are clear and easy to see across a room.

2. Place them in view of all audience members.

3. Keep them out of sight until they are ready to be used. Place them out of sight after they are used.

4. Try using different media. Try posters, overhead transparencies, actual objects, videotapes, slides, or computer generated graphics.

5. Practice with the visual aid so it can be used smoothly during the speech.

6. Face the audience and not to the visual aid when presenting.

Chapter *6*

THE SPEECH TO DEVELOP BODY LANGUAGE

Question: Is it all right to lean on the speaker's stand?
Answer: No. It makes you appear tired and uninterested in your subject.

Time limits: 4-5 minutes.
Speaking notes: 10-word maximum limit.
Sources of information: Two are required, preferably three. For each source give the specific magazine or book it was taken from, title of the article, author's full name, date of publication, and the chapter or pages telling where the material was found. If a source is a person, identify the the person completely by title, position, occupation, etc. List these on the outline form.
Outline your speech: Prepare a 75-150 word complete sentence outline.

PURPOSE OF THE SPEECH TO DEVELOP BODY LANGUAGE

Speaking is a total bodily activity. To be really effective a person has to speak with the entire body. Use your feet and legs, hands and arms, trunk, head, and eyebrows. Many beginning speakers do not realize this, despite the fact that they themselves use total bodily expression all the time in their normal conversation. One sees such speakers standing before a class very stiff and rigid making speeches. They move only their vocal cords, their tongue and jaws. Actually, they are half speaking (communicating) because they are using only half of their communication tools. If they would put all their communication power into action, they would include bodily action and gestures. A speech assignment of this kind is made because it will provide an experience which will demand that the speaker use bodily actions and gestures, and thus improve the speech.

EXPLANATION OF BODY LANGUAGE IN SPEECH

A speech to illustrate body language may be any kind, since bodily actions and gestures should be used in every speech with varying degrees. The purpose of your speech need not be influenced because increased body language is required. These activities will be aids in assisting you to communicate in a manner which fulfills your purpose, regardless of what it is.

Bodily actions may be defined as the movements of the body as it changes places. Gestures may be defined as movements of individual parts of the body, such as: raising an eyebrow, shrugging the shoulders, pointing. . . But all movements are body language.

It is nearly impossible to speak without *some* body language. Just because you may not be aware of all that goes on while you speak, in no sense means that you are not using some actions. Your nervousness and stage fright elicit certain gestures which tell the audience you are nervous. Now, if you substitute *meaningful* activity, you at once improve your communication and release many nervous tensions which accompany speaking. The point to bear in mind is that all speech communication should be accompanied by *appropriate* and *meaningful* body language which should not be interpreted to mean that you must employ constant bodily movements and incessant gestures. Such monotony of motion would be nerve wracking to an audience. Someone once said that moderation is good to practice in all things. This is true of body language.

HOW TO CHOOSE A TOPIC
FOR A SPEECH TO DEVELOP BODY LANGUAGE

Since the purpose of presenting this speech is to improve the use of body language, select a subject which can be demonstrated while talking about it. On the other hand, the purpose of the speech itself will be to inform the listeners. It will be wise then to choose a topic in which you are interested and about which you can find source materials. You must also adapt your material (your speech) to your audience; hence, it must be suitable to them as well as to you. Review the topics in Appendix A for suggestions.

In choosing your topic think about your sports activities and your hobbies. Ask yourself what you know how to do that others may not. After your choice is made, *stick to it* even though you discover it is more difficult to prepare than you had anticipated. Do not change topics just because you misjudged the amount of effort it would take for preparation. It is important that you make your selection of a topic without delay, for this speech will require considerable planning.

HOW TO PREPARE A SPEECH TO DEVELOP BODY LANGUAGE

In the speech to develop body language, your *communicative purpose* will be to inform your listeners in such a way that they *understand* what you are talking about. You will find out all about this type of speech by reading the chapter in this text, "The Speech to Inform." *Develop* your speech in the manner suggested for the informative speech.

In rehearsing this talk, practice bodily actions and gestures, as these will constitute a great part of this speech. These actions should not be memorized in detail, which would result in a mechanical performance. Instead, stand before a mirror while you practice. If possible, use a large mirror that reflects your whole body rather than just the upper half of it. A friend who will watch you and give helpful criticisms will provide an excellent means for improvement. Practicing with a video recorder will help also.

While you rehearse, your efforts should be exerted to create a well-organized set of spontaneous actions. As stated above, you must not memorize these actions. They must be motivated by the earnestness of your desire to make your listeners understand you. You must feel impelled to use your body and hands in expressing yourself. These actions of your body and hands need not be like those of anybody else – they are your own, the same as your walk and style of dancing are your own. All that you need to do is to observe yourself in practice in order to eliminate awkwardness, undesirable posture and foot positions, and distracting mannerisms.

The thought is that if you are willing to try and to undergo a little self-inflicted criticism, you can develop your own style of gesture and bodily action. In doing this, it is advisable that you read several references on body language. However, do not "program" or adopt gestures that look unnatural. It is important to remember that gestures and movement should be large and deliberate enough for the audience to see. Your posture should be one of alertness in which you *stand tall*. Keep your weight on the balls of your feet and on the *forward* foot.

Bodily action should be free, relaxed, easy. It should have tonicity, vigor and coordination, without the appearance of extreme nervous tension, which is characterized by shuffling feet and restless tiger-like pacing. In moving to the left, lead with the left foot; to the right, with the right foot. Avoid crossing your legs in order to get started. Move quietly without "clomping" heels and scraping soles. Be sure that the movement is motivated and acts as a transition between ideas, as an emphasis, as a device for releasing bodily tension and holding attention. Use bodily action deliberately until you habitually make it a desirable part of your speech, a part that communicates meanings and ideas.

HOW TO PRESENT A SPEECH TO DEVELOP BODY LANGUAGE

When you present this speech, approach the speaker's stand with the attitude of a person determined to win. Take pride in the fact that you are going to use your entire body in speaking. With this attitude you cannot lose.

When you actually present your speech, concentrate on one point which will make the audience understand what you are informing them about. They have to understand you, or you will not be getting your ideas across (communicating). Now, while you are earnestly presenting your ideas, try to make them clearer by demonstrating what you have to say. Do this by acting out certain parts as you talk. If you tell the audience that it is best to mount a horse a certain way, show them how to do it. If you say a baseball should be thrown a certain way, demonstrate it with all the force and energy you would use were you actually pitching. If your demonstration is so vigorous that it makes you short of breath, so much the better; you will have been truly trying to show, as well as tell what you have to say. You may exhibit pictures, charts, diagrams, write on the blackboard . . .If you do, be sure that your equipment is ready for exhibition before you begin.

Do not be afraid to try; do your best, and you will do a good job. Plan to continue using body language in your future speeches.

START CANOEING AND ENJOY YOUR WEEKENDS
A Speech Using Body Language by Joann Bopp

(The speaker's props were canoe paddles, an armless chair, and a small rug.)

Wouldn't you like to get more fun and relaxation out of your leisure time? Those two-day weekends could be spent away from the busy, hurried city life that most of us lead. Just put a canoe on top of your car and head for water. A canoe can float on as little as four inches of water. A quiet lake, stream, or pond may hold more fascination than you ever imagined. A canoe could also bring the thrills of shooting rapids of a swift running river, but this is for the experienced boatman.

I would like to give you a few rules and demonstrations to show you how to canoe in a very short time. Number one rule is getting in and out of a craft correctly. Canoeing is often thought of as being very dangerous but the danger usually occurs when getting in or out of the canoe. To get in, you step first to the center, lengthwise, and place the other foot behind (demonstrate on rug). Then lower yourself to a kneeling position which is the correct canoeing position (demonstrate by kneeling on rug). There are braces across the canoe to lean against. Once you have established this low center of gravity the canoe has great stability. Getting out is just reverse. Keep your weight to the center as much as possible (demonstrate by getting off the rug).

These are the paddles (show paddles), they are made of fir, a soft wood which holds up well in water and is lightweight. To select the paddle measure it to your height. It should come to about your chin (demonstrate). (Sit in the chair to demonstrate paddling strokes). To hold the paddle grip the end with one hand and with the other hand grasp it a little above the blade (demonstrate).

The basic stroke is called the "cruising stroke," or the "bow stroke." Extend the paddle in front of you (demonstrations follow), close to the canoe, and dip into the water, bringing it straight back to the hip by pushing with the top hand and pulling with the lower hand. Now bring the paddle back to repeat. The paddling is usually done by a two-person team called tandem paddling. In tandem paddling the person in front is the steerman who steers the boat. The person in the rear is the bowman and provides the power. The bowman uses the bow stroke most of the time (demonstrations follow). The steerman uses the bow stroke also, but often makes a hook outward on the end of the stroke to keep the canoe on course. This version of the bow stroke is called the "J-Stroke." The steerman also uses the "sweep stroke" for turning. It is a wide, sweeping, arc-like stroke made close to the water surface (demonstrate). To stop or go backwards the "backwater stroke" is used. Simply place the paddle into the water at right angles to the canoe and hold it firmly to stop (demonstrate). To go backwards reverse the "bow-stroke (demonstrate). (Rise to a standing position with paddles in hand.)

This is by no means all there is to know about canoeing, but if you can accomplish these things you will be able to have fun. So to enjoy the outdoors and take a break from a humdrum routine. I hope you will try canoeing.

Chapter 7

SPEECH OF SELF-DISCLOSURE AND STAGE FRIGHT

Question: How can you speak to an older group on equal grounds?
Answer: Know more about your subject than they. Older persons respect well informed students.

Time limits: None.
Speaking notes: Make a list of your "speech fears" if you wish.
Outline of speech: Prepare a list of your fears. Hand the list to your instructor when you rise to tell about yourself.

PURPOSE OF THE SPEECH OF SELF DISCLOSURE AND STAGE FRIGHT

The speech of self disclosure and stage fright is unique. It is also important because it does a great deal for the student. By carrying it through, a person sometimes achieves a mastery over self which before was thought impossible. The student sees that practically all inexperienced speakers suffer similar fears and physical reactions, including apathy, speechlessness, shortness of breath, dry mouth, weak knees, pain in the stomach, and nervous trembling. Because improvement so often is an immediate result of this speech experience, it is offered here with the thought that every student will gain much from it. As you will see, it is not a speech ever to be presented to a public audience.

EXPLANATION OF THE SPEECH OF SELF-DISCLOSURE AND STAGE FRIGHT

This speech is absolutely unrehearsed. It requires a maximum of honesty, sincerity, understanding of the other fellow, and straight-from-the-heart truth. Without complete honesty and frankness, many benefits are lost.

When it is your turn to speak, merely take the floor and honestly tell your audience about all the feelings you have when you talk to them. If your knees are shaking, you say so and go even further – you let them shake while you show your audience, without exaggeration, how they shake. In other words, tell everything.

You may be amused at your fears as you recount them. Your audience may be amused with you, but not at you. They undoubtedly have many of the same fears. After making known all your fears, the class will tell you voluntarily how they think you can overcome your various nervous tensions. After the class suggestions, it will be your turn again. You will honestly tell them how you feel at that moment. You will likely be surprised to find yourself calm, greatly relaxed, and poised. If not, you probably will not have told the group all your fears and will still be trying to hide certain feelings which you hope your audience will not recognize. If you feel "pretty good," then it is likely that you have told everything and no longer are trying to hide a great number of normal nervous reactions. Throughout this experience you will remain standing.

SUGGESTED TOPIC FOR SELF -DISCLOSURE AND STAGE FRIGHT

You need no specific topic for this speech. Just tell how you feel before speaking, when speaking, and after you finish a speech. Also tell what you think really caused your fears.

HOW TO PREPARE A SPEECH OF SELF-DISCLOSURE AND STAGE FRIGHT

You should think of all the many sensations and thoughts and insignificant reactions that have flashed into your mind during your past speeches. In order not to overlook anything, write out a list of these bothersome gremlins and study them carefully so that you may orally trade stories with other class members. If something funny has happened to you because of stage fright, plan to tell the group about it. You will enjoy a good joke on yourself and so will they. It will be good mental hygiene.

Your best preparation is to give yourself a definite "set of mind" in which you make a decision to tell all without reservation.

HOW TO PRESENT A SPEECH OF SELF-DISCLOSURE AND STAGE FRIGHT

This should be the simplest, most undramatic and sincere discussion you have made. It should come straight from the heart from start to finish – nothing more, nothing less. Your style should be you talking with a group of friends who will reciprocate. You do not need any notes unless they comprise a simple list of the fears and sensations you want to talk about.

The order of the speech should be these three steps:

1. Describe all your fears and sensations.
2. Ask your audience to tell you informally how they think you can improve yourself.
3. After the audience concludes their remarks, tell them exactly how you feel at the moment; then retire to your chair.

Chapter *8*

THE SPEECH TO INFORM

Question: Does one ever overcome nervous tension before giving a speech?
Answer: Probably not entirely. Without some nervous tension you might end up with a lifeless speech.

Time Limits: 4-5 minutes.
Speaking notes: 10-word maximum limit.
Sources of information: Two are required, preferably three. For each source give the specific magazine or book it was taken from, title of the article, author's full name, date of publication, and the chapter or pages telling where the material was found. If a source is a person, identify the source completely by title, position, occupation, etc. List these on the outline form.
Outline your speech: Prepare a 75-150 word complete sentence outline.

PURPOSE OF THE SPEECH TO INFORM

No one knows how many speeches are given each year. Neither does anyone know exactly what kinds of speeches are presented. We do know, however, that of the millions and millions of talks, many of them are made specifically to inform people – to tell them something they will find beneficial to include in their knowledge. While no one can foretell accurately what kind of speeches you may be called upon to present in the future, it is a safe bet that you will speak many times to inform people. Because so many speeches are informative in nature, you are offered here the opportunity to become acquainted with the informative speech.

EXPLANATION OF THE SPEECH TO INFORM

The speech to inform provides a clear understanding of the speaker's ideas upon a subject. It also arouses interest in the subject because the material which is presented is relevant to the lives of those who hear it. It is incumbent upon the speaker to provide this relevant material with its accompanying interest in order to inform intelligently. To accomplish the ends of informative speaking, one is obliged to select a subject of interest to the speaker and the listener. This can be done by an apt analysis of the audience – in this case your classmates. You, as the speaker, are charged further with the serious responsibility of knowing what you are talking about, knowing more about it, in fact, than anyone in your audience does. For this reason, your talk demands that you study not one but several (no less than two) sources of information. Under no consideration should you be satisfied to glance hurriedly through an article in a popular magazine, jot down a few notes, toss the periodical aside, and rush off, content with the world and a "sloppy" job of acquiring knowledge. This kind of preparation does not even begin to enable you to give an informative discourse.

Occasions for the informative speech are many. They occur on the lecture platform, in the pulpit, in the classroom, at business meetings; in fact, wherever you find reports being made, instructions given, or other ideas being presented by means of lectures and discussions. The point to bear in mind is that any time information is disseminated, an occasion for an informative speech arises.

HOW TO CHOOSE AN INFORMATIVE TOPIC

Study the list in the appendix carefully. Select something that interests you and that is appropriate to the audience you are to address or select a topic that you are curious about. Think of something that you read about or heard about on television that left you wanting to know more. Be sure that you can find information about the topic you select. Do not put off choosing a topic.

HOW TO PREPARE A SPEECH TO INFORM

To prepare for this speech, or any speech, you must know and follow certain fundamentals of preparation. These consist of the following steps: (1) choose your subject; (2) analyze the occasion; (3) analyze the audience; (4) gather your material; (5) organize and support your main points with evidence; (6) word your speech by writing it out in full, in part, or by rehearsing it from an outline; (7) practice aloud.

If you wish to organize your thoughts logically, you should decide early what objective you hope to attain and what reaction you want from this particular audience. Next, if you wish, you may divide your speech into three conventional parts: an introduction, the body, and the conclusion. To be more effective, some speakers break down their talks by using various combinations of the following steps: (1) gain attention; (2) make your audience want to hear your ideas; (3) present your ideas; (4) tell why this material is important to your listeners and how it affects them; (5) ask your audience to study the topic further or to take some action on it. The time required for any one division of a speech varies greatly; however, more time is given to the presentation of ideas than any other division of the speech.

The wording of your talk may be accomplished either by writing it out in full from the outline, or by considerable practice. In any event, rehearse before a mirror or with a tape recorder as many times as necessary (usually about four) to fix the proper steps and the order of their content, along with desirable stage appearance and bodily action. Give the speech for a friend or family member and get reactions. Do not memorize the words.

How to use notes is somewhat a matter of opinion. If you are adequately prepared, you will not need notes. You will talk extemporaneously, which is the most commanding method known. If you must refer to notes, they should be either short sentences, phrases, or single words which have a particular meaning to you. The notes you hold in your hands should be brief, concise, meaningful, and entirely familiar. A glance at your notes should be sufficient for you to gather their full meaning so that you may speak fluently yet logically. The notes should be on index cards.

One other point is important. The information you present must be accurate. For accuracy of information, acceptable sources of information written by reliable and competent authorities must be consulted. Your audience should know where you got your material. What is more, you are the person to identify these sources and authorities. You are expected to go even further in this matter of giving information: you are expected to offer your conclusions and views and evaluations of your information. All this entails the neat assimilation of all you have pulled together – that is, your entire speech.

A few hints might well be offered at this point. First, have only two or three main points to your speech. Support these well with examples, illustrations, analogies, and facts. Second, do not be afraid to inject humor and anecdotes into your thought to add interest. Be sure these additions are suited to your subject and audience. Third, be sure your speech moves ahead. Do not allow the speech to drag or become stalemated. Last, bend plenty of effort toward an interesting introduction and an equally effective conclusion.

OUTLINE YOUR SPEECH

Outlining your speech is necessary if you wish to secure organization, logical order of material, coherence, and unity. Without these rhetorical qualities, your thoughts will be a jumbled mass of words with little direction or a definite goal. An outline is to the speaker what a map is to a person taking a trip; it shows you where you are going and how to get there.

After neatly constructing a 75-150 word sentence outline, be prepared to hand the outline to your instructor when you rise to speak. Your instructor will undoubtedly wish to follow this while listening to your speech and may write suggestions on it for improvement. Remember that this outline is not to be used while you are speaking. State two or three sources of information within the speech presentation.

Read at least two references on outlining. Ask your instructor for assistance.

HOW TO PRESENT A SPEECH TO INFORM

Use an easy, energetic presentation. Be enthusiastic and original in what you have to say. Use your hands to demonstrate how to do things. Draw pictures, exhibit charts, in fact, do whatever is necessary to make your ideas understood and interesting. Take stage properly, utilize expressive bodily action, maintain direct eye contact, observe time limits, and stop when your speech is finished. Your conclusion should be as strong and appropriate and as well prepared as your beginning remarks.

THE WORLD'S GREATEST SPEAKER*
An Informative Speech by David Kensinger

Stop, for a moment, and think. Who was the greatest speaker of all time? Winston Churchill? Adolf Hitler? Alexander Hamilton? William Jennings Bryan? Martin Luther King, Jr.? All good answers, but when professors emeriti of speech from around the United States were asked that question in a 1983 survey over 40% responded with the same man, not among those previously mentioned. And a significant portion of the remainder placed him in their top five, while virtually all classified him as, "having had a major impact on the historical development of speech as an art." No guess?

Well what if I told you that he never spoke a word of English, had, by his own admission, terrible study habits, was born over 2,000 years ago, and rarely bothered to make transcripts of his own addresses because he usually spoke from memory anyway? Give up?

Well this one man lived in a time before recordings or videos but what scripts do exist of his speeches are so powerful and all contemporary accounts of his prowess so laudatory that he is nonetheless considered by many, bar none, as the greatest speaker who has ever lived.

Marcus Tulius Cicero was a Roman orator, philosopher, and statesman who lived from 106 to 43 B.C. He was born to a family of modest means, but, in spite of this, his father took him and his brother to Rome so that they could receive formal education. Upon completion of his rhetorical and legal training he was regarded as one of the premiere litigators of the Republic. But. . .

Surprisingly, he abandoned the profession three years later to pursue a career in public service saying his famous, "Civum bonum Romani primus sum." "I am first a good Roman citizen." This dedication to the glory and ideals that were the Roman Republic would guide him for the balance of his life.

Never was that dedication to be more sorely tested than when in 63 B.C., he was elected Consul of the Senate and the second place finisher, the patrician Cataline, planned his untimely demise. Cataline and a group of conspirators plotted to assassinate Cicero and declare themselves rulers of a new Roman Order.

Warned of the attempt just in time, Cicero fled to the relative safety of the Senate Chamber and awaited Cataline's return so he could begin the prosecution. Cicero presented his neatly scripted and practically incontrovertible case, but Cataline, in response, puzzlingly refused to even offer a defense of himself. As a bewildered Cicero took the rostrum for his closing argument, he was informed by an ally that of the 179 jurors presiding over the trial, approximately 150 had been bribed by Cataline's wealthy father so he might as well give up. But such was not his nature.

Discarding his prepared script, Cicero launched into a four hour extemporaneous oration on the abhorrence of crimes against the State. His reasoning was that a thief or a murderer commits his crime against only one man but a traitor betrays the entire state and his crime is therefore multifold more despicable because it was perpetrated against every citizen of Rome. He concluded that the only crime as reprehensible had to be the profaning of the pubic trust by the acceptance of bribery. As he took his seat, even the bribed jurors were so racked with guilt and moved by the force of his argument that the final vote was 176-3, guilty. The dissenting votes were Cataline, his father, and his brother. And so Cataline was executed, the conspiracy crushed, and the Republic saved, for the time being.

But the increasing popularity of the upstart General Julius Caesar would pose an even more serious threat to Cicero's vision of a noble and just Rome. Cicero warned that Caesar wanted to become a god-king and transform Rome into an empire, but his dissent of reason was drowned out when Caesar returned to Rome as a conquering hero. In a gesture of goodwill, Caesar offered Cicero a place in the First Triumvirate but he instead opted for exile in Tusculus.

With the Triumvirate collapsing in 44 B.C., Cicero was recalled by his friend Pompey; if not to speak in favor of the Triumvirate, then at least to salvage the reputation of this particular member. His timing was unfortunate, however. On the Ides of March in 44 B.C. Caesar was assassinated and Cicero was the chief suspect. He spoke valiantly in his own defense but was nonetheless returned to exile for mere suspicion.

Once the true assassins had been discovered, he returned to Rome for one last time as the sage of the Roman Senate, at the grace of Caesar Agustus, and with the proviso that he not speak against the new empire. In a decision of conscience, Cicero resolved that he could not sit idly by while the Constitutional Republic he had fought so hard to lead and to defend disintegrated into Empire. Entering now his mid-60s he nonetheless delivered a blistering torrent of speeches that were as damning for him as they were for the Empire. This sedition could not be tolerated, and in December of 43 B.C., by the order of Anthony and Agustus, Cicero was beheaded.

And so this one man, this, "greatest speaker who has ever lived," this philosopher, translator of Greek, and defender of tradition was executed by the edict of two men arrogant enough to call themselves, "Emperor." With him, died the last vestiges of the Roman Republic.

If Cicero is not among the most celebrated or successful of Roman Statesmen it is because he always chose principle over expediency, righteousness instead of ease, and means as opposed to ends. During his periods of exile he wrote prolifically: *On Friendship, On Moral Duties, On Old Age, and On the Character of the Orator.*

Among the more memorable passages from Cicero are. . .

"Cui bono?" "To whose profit?"

"Cui resultum?" "To what ends?"

"Ab naturo civitas viros altissimus virtui compellendi est, tandem illos non perficio." "By its nature, politics must attract men of the highest conviction and then bitterly disappoint them."

For those who lament the lack of passion or conviction in contemporary politics or bemoan the decline of political oratory as a recent issue of *The New Republic* has, there is truly a man to admire in Marcus Cicero.

It is curious to ponder how a man of such high-minded ideological austerity and long-winded rhetorical prowess would fare in the world of soundbites and special interest politics we now call American government. Perhaps not very well, but be sure of this. Had he been born a thousand years earlier or ten thousand years later, Marcus Tulius Cicero would be remembered as the greatest speaker of all time.

*This speech won first place in the Kansas State Speech championship for Informative Speaking in 1989.

Chapter *9*

SPEECH TO PERSUADE

Question: Should a speaker talk down to the audience?
Answer: Never. Use understandable, nontechnical
language. Audiences are intelligent.

Time limits: 5-6 minutes.
Speaking notes: 75-word maximum limit.
Sources of information: Two are required, preferably three. For each source give the specific magazine or book it was taken from, title of the article, author's full name, date of publication, and the chapter or pages telling where the material was found. If a source is a person, identify the source completely by title, position, occupation, etc. List these on the outline form.
Outline your speech: Prepare a 75-150 word complete sentence outline.

PURPOSE OF THE SPEECH TO PERSUADE

A speech to persuade is used so widely that we are probably unaware of its frequency. Actually, very few persons do what someone else suggests unless they are convinced. The most common method used in convincing someone is a system of talking. The pattern of ideas employed is not always known to the person who uses it but, generally, the speaker uses certain techniques to gain conviction.

It is probable that you will be asked to present ideas and arguments at some future date. When this time arrives, you will find it a much easier speech assignment once you have practice in the art of convincing an audience.

EXPLANATION OF THE SPEECH TO PERSUADE

The speech to persuade is one which causes the audience to change, adopt, modify, or continue a belief or action. You must present sufficient logic and evidence to swing the audience to your position on a debatable proposition. This usually means that you will also ask them to take the action which you suggest. It is usually wise and necessary to appeal to emotions that accompany attitudes and decisions which you desire from your audience. These basic emotions may be reached by certain basic appeals such as, wealth, love of country, self-preservation, desire for recognition, desire for new adventure, loyalty, political beliefs, religion, and the like. This necessitates a thorough analysis of your audience so that you may base your appeal on their beliefs and attitudes. It also means that you must present your logic and evidence in such a way that it directs the audience's thinking through channels they readily follow.

The speech to convince is utilized on many kinds of occasions. At most popular gatherings, such as political meetings, lecture forums, charity drives, community drives, church services, and other civic gatherings, an effort is made to convince. Business meetings involve conviction any time differences of opinion prevail. Decisions are reached by persuading someone. Any time that a debate is in progress, be it a formal argument between two rival schools, within a legislative body, among three friends, or in court proceedings – the statements of the speakers involve persuasion through logic, evidence, and emotion. (Could it be that the last time you asked your parents for a special type of clothes you gave a most convincing argument containing much logic, considerable evidence, and some emotion by stating why you should have it?)

HOW TO CHOOSE A PERSUASIVE TOPIC

Examine the topics in the appendix. If you do not select one of them, be extremely careful in the choice of a topic of your own. The points to watch are the ways you word your topic and what you propose to persuade your audience to believe. In wording your topic *be sure* you propose to your audience that they *should* adopt a certain debatable proposition. For example, if you decide to convince your listeners that "All school books should be free," notice the word "should." It implies "ought to be." So your purpose is to persuade your audience *to believe* this is a sound idea and it will be beneficial *if carried out.* You are not asking them to carry it out by standing behind a book counter and handling out free textbooks.

A *sales talk* is not appropriate for this assignment because your purpose is to make your listeners reach down in their pocket, pull out money, and give it to you. This *requires* them to do something. Naturally a certain amount of convincing will precede your request for money, but your *actual purpose* is to cause them to hand you one hundred dollars. This type of speech is discussed in Chapter 11. We may conclude then that a speech *to convince* is not a sales talk, it is not primarily to motivate to action, but it is one in which your purpose is to *change a person's mind* about something on which there is definite disagreement.

Your topic must be a proposition which is specific and which offers a debatable solution to a controversial problem. It is not adequate to propose the subject "We should all drive more carefully." We agree on this already. If you wish to do something to make us more *careful drivers*, suggest a definite and debatable *solution*, such as: "The legislature should pass a law limiting speed on the highways to sixty miles per hour," or "All persons who are convicted of traffic violations should be compelled to attend a driver's school for two weeks." These are proposals about which people disagree. We can readily say *yes* or *no* to them. We can *debate* them, but we cannot debate the subject that "We should all drive more carefully," since we agree on it. Examine your topic closely to be certain you have a correct topic on which to base your speech to convince. If you are in doubt, consult your instructor.

HOW TO PREPARE A SPEECH TO PERSUADE

In preparing the speech to persuade remember that your purpose is to swing people over to your beliefs. This is obviously not an easy task; however, it is not at all impossible.

To achieve the "convincing effect," you need to look carefully into the organization of your speech. Briefly, it may be as follows:

1. **Present a history of the problem.** Discuss the events leading up to the present time that make the topic important. Tell why it is significant that the audience hear the discussion you are about to present. (Do not spend too much time on the history – you have other points to cover.)

2. **Discuss the present day effects of the problem.** Give *examples, illustrations, facts,* and *views of authorities* that clearly demonstrate the situation you are talking about. These are *musts* if you wish to be convincing.

3. **Discuss the causes that brought about the effects you listed in point 2.** Here again you must present *examples*, illustrations, facts, and views of authorities to prove your points. Be sure you show how the causes have and are bringing about the effects you mentioned. For example, if you say your car died (effect) because of a blowout (cause) you must definitely establish this *cause* rather than permit your audience to believe that the car *may* have died because the steering mechanism on the car suddenly broke.

4. **List possible solutions to the problem**. Discuss briefly the various alternatives that could be followed but show they are not effective enough to solve your problem. *Give evidence for your statements; examples, illustrations, authorities' views, facts and analogies.*

5. **Give your solution to the problem.** Show why your solution is the best answer to the proposition you are discussing. *Present your evidence and the reason for believing as you do.* This must not be simply your opinions. It must be logical reasoning backed up by evidence.

6. **Show how your proposal will benefit your audience.** This is the real meat of your entire speech if you have thoroughly fulfilled each preceding step up to this point. Here is that part of your speech where you must convince. You definitely have to show your listeners how they will benefit from your proposals. For example: How they will make more money, how they will be safer from an enemy, how they will live longer, how they will be happier, how they will get better roads, better schools, lower taxes, cheaper groceries. . . In other words, your listener must see clearly and vividly that your proposal will help.

If you do not care to follow the preceding organization of a speech to convince, here is one which accomplishes the same end but is described differently:

1. State your proposition in the introduction.

2. Present a history of the problem which brought up the proposal you are asking for adoption.

3. Show that your proposal is *needed.* Offer evidence which establishes a *need* for *your* proposal. No other proposal (solution) will do.

4. Show that your proposition is *practical.* Give evidence to prove that it will do what you say it will do. In other words, show that it will work.

5. Show that your proposition is *desirable.* This means to give evidence showing that what it will do will be *beneficial* rather than harmful. For example: Concerning the desirability of military training people say, "Yes, military conscription will work, but it is *undesirable* because it will bring a militaristic control of our government."

6. Conclude your speech with a final statement in support of your proposal.

Note: If you are opposed to a certain proposal, you may establish your point of view by offering arguments which show any one of the following to be true:

1. The proposition is not needed. (Give evidence.)
2. The proposition is not practical. (Give evidence.)
3. The proposition is not desirable. (Give evidence.)

Of course, if you can establish all three of these points, you will be more convincing than if you prove only one.

You should be warned that you will face untold difficulty from your audience if you fail to have the body of your speech properly organized and all your points supported by evidence. The best guarantee of success is careful preparation. In addition to a well-organized speech with its points supported by evidence, you must have a well-constructed introduction and a powerful conclusion. Besides these considerations in relation to the materials of the speech itself, your oral practice will determine whether or not you are actually prepared to present a convincing speech. Even though you possess volumes of evidence, clear-cut organization, and vivid language, *you must deliver the speech confidently and well*, without excessive use of notes if anyone is to be convinced that you yourself are convinced of your own proposal.

Materials for preparing your subject can be secured from your library. Encyclopedias, reader's guides, magazine and newspaper guides all offer excellent sources. Check with your instructor and librarian for assistance.

HOW TO PRESENT A SPEECH TO PERSUADE
In general a frank, enthusiastic, and energetic presentation is desirable. A reasonable amount of emotion should be evident; however, it should not be overdone. Your bodily action should suit the words you utter and be such an integral part of your overall presentation that no attention is directed toward it. Vigor and intensity should characterize your bodily action. You must show by your actions that *you* are convinced. Your voice

should reflect a sincere belief in your views, and through inflections and modulations, carry the ring of truth and *personal conviction*. Sufficient force should be utilized to convey sound and meaning to all who listen.

Naturally, your presentation must vary according to your audience, the occasion, the size of the room, its acoustics, and the type of meeting before which you present your speech. You would not speak to a small group of business people in the same manner that you would address a large political gathering.

If you use notes, know them thoroughly. Do not try to hide them. Hold them high enough when looking at them that your head is not bowed or place them on the podium. After the conclusion of your talk, remain standing at least two to three seconds before you return to your seat. Check with your instructor to see if there will be time to take questions.

ON WOMAN'S RIGHT TO VOTE
by Susan B. Anthony

FRIENDS AND FELLOW CITIZENS: I stand before you tonight under indictment for the alleged crime of having voted at the last presidential election, without having a lawful right to vote. It shall be my work this evening to prove to you that in thus voting, I not only committed no crime, but, instead, simply exercised my citizen's rights, guaranteed to me and all United States citizens by the National Constitution, beyond the power of any State to deny. The Preamble of the Federal Constitution says:

"We, the people of the United States, in order to form a more perfect union, establish justice, insure domestic tranquility, provide for the common defense, promote the general welfare, and secure the blessings of liberty to ourselves and our posterity, do ordain and establish this Constitution for the United States of America."

It was we, the people, not we, the white male citizens; nor yet we, the male citizens; but we, the whole people, who formed the Union. And we formed it, not to give the blessings of liberty, but to secure them; not to the half of ourselves and the half of our posterity, but to the whole people – women as well as men. And it is downright mockery to talk to women of their enjoyment of the blessings of liberty while they are denied the use of the only means of securing them provided by this democratic-republican government – the ballot.

For any State to make sex a qualification that must ever result in the disfranchisement of one entire half of the people is to pass a bill of attainder, or an ex post facto law, and is therefore a violation of the supreme law of the land. by it the blessings of liberty are forever withheld from women and their female posterity.To them this government has no just powers derived from the consent of the governed.To them this government is not a democracy. It is not a republic. It is an odious aristocracy; a hateful oligarchy of sex; the most hateful aristocracy ever established on the face of the globe; an oligarchy of wealth, where the rich govern the poor.An oligarchy of learning, where the educated govern the ignorant, or even an oligarchy of race, where the Saxon rules the African might be endured; but this oligarchy of sex, which makes father, brothers, husband, sons, the oligarchies over the mother and sisters, the wife and daughters of every household – which ordains all men sovereigns, all women subjects, carries dissension, discord and rebellion into every home of the nation.

Webster, Worcester and Bouvier all define a citizen to be a person in the United States, entitled to vote and hold office.

The only question left to be settled now is: Are women persons?And I hardly believe any of our opponents will have the hardihood to say they are not.Being persons, then, women are citizens; and no State has a right to make any law, or to enforce an old law, that shall abridge their privileges or immunities. Hence, every discrimination against women in the constitutions and laws of the several States is today null and void, precisely as in every one against negroes.

Delivered in 1873 after she had been arrested, put on trial, and fined one hundred dollars for voting at the presidential election in 1872. She refused to pay the fine and never did pay it.

Chapter *10*

THE SPEECH TO MOTIVATE

Question: Should a speech be long or short? Answer: Speeches today seem to be growing shorter. Leave an audience wanting more rather than having had too much.

Time limits: 4-5 minutes.

Speaking notes: 50-word maximum limit.

Sources of information: Two are required, preferably three. For each source give the specific magazine or book it was taken from, title of the article, author's full name, date of publication, and the chapter or pages telling where the material was found. If a source is a person, identify the source completely by title, position, occupation, etc. List these on the outline form.

Outline your speech: Prepare a 75-150 word complete sentence outline.

PURPOSE OF THE SPEECH TO MOTIVATE

It is an accepted truth that people need to be stimulated or aroused if they are to be concerned about a proposition or problem that is laid before them. Often a speaker appeals to the audience to do something, to change their minds, to give consideration to an idea, but does not stir them sufficiently to make them willing to be more than mildly interested. As a speaker it is to your advantage to learn the methods and approaches that cause audiences to be stimulated by speech. This assignment will provide an experience for the speech to motivate so that you will be fully aware of the importance of this type of speech.

EXPLANATION OF THE SPEECH TO MOTIVATE

The speech to motivate an audience is one that does just that – it stimulates some action. It makes people want to do something, perhaps generalized, to correct a problem, although a specific action may not be in mind. If its purpose is fulfilled, it touches the emotions and influences the intellect of the audience sufficiently that they feel impelled to adopt new attitudes and/or take action suggested by the speaker. The basic features of this speech are these: use of vivid language, obvious sincerity and enthusiasm on the part of the speaker, and appeals to basic drives that all persons possess. Much of the persuasion is achieved by utilizing catchy slogans, concreteness, specific examples, illustrations, and facts. Contrast is stressed by playing the big against the little, the bad against the good, the money that can be earned against that which will not be earned, the sick against the well.

Best known occasions for the speech to persuade are anniversary memorials, dedications, commencement exercises, religious gatherings, conventions, rallies, pep meetings, sales promotions, and between-halves situations in which a coach arouses the team to a high pitch of fury accompanied by a will to win.

The speech demands that the speaker be aroused and vigorous. It calls for enthusiasm, energy, force, power, and spirit – the quantity and quality depending upon the response sought from the audience. But most of all it requires that the speaker be sincere.

HOW TO CHOOSE A TOPIC TO MOTIVATE AN AUDIENCE

Regardless of what kind of speech you present, it should always possess *sincerity*. Of all the many kinds of speeches there is none that demands sincerity from the speaker more than the speech that is intended to motivate. Therefore, in choosing a topic from the above list or in formulating your own topic, place sincerity foremost in your thinking. Do not try to find a subject that is suitable for the national congress or for presentation over a national radio network. Find a discussion suitable for your audience, in this case, your classmates. It does not have to be something big, something startling or overwhelming. The occasion does not call for such a speech. It does call for a speech appropriate to your situation, your audience, one within the scope of your experiences, and, above all, one in which you are sincere. Examine the topics in the appendix for ideas.

HOW TO PREPARE A SPEECH TO MOTIVATE

Basically, you will prepare this speech according to the steps followed in preparing any speech. It is essential that you give more than passing attention to your purpose to stimulate or arouse. This purpose will be behind every statement you utter. It will be superimposed over your entire construction, hence it will receive first consideration.

Having made yourself keenly aware of your purpose, you will next set about achieving this purpose. Naturally, your attention turns to organization. We will assume that you have gathered your materials and are ready to arrange them under the various divisions of your organization. First, as always, you will think of your introduction. It may be that you will construct it or alter it after certain other parts of your speech are completed, but certainly you will give it close attention before you are ready to state that your speech is prepared. In arranging and organizing the main body of your remarks, the language will undergo considerable scrutiny. Vivid phraseology, word pictures, graphic illustrations, all aptly told must be presented with words that contain acute meanings and definite associations in the minds of the listeners. You may also offer slogans and catchy phrases to make your ideas stick and remain with your listeners.

You will also be concrete and specific by naming certain persons and definite places that the speech calls for. You will avoid the abstract and intangible when giving examples, illustrations, and facts. This does not mean that you are to employ needless detail, but it does mean that your ideas must be aimed to hit their mark and make a strong impact. If you do not do this, it will be like trying to drive a spike with a tack hammer. As was stated in the paragraph entitled "Explanation of the Speech to Motivate," you will use contrast as a means of clarifying your thoughts and pointing up their significance. And last, you will stimulate your audience because throughout your entire speech you will have appealed to the basic drives in people: security from enemies, saving or making money, keeping their homes intact, gaining recognition, enjoying social prominence, having a cleaner city or town, knowing new experiences...You will have touched your listeners' pride, their pocketbooks and bank accounts, their sympathies, their families – yes, even their fighting spirit. Once you have stimulated your audience, thoroughly aroused them, if the speech demands it, be sure to tell them what to do or what action to take, whether it be to think or perform. If you do not do this you will be generated power but failed to use it.

As usual, there is no better source of materials for a speech than the media center. The librarian and your instructor will assist you in locating materials. There may be persons on the faculty or friends you know who have special knowledge that you can use. Do not overlook interviews with them.

The last step in preparing this speech will be rehearsal. Be sure you rehearse enough that you know from memory the sequence of ideas, not words, that you plan to present. Practice before a mirror and/or friends until you feel competent to stand before an audience.

HOW TO PRESENT A SPEECH TO MOTIVATE

A forceful, dynamic, and energetic presentation should be used unless you are speaking on a solemn occasion involving reverence, devotion or deep feeling. In such cases your voice and manner should be animated and sincere with projection of your ideas accompanied by appropriate bodily action and gestures. On other occasions, indications should show that you are alive with your subject, full of it, and eager for others to share it. Above all, you must be sincere and earnest. Remember that your audience will reflect your activity and eloquence. They will be just as lively or solemn as you stimulate them to be. The use of appropriate diagrams, charts, and demonstrations can add much to your speech.

BURIED ALIVE*
by Kimberly L. Jones

There's something in the air that is wearing away at the tombstones in Jacksonville, Arkansas; it's causing dime-sized holes between the nostrils of workers in Newark, New Jersey. In Staten Island the snow is turning red. In rural Michigan, geese are born with their wings on backward; and in Tennessee, the Blue Ridge Mountains are turning brown. Why? Maybe you've read about it; maybe you've only heard about it, but the fact of the matter is, we all know very little about this deadly culprit. What is it that looms ahead, overshadowing our future health and our environment? It's hazardous waste.

In 1977 the residents of a suburb of Niagara Falls realized that out of sight, out of mind does not often apply. Between 1942 and 1953, Hooker Chemicals dumped more than 21,000 tons of highly toxic waste into an old excavation known as Love Canal. Hooker then sold the canal area to the Niagara School Board for $1.00 on the condition that they would not be held liable for any future injury or damage. An elementary school and several housing projects were then built on the clay capped dump site ignoring all warnings concerning its dangers. By 1976, complaints of chemical burns and smells were constant, but ignored by city officials. Within one year chemicals from badly corroded barrels began leaking into the sewers, gardens, and basements of nearby homes. As the topsoil began to settle, rains surfaced barrels and their deadly contents to contaminate the entire area. Following health studies revealed an usually high rate of miscarriages, birth defects, cancer, and deaths. Although the memory of this tragedy has faded with time, we have yet to reveal the long term effects.

It is a vivid reminder that we can never throw anything away. This event triggered the realization that one of our country's primary environmental concerns is dealing with the large amounts of hazardous waste produced today, as well as coping with what is stored in the some 50,000 sites before any security or regulation.

We've forgotten about Love Canal maybe because we couldn't relate to the victims, or maybe because miscarriages and cancer have become an everyday, almost blasé tragedy. But what we must admit is that it's not over yet. No one knows the long term effects of contamination on anyone. Are we talking about more cancer? Widespread disease? Deaths? Mutant babies? Or perhaps no babies at all?

Why hasn't something been done? How can we sit here and listen to this, and yet allow it to continue? Maybe because it is far easier to avoid an issue than it is to address it and display the ignorance and laziness at the root of the problem. As of now, many states are not even required to monitor all of their hazardous wastes. A 1984 study by the National Academy of Scientists, revealed that only about 20% of the 710,000 chemicals in commercial use have ever been subjected to extensive toxicity testing, and one-third of them have never been tested at all.

In Massachusetts, because there are no waste facilities, they opt to ship out their hazards to states as far away as Alabama. Now maybe this doesn't sound like such a bad idea, but what we must realize is that between 1980 and 1985, 7,000 accidents occurred when waste was transported from one place to another. It involved the release of 210,000 tons of chemical waste, it killed 139 people, and caused at least 50 million dollars in property damage. But safely storing and transporting materials is hardly even a significant issue anymore, because today we have no place to store it at all. With each of us producing 1.1 tons of it per year – 292 million tons for the nation, the most optimistic of figures claims that we will reach commercial capacity in another 10 years at best. Sure, it is one thing to hear about a dump across town, yet quite another to be warned not to drink the water from your town tap. Well, it is happening. It has contaminated the drinking water drawn on by some 3 million people in Long Island.

In Atlantic City, New Jersey, the city was forced to shift its well field in an effort to escape chemicals leaking from a chemical waste site only a mile away. But rather than an urgent address, our government at all levels has avoided the issue and in some cases made it worse. Recently the FDA has encouraged widespread use of poly-vinyl chloride, a tough plastic used in the production of shower curtains and rain coats for packaging food and beverages. Not only do plastics constitute the most serious of our toxic pollution due to chlorine level, but this throw away convenience we suddenly cannot do without is being tossed at intolerable rates into our fragile environment. What is it? It's yesterday's newspaper, it's our Styrofoam coffee cups, and our disposable diapers. Once this so called convenience is placed into our environment it becomes just as hazardous as any chemical waste.

Each year the U.S. produces more than 5.1 billion tons of solid refuse averaging out to 115 pounds a day for each of us. We've thrown it into the oceans, we've burned it in incinerators, and we've dumped it into landfills. We even look proudly to a ski resort built around a dump in Colorado.

Well, this is ridiculous, and enough is enough! It is time to recognize the significance of this problem. In the next decade this nation will be buried alive under a mountain of trash and left to die. It has become a personal problem. But where does our involvement end? Too many of us don't understand that it doesn't end as soon as we bag up the motor oil and the plastic sandwich bags. Nor does it end when the Hefties are picked up from the curbside to be hauled away.

Each of us can reduce our own exposure to contamination by insisting that existing laws are expanded and this time enforced. We must also ensure that protection agencies are adequately staffed and funded. But most importantly, there must be a public outcry for recycling. This simple act is perhaps the solution to our crisis. But recycling will only become widespread if there is a large market for it. Providing favorable tax incentives and transportation rates for secondary materials will help, but they are not enough. Local, state, and federal procurement policies and laws must be changed to require that a percentage of all materials our government purchases be made partially from totally recycled materials.

There is also enormous potential for both waste recycling and waste trading – yet we have done little to advance technology in this area. It is actually possible to use both the chemical and solid waste from one company, and convert it into useable material for another company's production.

Each of us can do little things. Individual acts such as consumption and litter have contributed to the problems because we allow ourselves to rationalize that this little bit won't hurt. Multiply that by 250 million Americans saying the same thing. Recycling an aluminum can, writing on both sides of the paper, and refusing to buy grocery products with packaging inside of packaging are all very significant acts. This environmental crisis is not only more complex than we think, but it is more complex than we could ever think. Certainly our involvement could never end if our land, our air and our groundwater become too contaminated to use for basic survival.

*This speech placed first in 1990 at both the Kansas State Championship Tournament for original oratory and the Flint Hills NFL qualifying tournament for nationals.

HOW CAN I ORGANIZE A PERSUASIVE SPEECH?

Use a five step sequence of ideas to help motivate your audience to action developed by Alan Monroe.

1. Attention. Get the attention of the audience and state your topic.

2. Need. Explain why there is a problem or why something needs to be done.

3. Satisfaction. Provide a solution that will satisfy the need.

4. Visualization. Help the audience see what it would be like if we did what you ask or what it would be like if we did nothing.

5. Action. Explain to the audience what specific actions they can take to solve the need.

Chapter *11*

THE SALES TALK

Question: Should a person vary the rate of speaking?
Answer: Yes, but be natural. Variety is a prerequisite of good speech.

Time limits: 5-6 minutes.
Speaking notes: Do not use notes when trying to sell something to an audience.
Sources of information: Two are required, preferably three. For each source give the specific magazine or book it was taken from, title of the article, author's full name, date of publication, and the chapter or page telling where the material was found. If a source is a person, identify the source completely by title, position, occupation, etc. List these on the outline form.
Outline your speech: Prepare a 75-100 word complete sentence outline.

PURPOSE OF THE SALES TALK

The sales talk is something you may be called upon to present much sooner than you now expect. It involves a situation in which you usually try to trade or sell a group of persons an article in exchange for their money. Sometimes this is a difficult task. Many persons have had little or no experience in this particular type of speaking and selling. This one experience is not intended to make a sales expert out of anyone, but certainly it will help the person who later finds it necessary to sell something to a group.

EXPLANATION OF THE SALES TALK

A sales talk is a speech in which you will attempt to persuade a group of people to buy a product from you now or at a later date. In some instances, you will actually take orders at the conclusion of your remarks; in other cases, you will merely stimulate an interest in your goods so that prospective customers will buy from you later. But in either case, your purpose is to sell by stimulating the customer to want what you have and to be willing to part with money to acquire the goods you have for sale.

The sales talk makes special demands on the speaker. You must be pleasing in appearance, pleasant to meet, congenial, and friendly. You must be thoroughly familiar with the product and be conversant with all matters pertaining to it, including many details.

The speaker should, by all means, be able and willing to answer questions regarding the production, the manufacturers (or the company sponsoring it, such as an insurance company), the cost, terms of selling, guarantees, repairs, cost of upkeep, and other such matters about the product. The speaker should know how to meet objections, questions, or comparisons made relative to the product, as opposed to a competitive product.

Occasions for the sales talk are many. We might say that any time a speaker appears before one or more persons with the purpose of selling, it is a sales talk. Think about occasions where you have heard a sales pitch – someone at your door selling Girl Scout cookies, someone at a fair showing you the latest kitchen gadget, or someone at your school telling you about class rings. The main idea is that prospective customers can be any kind of people and be met anywhere and at any time.

HOW TO CHOOSE A TOPIC FOR A SALES TALK

Choose a product for sale that you believe in; then build your talk around it. Be sure to select something your audience needs and can use. Some natural topics are athletic equipment, computers, food, school books, a movie or play. For additional suggestions, ask your instructor.

HOW TO PREPARE A SALES TALK

First of all, follow the regular steps of preparation used for any speech. You know these. Pay particular attention to diagnosing your audience. It would be fatal to misjudge your prospective buyers. You should know as much as possible about these items concerning their personal situations: probable incomes, credit ratings, occupations, religions, education, local beliefs, and anything else that concerns them.

A wise salesperson will find out what other salespersons have sold or tried to sell the group in the way of competitive products. The salesperson will also be familiar enough with these products to make comparisons favorable to their own.

It will be advisable in all cases to demonstrate whatever you are selling. This means that you must know how to show it to the best advantage. Be sure, very sure, that it is in good appearance and working order. Let your customers try it out. If it is candy, pass samples around. If it is a computer, let them work on it.

It is essential that you be ready to sign order contracts. This will necessitate your having pen and ink, order forms, credit information, checkbooks, and receipts for use. Do not make buyers wait if they are ready to buy.

Another point is to be prepared to greet the audience promptly. Go to the designated meeting place early. Have everything in proper and neat arrangement before your audience arrives. After you think you have every display most advantageously placed, all sales forms in order, and everything in tip-top shape, go back for a final check. If you have omitted nothing, then you are ready.

As for your speech, have it well in mind. Do not use notes. It would be foolish to attempt to sell something while referring to notes in order to discover the good points of your product.

The organization of your speech should be well thought out. One plan which can be recommended is the one that follows.

1. Give a friendly introduction, stating your pleasure in meeting the audience. Be sincere.

2. Present information about yourself and your product. Who are you? What position do you hold? How long have you been with this company? Why did you choose to work for your particular company? What is the name of the company? Hold old is it? Is it a nationwide organization? Is it financially sound? Is it reliable? Does it stand behind its products? Does it guarantee its products? Does it quibble over an adjustment if a customer asks for one? Does it have a larger dealer organization? Can you get parts and repairs quickly if these are needed? Does the company plan to stay in business? Does it test all of its products before placing them on the market? How large is its business? What special recommendations does the company have? Of course, it may not be necessary to answer all of these questions; however, many of them will have to be answered by giving information which establishes you as a reputable salesperson and your company as a reputable firm.

Now that you have laid the groundwork, you are ready to show and explain the goods or services you have for sale. The nature of what you are selling will demonstrate how you do this. Probably, the first thing you will do will be to explain the purpose of your product; that is, you will tell what it is for.

Next you will explain and demonstrate how it operates. In doing this, be sure to play up its advantages, its special features, new improvements, economy of operation, dependability, beauty, ease of handling, and the like. Give enough details to be clear but not so much that you confuse your listeners.

At this point you have established yourself, your company, and you have explained and demonstrated your product. Your next step will require careful analysis of your audience. This is done to show how your product will benefit them. You must know their wants and needs and let them see vividly how your products will benefit them. If the article is a box of chocolates, the buyer will delight family and friends by serving them. If the salesperson is offering a correspondence school course, the buyer will make more money, gain prestige, secure advancements by buying the course.

Whatever the sales item, you must show the advantages and benefits of the ownership of it. Sometimes it is helpful to mention the names of other persons who have bought the product from you and are now benefiting from ownership of it.

And now comes the last step. How may they buy it? Where? When? Who sells it, if you carry only samples? How much does it cost? Do you sell on the installment plan? What are the interest charges? How much do you require as a down payment? How many months are allowed in paying for it? What is the amount of the monthly payments? Or is it cash? Is any discount allowed for cash? What special inducement is offered to those who buy now? How much can they save? Will future prices be higher? Do you take trade-ins? How much allowance is made on a trade-in?

Make it as easy and simple as possible to buy the goods you are selling. Be sure that your explanations are clear and exact. Do not use misleading terms or glib wrong impressions. If your sales ability will not withstand a full, complete, and candid examination, you will be wise to change your policies or change your vocation.

To be able to present the above information effectively, to demonstrate the product, to show the prospective customers how they will benefit from owning your goods, and how they may buy it, you will rehearse the demonstration and accompanying speech aloud many times. Do this until you have attained complete mastery of the entire speech.

HOW TO PRESENT A SALES TALK

Look good; be good. In other words have a neat and pleasing appearance, plus a friendly and polite attitude. These points are extremely important. Your own good judgment will tell you what is appropriate dress. Your common sense will provide the background for the right attitude. Generally, you should begin your speech directly, if this procedure is appropriate to the mood of your listeners. Avoid being smart or using questionable stories to impress your listeners. Put the group at ease and get on with the speech.

Your manner should be conversational; your voice should be easily heard by all but not strained. Your bodily action should be suitable for holding attention, making transitions, and demonstrating what you are selling. Your language, of course, should be simple, descriptive, vivid, and devoid of technical terms.

In using charts, pictures, diagrams, or the sales article itself, your familiarity with these should be so great that you can point out any information or refer to any part of the product while retaining a posture that permits focusing your attention on the audience. In answering questions you should be as clear as possible and sure that your questioner is satisfied with the information you give. Avoid embarrassing anyone. An alert and enthusiastic yet friendly attitude is most desirable.

SPECIAL HINTS

Do not knock your competitors or their products; it is better to praise the opposition. If you have any special inducements to encourage the buying of your product, be sure to present them at the appropriate time.

After concluding your talk allow your audience time to ask questions. It may be that some of them will wish to ask questions during your speech. If this is the case, be sure to answer them clearly; however, do not turn the meeting into a question and answer occasion before explaining your wares.

THE JAYHAWK MUG
A Sales Talk by Margie Hapke

Good Morning . . . Excuse me. . . Just a minute. . . Oh man, I hate it when it happens . . . You know what the problem is. It's these styrofoam cups. They are so flimsy and unreliable. I'm sure it's happened to you too. It happens to everyone at some point in time or another. These styrofoam cups are just worthless. But today I've got a product here to show you that will solve the problem of the flimsy and unreliable cups forever.

It's the Jayhawk Mug. Now the Jayhawk Mug has numerous features that give it a definite advantage over styrofoam and paper cups, and produces benefits not only to you the user, but to the environment as well. Now the Jayhawk Mug is made from hard plastics that are guaranteed not to split or crack, eliminating the problem that you all just witnessed. The mug also features double wall construction that provides it with thermal insulation keeping your hot drinks hot and your cold drinks cold without changing the outside temperature of the mug. How many times have you filled a styrofoam cup with hot coffee only to find out it's so hot you can't hold on to it? And what about in the summertime when you have the styrofoam cup full of ice and Coke and the thing sweats and gets your hand all wet and drips all over your shoes? It's really a nuisance. The Jayhawk Mug's double wall construction eliminates that problem – a definite advantage.

Another benefit of the mug is a reduced charge for refills offered at all the Kansas Union concession outlets. This mug holds 32 ounces of any beverage like Coke, coffee, iced tea, and can be refilled with any beverage for just 60 cents. That same amount of product in a one-time use styrofoam cup would cost you at least a dollar .

And speaking of one-time-use-only, that's probably the biggest benefit of using the Jayhawk Mug – the benefit to the environment. Styrofoam is a hazard in our landfills because it just doesn't bio-degrade . By reusing the Jayhawk Mug you can help significantly reduce the amount of non-degradable styrofoam that the KU campus sends to landfills each week.

Now, how can you get your very own Jayhawk Mug? It's easy. You just stop in at any one of KU's concession outlets. The Mug sells for two dollars and fifty cents. It's a great price. It's affordable. And a savings from just six refills pays for it. So run across the street to the Wescoe Beach and pick yourself up a Jayhawk Mug today. You'll never walk around with a wet T-Shirt again.

Chapter **12**

THE SPEECH TO ENTERTAIN

Question: Should a person learn to tell good jokes?
Answer: Yes. You will enjoy it and so will others.

Time limits: 5-6 minutes.
Speaking notes: 10-15 word maximum limit.
Sources of information: Two are required, preferably three. For each source give the specific magazine or book it was taken from title of the article, author's full name, date of publication, and the chapter or pages telling where the material was found. If a source is a person, identify the source completely by title, position, occupation, etc. List these on the outline form.
Outline your speech: Prepare a 75-150 word complete sentence outline.

PURPOSE OF THE SPEECH TO ENTERTAIN

Many persons try to be entertaining when giving speeches. Some succeed and some do not. There is a common misconception about the difficulty of presenting a speech to entertain: the idea is current that the speech to entertain is a "breeze," that nothing is difficult about it, and that a series of risque stories or jokes meet the requirements for a speech to entertain. This is far from the truth: a humorous speech is one of the most difficult to present effectively. Because of this difficulty and for the reason that you may be called at a future date to deliver a humorous speech, this assignment is presented.

EXPLANATION OF THE SPEECH TO ENTERTAIN

A speech to entertain utilizes humor. It may rely on words, anecdotes, bodily actions, gestures, voice, speech construction, special devices, demonstrations, unusual situations, pantomimes or a combination of any or all of these.

Its purpose varies both in relation to the amount and type of humorous response the speech is planned to elicit from the audience. Some speeches make listeners laugh gaily and loudly; others produce only chuckles and snickers; and others bring forth only grins and smiles of amusement. It is important for a student to understand that a humorous speech does not need to be uproariously funny to entertain. We might be better understood if we were to call this speech a speech to amuse.

The special feature of a humorous speech is that it does not demand that a speaker do more than catch the attention and interest of an audience and then hold these by developing a *trend of thought* or *an idea*. The speaker is not required to make the audience feel that they are closely related to the subject and that they must derive a moral or new philosophy from the remarks. Nor does the speaker have to ask them to take any action. It should be understood at this point, however, that a humorous speech *may* do more than simply entertain. There is nothing to prevent its being informative, stimulating, or convincing, provided none of these goals becomes the chief aim of the speaker. The chief aim of the speech is to entertain. The thought or ideas presented are the core of the speech around which humor is built. The overall effect is one in which the audience finds a definite trend of thought and philosophy presented delightfully and entertainingly.

Occasions for humorous speeches are found ordinarily at dinners, club meetings, special assemblies, parties, and gatherings at which weighty discussions are inappropriate and out of harmony with the mood of the occasion.

HOW TO CHOOSE A TOPIC FOR A SPEECH TO ENTERTAIN

In selecting a topic for a humorous speech, keep in mind the five necessary considerations that govern the selection of any speech topic, that is, the audience, the occasion, the speaker, the speech itself, and the surroundings in which the speech will be given. Your choice of a topic must be keyed to controlling factors. It is important to note that you may have a mixed audience with a widespread interest or taste. You must consider the probable speaking environment. Of course, since you will be the speaker, the subject that you choose must be one which you can present acceptably.

The topic should be viewed from the standpoint of the time allowed for preparation, the availability of materials from which to build the speech, your own personality, your position in the community, your ability to present certain kinds of material and ideas, and your type of presentation. You should make your choice of topic with all of these considerations in mind. The topic ideas in the appendix should stimulate your thinking.

HOW TO PREPARE A SPEECH TO ENTERTAIN

As in the preparation of any good speech, particular attention much be paid to organization of points, the arrangement of materials, and the rehearsal of the speech. The purpose, to entertain, should be clearly in mind; the purpose is assisted by a thorough understanding of the methods to be used for fulfilling this purpose.

This type of speech requires a considerable study of references and some consultation with your instructor. In addition to the factors of good speech preparation previously studied, ample rehearsal is positively necessary. It is difficult to imagine anything more grotesque than a speaker's attempt to present a humorous speech and constantly referring to notes, because of inadequate preparation of the speech. Timing is important in securing a humorous response, and practice improves timing.

The humorous speech should not degenerate into a series of unrelated funny stories, nor should it merely consist of the telling of one story. Exaggerations or episodes used as illustrations must apply to the theme of the speech or in some way assist the speaker in making the point. Only careful preparation and rehearsal will assure one that they are using illustrations properly.

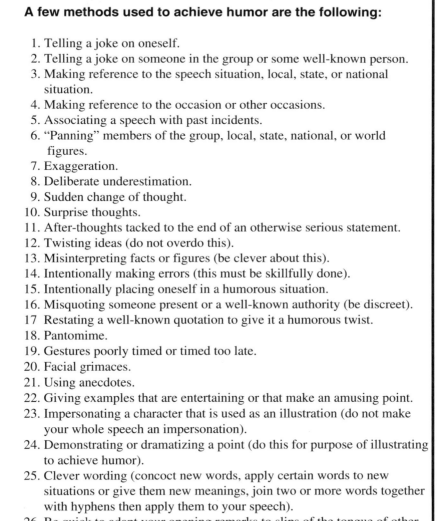

A few methods used to achieve humor are the following:

1. Telling a joke on oneself.
2. Telling a joke on someone in the group or some well-known person.
3. Making reference to the speech situation, local, state, or national situation.
4. Making reference to the occasion or other occasions.
5. Associating a speech with past incidents.
6. "Panning" members of the group, local, state, national, or world figures.
7. Exaggeration.
8. Deliberate underestimation.
9. Sudden change of thought.
10. Surprise thoughts.
11. After-thoughts tacked to the end of an otherwise serious statement.
12. Twisting ideas (do not overdo this).
13. Misinterpreting facts or figures (be clever about this).
14. Intentionally making errors (this must be skillfully done).
15. Intentionally placing oneself in a humorous situation.
16. Misquoting someone present or a well-known authority (be discreet).
17 Restating a well-known quotation to give it a humorous twist.
18. Pantomime.
19. Gestures poorly timed or timed too late.
20. Facial grimaces.
21. Using anecdotes.
22. Giving examples that are entertaining or that make an amusing point.
23. Impersonating a character that is used as an illustration (do not make your whole speech an impersonation).
24. Demonstrating or dramatizing a point (do this for purpose of illustrating to achieve humor).
25. Clever wording (concoct new words, apply certain words to new situations or give them new meanings, join two or more words together with hyphens then apply them to your speech).
26. Be quick to adapt your opening remarks to slips of the tongue of other speakers. Do not overwork this device or it will become tiresome and trite; be approipriate.
27. Persons in public life, international situations, recent happenings in the news. . . all offer excellent opportunities for entertainment. Think about the strategies talk show hosts employ in their monologues.

In actually setting up the speech to entertain you will follow the principles laid down for any speech; you will construct a clever and interesting introduction; you will develop your remarks point by point in logical order; you will bolster these points with examples, illustrations, facts, quotations from authorities, analogies, and conclusions, which you will draw from the material you present. Lastly you will have a conclusion to your speech which is appropriate to all you have said. It becomes evident that a speech to entertain simply does what every other speech does, and in addition – this is important – it utilizes materials that in themselves carry and imply humor. The selection of these humorous materials, their arrangement in the speech, and the words used to present the ideas are what achieve the effect of entertainment.

Now, you ask, "How do I know my speech will be entertaining?" The answer is that you do not. The only assurance you can get is from your preparation. Frankly this is dependent entirely on your own effort and ability. It is difficult, very difficult, to select, to organize, to word, and to rehearse a speech to entertain, but you must do these preparations, nevertheless. Your own ingenuity and your own intelligence are the only assets you can have in preparing the humorous speech for presentation. Use these inherent personal resources well and you will have little to worry about. There simply is no quick, easy way to prepare an entertaining speech – or any other for that matter. Any student looking for a short cut, would be wise to end the search and to apply the time to preparation. That is what is necessary in the end anyway, if anything more than a mediocre speech is to be prepared for presentation.

HOW TO PRESENT A SPEECH TO ENTERTAIN

The humorous speech is characterized generally by a lively presentation. The speaker may be whimsical, facetious, gay, jovial, or may present a mixture of these moods. The speaker should be pleasant, of course. Bearing and decorum should reflect visibly the feelings and tenor of the remarks.

The speech should progress with a smooth forward motion. Delays and hesitations should be avoided, excepting those employed for a special effect. If laughter is incited, the speaker should carefully refrain from resuming the talk until that moment just before all laughter has stopped. Speakers should never laugh at their own jokes or indicate that they know they are funny.

It is necessary, however, that the speaker obviously enjoys the audience and occasion. One of the greatest dangers is that the inexperienced speaker will prolong anecdotes, the jokes, or the whole speech. Try to hit the punch lines when they are hot and then to move on to the next ones.

There is one last word of caution: watch your posture; use appropriate bodily actions and gestures; speak loudly enough to be heard by everyone; articulate well; and use good English.

THE PLIGHT OF THE ONION
A Speech to Entertain by John E. Koch

Ordinarily, Ladies and Gentlemen, I am a very peaceful individual. It requires an event of great importance to stir my peaceful nature. Lately, such an event has come to pass. I must speak out in defense of my convictions, for silence would prove me a traitor not only to my own generation, but to generations to come. I cannot display indifference when the issue demands enthusiasm.

Just what is this issue that stirs the hearts of men to take arms against that sea of troubles and by opposing, end them? I do not feel that I am unique in being affected by this onslaught on human liberty. You, Ladies and Gentlemen, have also been touched by this debasement of our customs and traditions. What is this menace of which I speak that poses such a threat to all that we hold so dear? Is it a green-eyed fire-spouting monster from Mars, or a creature from the moon. No, it is not. It is one of our own kind. It is referred to as a scientist.

It will suffice to mention no names since we must judge them by their works. The intrusion of these people on our liberties has caused many to sound the call to arms; for when we are enveloped by that sea of troubles, we must fight back or swim.

The scene of attack is Idaho State University. There, a group of scientists, as they call themselves, have been secretly experimenting, unbelievable as it may seem, to deprive the onion of its cooking odor. In some secret cache are hidden away thousands of odorless onions, the first line of odor-free American vegetables.

Picture the onion without its smell, and you deprive millions of Americans of a familiar fragrance that signals the secrets of the coming meal. To remove its odor is to destroy all that is dear to it – its personality. The thought is enough to cause tears to one's eyes.

Although this is bad enough, the scientists will not stop here. They will not remain content with having removed the odor from the onion, but with their long tentacles they will reach out farther into the realm of life. What will be next – the smell of cooking cabbage, the grit of spinach, the hot of peppers, and soon the removal of color and taste? Will our diet become a mass of odorless, tasteless, colorless nourishment? It might, if we do not arise and take arms to prevent this calamity. I beg you to rally defenders to the cause of the onion.

As Americans, we must demand the onion with its odor, the spinach with its grit, the pepper with its hot. Let us not sit here idly any longer. Arise and carry that plea to all Americans. Keep the scientist out of the kitchen; keep the onion out of the college.

HOW SHOULD MY SPEECH BE ORGANIZED?

1. *Chronologically.* Arrange the information according to how it happened in time.

2. *Topically.* Arrange the information according to the different topics you will cover.

3. *Spatially.* Arrange the information how it physically appears in a certain space.

4. *Problem/solution.* Present the problem, then the possible solutions to the problem.

5. *Cause/effect.* Identify the cause of something, and then identify its effect.

Chapter *13*

AFTER DINNER SPEAKING

Question: What is the best type of speech for a beginner?
Answer: Generally an informative speech. Don't avoid other kinds, however.

Time limits: 3 minutes –This time limit is necessary in order that each person may be permitted to speak. Longer speeches may extend the time too much.
Speaking notes: 10-word maximum.
Hint: Although you are not required to prepare an outline or to read source materials, it will be wise to do both for your own benefit.

PURPOSE OF AFTER DINNER SPEAKING

One of the best ways to learn anything is actually to experience it. From the experience of preparing this speech assignment, you will gain first-hand knowledge of after dinner speaking. You will see how the program is arranged, how the order of serving is coordinated with the speeches, and how the toastmaster must carry on and keep events moving. You will acquire much other valuable information concerning after dinner speaking. You will learn it because you will help build the entire program and because you will be a speaker at the dinner.

This experience is proposed so that you may broaden your knowledge of the various types of after dinner speeches and their related activities.

EXPLANATION OF AFTER DINNER SPEAKING

After dinner speaking is giving a speech following a meal at which a group has gathered. The speech may have a serious purpose or it may be designed to give entertainment and pleasure. The type of speech which you present depends on the purpose of your talk. The type of speech is governed also by the occasion, its objective, and the reason for your remarks. After dinner speeches require that the speaker follow closely all the rules of organization previously noted, particularly those for serious talks.

Occasions for the after dinner speech are many. They may be business luncheons, club dinners, committee meetings, special breakfasts, promotional gatherings, campaign inaugurations, socials, celebrations, anniversaries, or any one of a dozen other occasions.

HOW TO CHOOSE A TOPIC FOR AFTER DINNER SPEAKING

Decide on the purpose of your speech. Be sure you can develop your topic to fulfill that purpose. Select something suitable and interesting to you , yet adapted to the occasion and audience. Adapt the theme, if there is one, for the occasion. As with any other speech, plan your topic well in advance. Appendix A has additional suggestions.

HOW TO PREPARE AN AFTER DINNER SPEECH

First of all, study this assignment carefully to learn fully the requirements of successful after dinner speaking. Follow previous information relative to speech organization, wording, and practice. Plan to use no notes. If you are a toastmaster, knowledge of and preparation for your task are the only assurances of a satisfactory performance.

The speaker's obligations: The preparation for this talk is no different from that of any other speech of the type you intend to present. Possibly your thoughts will be to entertain. If this is true, of course you will prepare a speech to entertain. Should you not be familiar with the requirements of this kind of speech, turn to Chapter 12. Follow this procedure for any type of speech you wish to deliver whether it be the speech to convince, to inform, or to motivate.

Having ascertained your subject and the manner in which you will treat it, complete the preparation of your speech carefully. Before you consider yourself fully prepared, find out all you can about the program, when you will speak, who will precede you, and who will follow you. Then be sure that your speech is in line with the occasion.

It is not necessary and certainly not always advisable that a speaker plan to tell a joke on the toastmaster, regardless of what the toastmaster may do in the way of introduction. If the occasion calls for humor, a person should be ready to meet it. If it is doubtful what to do, play it safe. Good taste never offends. As far as risque stories go, leave them at home. The world has a great storehouse of humor and stories for all who want them, and these are excellent for after dinner speeches.

To complete the preparation of your after dinner speech, practice it aloud several times before a mirror or tape record. It is a splendid idea to ask a friend or friends to hear you in rehearsal. Before you accept their advice or criticisms too literally, give some thought to their suggestions and the reliability of their advice.

The toastmaster's obligations are to see that everything is ready to go, to open the proceedings, to keep them going, and to close the meeting. Let us examine these duties separately.

First, to arrange everything, you should arrive at the meeting place early, at least by an hour. Then perform the following chores: (1) advise the servers in detail as to how the meal is to be served; (2) note the arrangement of the banquet room and suggest any changes desired; (3) inquire about a checkroom or other space for coats and make certain it is available and ready for use; (4) locate restrooms and be ready to direct persons to them; (5) shortly before serving time, personally check place cards on the tables to be sure that the right number is available; (6) keep careful check on the guests as they arrive so that you will know when everyone is there; (7) indicate to the group when they are to go into the dining hall, that is, if they have been waiting in a lobby. If everyone has previously gathered in the dining room, be the first to seek your chair as a signal that the others should follow suit; (8) your general duty will be to see that guests are welcomed by yourself or another designated person, that they are introduced, their coats properly disposed of, and that they are entertained and put at ease; (9) during the banquet, constantly remain alert to see that all goes well, and (10) see that the committee pays for the banquet or makes definite arrangements to settle the account later. Also see that a tip is left for the servers. Of course, when there are several toastmasters, these duties may be divided among them. Everyone should know specifically what they are to do and should carry out each obligation conscientiously.

In regard to the actual work of introducing the speakers, considerable information must be gathered and set up several days early. This includes these necessary items: (1) The names of the speakers; (2) their topics; (3) data concerning speakers that will be suitable to use when introducing them; and (4) the order of the speakers. All this must be drawn together at a toastmasters' meeting and definitely agreed on by mutual consent. The act of introducing the speakers requires ingenuity and planning. A toastmaster should learn early that they are not to make speeches. This pleasure belongs to the after dinner speakers. The toastmaster merely presents each speaker by giving a short introduction. Thirty seconds usually suffices, sometimes less, but never more than a minute or two, at the maximum. At this banquet the thirty second limit should prevail. The introduction may be a clever statement or two about the speaker, their name, and topic. A fitting anecdote is in order if the occasion demands it. After the speaker concludes the speech, the toastmaster should get on with the show and not take time out to offer a rebuttal to some remark made by the speaker.

Throughout the evening's performances, the toastmasters should agree on matters such as when and whom to applaud and any other activities or procedures that should be initiated by the toastmasters.

HOW TO PRESENT AN AFTER DINNER SPEECH

Your presentation should reflect the type of speech you deliver. Generally speaking, a simple organization, graphic word pictures, sufficient humor, lively and animated delivery, and a forward motion of ideas characterize after dinner speeches.

Voice and bodily action should be in harmony with the speech occasion and environment. The chances are that you will not need to talk loudly to be heard, nor will you be permitted much bodily action because of room accommodations and arrangement. Care should be exercised when rising to speak, or your chair may scrape noisily on the floor making you appear awkward. To prevent this, see that your chair is far enough from the table that you may rise freely without moving the chair. When the chairperson, toastmaster, or president introduces you, rise and address them according to the position they hold; such as, "Mr. Toastmaster," "Madam President," and the like.

If during the program some person appearing ahead of you unknowingly steals your speech, the best thing for you to do when you speak is to refer to their remarks in support of your statements. You can go ahead then with your own thoughts and elaborate on them as necessary and as has been planned. "Ad lib" and improvise as the situation demands. Retain a sense of humor; use it if it is appropriate, and observe time limits. Remember that the program committee allotted only a certain amount of time to you.

GROUP PLANS TO BE MADE

To make this experience real, you should by all means hold this meeting at a local hotel, cafe, school cafeteria or other place where the class can meet and eat without crowding. The atmosphere should be absolutely real, no make-believe.

In order to prepare successfully for this dinner, the following arrangements should be completed by separate committees:

Committee No. 1:

The reservation and menu committee should set a date for the luncheon and reserve a suitable place to hold it. Committee members should check carefully the size of the room and whether or not there will be extra charge for the use of the room. Serving facilities should be ascertained and assurance should be received that the group will not be disturbed by customers, if they are in a public restaurant. It is to be noted also if there is lobby space in which to gather and check coats before going into the dining room. At least three different menus and their respective costs should be investigated and submitted to the class. One menu should be adopted and a price limit established. The time the meal will be served should be announced. It may be a noon or evening function, but preferably an evening one.

Committee No. 2:

The decorations committee decides what, if any, decorations are to be used. A fund must be established to cover any costs. Expenditure must be kept within the limits of this fund.

Committee No. 3:

The toastmaster's committee, approximately twenty-five percent of the class, will act as toastmasters. They should be elected by secret ballot. Each class member will write on a piece of paper as many names as there are to be toastmasters. If five is the number of toastmasters, then the five persons whose names are written the greatest number of times will be declared elected. They in turn, will meet as a committee to decide the order in which they will preside and the order of those they will introduce. They will learn in advance the topic of each speaker, thus preventing overlapping talks. Each toastmaster should plan to introduce a series of speakers, after which they will present the next toastmaster who will continue in the same manner. The first toastmaster will open the meeting and introduce guests. This may be done just before starting to eat, or it may be done at the first part of the program following the dinner. The last toastmaster, after introducing the speakers, should make appropriate closing remarks and adjourn the meeting. It is often embarrassing to everyone present if the last toastmaster does not make it absolutely clear that the banquet is concluded.

This use of several toastmasters may be somewhat unconventional but this arrangement gives more persons the experience as toastmaster. It adds variety to the program, provides opportunity for originality, and generally enhances the experience. It also suggests a basis for comparison of ideas as to what makes a good toastmaster.

Committee No. 4:
The collection committee is responsible collecting in advance the proper amount from each class member. They will divide and deliver this money to each committee chairman whose group has incurred a debt which must be paid immediately following the dinner. Persons who have a plate reserved at the dinner but who do not come should expect to forfeit the price of the meal. Most hotels will charge for the places set.

SUMMARY
Needless to say, all of the above committees must coordinate their efforts and work as a unit. Each reports its activities so all may know what progress has been made. It is likely your instructor will act as coordinator. It will be wise to seek advice besides reading numerous references pertaining to banquet procedure.

The group may or may not wish to invite guests. It is highly desirable that parents, friends, teachers, or dates be invited. This makes the affair a real banquet. While it is advisable to bring guests, those who do so should remember that they will be expected to pay for the guests' dinners.

Here are several points to investigate:
1. How early should you arrive? (A minimum of five minutes early.)
2. What clothes should you wear? (Hint – better make this dinner informal.)
3. What is the proper etiquette? (Good manners and willingness to make conversation – do not "freeze up.")
4. When and whom should you applaud? (Follow the toastmaster's lead.)
5. What are the toastmaster's duties? (To set the pace for the entire banquet.)
6. When should the food be served? Between speeches? Just how? (Hint – better settle this point definitely and be sure your servers are correctly informed. It is desirable that speeches come after dessert.)
7. What should you do if you make a blunder? (Do nothing; go on.)
8. Supposing someone is late; what then? (Wait a few minutes then start the banquet.)
9. What if you should forget your speech? (Hint – do not ever memorize it. Have your main points in mind. Rehearse.)
10. How and when should you seat yourself? Where? (If there are no place cards, find your own seat.)
11. What should you do when the toastmaster dismisses the group? Linger? Just what? (Go home, unless other arrangements have been made.)

WHAT IS MOST IMPORTANT
An After Dinner Speech by Tim Borchers

I was walking down the street one day when this weird looking bearded guy wearing a toga approached me, "You may be just the person I am looking for to carry out my quest." I walked faster, but he chased after me, "You are to tell the world of terrible destruction. The citizens of the world don't know how to think anymore." He looked real intense and kind of sad, so I let him continue. "The citizens believe everything told to them by bad people. There is only one way to save the world from pending doom. Someone must teach the world how to think again." I was wary. "Can I do that?" I asked. He replied, "You must at least try."

My buddy Plato once theorized people would blindly accept society's versions of importance, truth and reality without critically evaluating these ideas. Unfortunately, we do. Now we must begin to examine what we often take for granted. We must understand, first, how we allow capitalists to tell us what is important; second, how we permit society to tell us what is true; and finally, how we rely on the media to tell us what is happening in the world.

I was sitting in my civics class one day and, in between naps, I caught the teacher asking, "Anyone, anyone. Who can tell me the implications of the Supreme Court case *Mapp vs. Ohio.*" The guy sitting next to me, wearing a "Property of the Football Team" sweatshirt, raised his huge hand and said, "Uh...15 yards and a loss of down?" I thought, "football player, he's dumb." Then I thought for a minute. "In six years, he will have been drafted by the pros, making a million dollars a year. I'll be graduating from college, $50,000 in debt. I'm dumb!" Then I started to question our society – "Why do Madonna, Bill Cosby, Donald Trump, and Ryne Sandberg all make more money than our teachers?"

In the beginning of time, or when TV was invented, same difference, these other people became famous by appearing on the tube. As soon as they became famous, they started advertising products for capitalists. Advertising for capitalists made these people rich and consequently important. Let's face it, since teachers are never on TV or in the movies, they don't get corporate endorsements, and voila! aren't important. Could you imagine? "Hi! I'm Tim Borchers, former student, now I'm a teacher. When it comes to shoes, I wear Nike Wing Tips. When it comes to education, Just Do It!"

By now you're asking, "I can't play football and I'm not a money-grubbing unethical capitalist swine. So how do I know what's important?" First, we need to write our Representatives and Senators. Tell them to support legislation abolishing capitalism! I don't suppose that will work, so let's make it simple: think! Don't accept the societal hierarchy created by capitalists. Stand up and say "Teachers are more important than football players." Establish for yourself what is important.

Knowing what's important is not enough, we must also see how society is full of them. . it. . stereotypes – society's statements of truth. I asked Plato when stereotypes started. He said he didn't' know. So I turned to Dr. Seuss. Dr. Seuss said, "Once there were two kinds of people in the world. The star bellied sneetches had bellies with stars. The plain-bellied sneetches had none upon thars. When the star-bellied sneetches went out to play ball, could a plain belly get in the game? Not at all!" We haven't advanced very far from the days of the sneetches. Television and movies perpetuate stereotypes until we don't know what's true.

Fortunately, there is a solution. Critically evaluate what society says. That's right, we have to think. Don't start stereotypes, don't repeat stereotypes. And if you hear someone repeating a stereotype, tell them to knock it off. Tell them to solve the greenhouse effect, make world peace, or go read a book.

You're asking, "What's the final thing we do without thinking?" It is this: we accept the media's perspective of what's happening in the world. Trying to figure out what was happening in the world, I bought a recent *Newsweek*. I was flabbergasted: on the cover, Wayne's World!! No Bush, no congressional sleaze stories, not even a measly story on world trade. *Newsweek* was an anomaly, I thought, so I bought a *Time*, long known for its in-depth reporting. Not! Again, Wayne and Garth.

Doris Graber, in her book *Mass Media and American Politics*, argues that the press indicates how much importance we should attach to public issues. This is called the media's Agenda-Setting function. So if all we hear is Wayne's World, we think it's important, if all we see is the Bush presidency, we think it's important, and if all we see is news about free trade, we think it's important.

You won't know what's going on in the world by reading news magazines, so you must determine what's important based on what you think and not the amount of press an issue gets. A social studies instructor of mine once said, "Develop your perception of reality based on information-gathering from a cross-section of media." Sorry, spending five minutes a day reading *USA Today* won't work.

We've reached a point where we don't know what's important, "true" or "really" happening in the world. Rather depressing, but here's some advice: Don't let the Donald Trumps of the world think for you. Cognate, muse, ponder, meditate, create, don't watch so much TV, read a book, don't eat sweets, wear your seatbelt. And above all, remember the ideals that make our country great – knowledge, discipline, and individuality.

Chapter *14*

IMPROMPTU SPEAKING

Question: Are impromptu (unprepared) or extemporaneous speech (well prepared but not memorized) more effective ?
Answer: The extemporaneous speech (well prepared but not memorized) is the most effective known.

Time limits: 2-3-4 and 5 minutes. (Start with two minutes. Increase the length of speeches until a student can talk five minutes.)
Speaking notes: During the first two experiences you may use notes which designate a "method." After this, memorize your method and apply it as you speak.

PURPOSE OF THE IMPROMPTU SPEECH

This speech experience is for the purpose of further enlarging your speech knowledge. It is to expose you to impromptu speaking and to provide you with a rudimentary acquaintance with the difficulties and nature of unprepared discourse. Many students assume that impromptu speaking is easy. Nothing could be further from the truth. In reality impromptu speaking is extremely difficult. It is used effectively only by experienced speakers. There are methods, however, which if properly used, will enable a person to perform acceptably on the spur of the moment. This assignment will assist you in learning these methods.

EXPLANATION OF IMPROMPTU SPEAKING

Impromptu speaking is giving an unprepared talk. A person simply takes the floor, selects a subject, and begins. Various methods are used to conduct impromptu expression. A common procedure is one in which the speaker takes the floor after being asked to talk on a certain subject about which something may or may not be known. This is another method: one topic is suggested by each of several persons in the audience; a few seconds are permitted the speaker to choose a topic from the list of topics on which they feel best suited to expound; then they begin conversation. Differences in the manner of selecting a topic are many; however, in any case, one fundamental principle is that the ideas voiced are unrehearsed and unprepared.

The purpose of presenting the speech is the same as that for any other type of speaking. The distinctive feature is the unprepared delivery and the suddenness with which a person is confronted with a speech situation. Impromptu speaking is often required at those times when a person is called upon without warning "to say a few words" at a luncheon, special meeting, social gathering, or other occasion.

SUGGESTED TOPICS FOR IMPROMPTU SPEECHES

Write three suggestions on a paper. They should be suitable to those who will be asked to use them as subjects. Avoid those such as: "What Did You Do Last Night?" or "A Trip to Yellowstone Park." Your instructor will ask you to supply a topic from time to time as needed during the class. Examples of suitable topics for impromptu speaking are: dancing, movies, what is your opinion about (1) recycling, (2) minimum wages, (3) state operated lotteries, ((4) traffic laws, (5) music videos.

HOW TO CHOOSE A TOPIC FOR IMPROMPTU SPEAKING

There is one general rule to follow in selecting a topic, if you have a choice. This rule is: choose the one on which you are best fitted to speak. Consider your audience and the occasion when you are making a choice of topic.

HOW TO PREPARE FOR AN IMPROMPTU SPEECH

Naturally you cannot prepare for an unknown topic, but you can prepare a method of attack on surprise offerings from your audience. One system of doing this is to have in mind various orders by which to develop your ideas.

One order might be the time sequence in which events occur by the hour, day, month, or year, moving forward or backward from a certain time. This example will illustrate the principle involved: Topic – Houses: (1) Give the history of houses from a definite date; (2) Tell which part of the country houses were first built in and their subsequent westward movement with time; (3) Describe how with time the types of houses change, 1620-1700-1775-1800, and the like.

A space order would take you from east to west, top to bottom, front to rear. For example, take the topic houses, then develop the speech in space order, giving the items in this way: (1) Specify the location of houses and their types, starting in California and traveling east; (2) Locate various classes of houses found in a city, starting at a slum area and moving to the wealthy outlying district, (3) Describe houses according to locations in various parts of the world.

Using causal order, you might discuss certain forces and then point out the results which follow. Using houses: (1) Eskimos live in igloos. Why? Give reasons (causes). Or you might mention that South Pacific tribes dwell in grass and mud huts. Why? Give reasons (causes). (2) Prefabricated houses are now being built. Why? Give the causes that led to their development. (3) There are many hundreds of styles of houses of different architecture. Why? Give causes for this great diversification.

A special order is one of your own devising. For example take the same topic – houses – and: (1) Tell how to build a house or different kind of house. (2) Give the legal aspects of house construction – such as, wiring, sewage disposal plants, plumbing, type of dwelling in restricted areas, distance from street,...(3) How to contract for house construction.

Another method which may be effective is given below. It should be borne in mind that any method a speaker elects to use is not self-propelled. The person who applies the method will need to keep their wits about them and utilize only those portions of the device which are adapted to the particular speech, the occasion, the audience, and their own background and knowledge. The speaker may find it necessary to literally memorize the points which follow. If they do this and then develop the topic in the order of the various headings, they will make a logical discussion.

I. Why is this topic important to your audience? To you?

II. Give a history of important events which will show the background and development of your subject.

III. What are the overall effects of your topic (such as, gambling) on your audience, the state, the nation, the world?
    A. What are the effects geographically?
    B. What are the effects politically?
    C. What are the effects economically?
    D. What are the effects socially?
    E. What are the effects religiously?
    F. What are the effects educationally?
    G. What are the effects morally?
    H. What are the effects agriculturally?

IV. What caused these effects? (Give as many causes as you can which will explain the effects you have enumerated. You may do this by discussing an effect and then by giving the cause of it immediately after.)

V. What are the different solutions to the problems? (You have told what is happening (effects) and you have told what brought them about (causes). Naturally, you must tell now what you propose to do about the problem or problems. Thus, you will have offered several different solutions.)

VI. Discuss the advantages and disadvantages of each solution you propose.

VII. Select one or two solutions which you think are best. Tell why they are best.

VIII. How do you propose to take action on these solutions? How may you and your audience go about putting your solutions into practice? Mention one or more ways to do this.

IX. Conclude your speech.
    A. You may summarize.
    B. You may appeal to your audience.
    C. You may ask your audience to do a specific act. Example:
        Write to your congressman or congresswoman,
        Vote against_____,

HOW TO PRESENT AN IMPROMPTU SPEECH

In presenting an impromptu speech your attitude is a deciding factor in determining your effectiveness. First of all, you must maintain poise. It does not matter how surprised you are or how difficult your topic is. It does not make any difference what happens when you receive your subject or while you are speaking or after you have concluded your speech, you still must maintain poise. It is impossible to over-emphasize the importance of poise. Now you ask, how do you maintain poise? Here are a number of suggestions and answers: (1) Do not fidget around at your seat before you speak, just because you know you will soon be "on the spot." (2) When you are called on to speak, rise calmly and take your place before your audience. (3) If you know your topic when you take the platform, begin your remarks calmly, without hurrying (have some vigor and force), and be sure that you have a plan in mind by which you will develop your thoughts. Do not apologize to your audience in any way, by word or action. (4) If you do not know your topic when you rise to speak but are offered several choices after obtaining the floor, simply stand calmly before the group and listen carefully to the suggestions which are made. You should ask that a topic be repeated if you do not understand it. After you have received all of the proposed subjects, either stand calmly or walk calmly back and forth a few seconds while you decide which offering you will talk about. Ten seconds should be the maximum time taken to decide.

Once your selection is made, decide immediately what method or plan you will use in developing it. This plan should have been committed to memory before you ever attended class or placed yourself in a position where you might be asked to give an impromptu speech. After you have chosen your method of development, you will make your introductory remarks by telling why the subject is important to your listeners. When you begin to speak, do not make any apology of any sort whatsoever. Get on with your speech.

In actually delivering an impromptu talk, it is wise not to start too fast but rather to pick up speed and power as you go along. Aside from this, you should observe bodily actions and gestures which are in keeping with the speech situation. Your voice should be filled with meaning and easily heard by all. Naturally, your articulation, pronunciation, and grammar will be of high standard.

There is little to fear from impromptu speaking if you follow a preconceived method of attack on your subject. The way to do this is to refuse to allow yourself to become panicky, to recognize that some nervousness is a good sign of readiness, and to realize that your audience will expect nothing extraordinary from you because they, too, will know you are speaking impromptu. Actually, they will be "pulling for you." If you go about your task with poise and determination, your chances of success are exceedingly good. A well-rounded knowledge attained from a strong reading program will assist immeasurably.

Chapter *15*

A SPEECH TO GAIN GOODWILL

Question: How long does it take to prepare a good five-minute speech?
Answer: Three to five hours would not be too much. Short speeches require proportionately more preparation time than long speeches.

Time limits: 6-7 minutes. Observe your time limits!
Speaking notes: Do not use them – your speech should be in you, not on paper.
Sources of information: Two are required, preferably three. For each source give the specific magazine or book it was taken from, title of the article, author's full name, date of publication, and the chapter or pages telling where the material was found. If a source is a person, identify the source completely by title, position, occupation, etc. List these on the outline form.
Outline your speech: Prepare a 75-100 word complete sentence outline.

PURPOSE OF A SPEECH TO GAIN GOODWILL

One type of speech being utilized many thousands of times each year is the kind that secures goodwill from an audience. The popularity and usefulness of goodwill speeches are not likely to decline, but rather to grow. Your place in society may at any time demand that you join the parade of those who present speeches designed to secure goodwill. Because this type of speech occurs so often, you should, by all means, have experience with it. This assignment provides such an opportunity for you.

EXPLANATION OF THE SPEECH TO GAIN GOODWILL

A speech to gain goodwill is one in which the purpose is to secure a favorable attitude toward the speaker and the group being represented. Normally this speech is presented to a friendly audience, which necessitates the presentation of what might easily be called a speech to inform. This will be the apparent purpose, as far as the audience is concerned. However, the thought behind the presentation of information is this: by causing listeners to understand and appreciate the group they represent, the speaker will secure goodwill from them.

Occasions for goodwill speeches occur at luncheons, club meetings, special demonstrations, school meetings, religious gatherings, conventions, business meetings. Any group that convenes to hear a speaker give them information, whether it be a straight informative talk, an illustrated lecture, the showing of a film, or the demonstration of a new product, likely will be the recipient of a goodwill speech. One might classify a goodwill speech as a very subtle or indirect sales talk.

HOW TO CHOOSE A TOPIC FOR A GOODWILL SPEECH

As always, choose a topic that has a compelling interest for you. Choose one you know something about, one about which you can get more information. Construct a goodwill speech in which you represent a certain group on a definite occasion. For example: (1) represent a nuclear power plant to an environmental club; (2) represent a police officer at a neighborhood watch meeting; (3) represent a college to a high school; (4) represent the city at groundbreaking ceremonies for a new business.

HOW TO PREPARE A SPEECH TO GAIN GOODWILL

First of all, remember that your purpose is to secure goodwill. Keep this in mind. Second, do not forget that your remarks will be necessarily of an informative nature. We will assume that you have analyzed your audience and selected your topic.

Naturally, as soon as you have done this, you should gather your materials. Practically all large companies and corporations will gladly send you information if you will write for it. Many local businesses and Chambers of Commerce will provide pamphlets and brochures. Encyclopedias and Readers' Guides are excellent sources. If you are willing to show a reasonable amount of initiative, you will have no difficulty in locating materials to supplement your own knowledge. If you reach an impasse, ask your instructor for assistance.

After you have gathered your material, you will need to organize it logically so that it can be easily followed. You must decide on the order, the arrangement, the illustrations and examples, an effective introduction, and a strong conclusion. In other words, the entire pattern of your speech must be worked out carefully.

There are several characteristics of the goodwill speech which you should note. First, be sure you have interesting facts, new material – the novel or out of the ordinary subject matter that the listeners have not heard before. Another point is that you should show a definite relationship between your corporation, institution, profession and the lives of your listeners. They should be made to see that their happiness and prosperity are tied in with your activities or those which you represent. In making this point do not be so bold that you ask their approval or request their approbation. You should take it for granted that they already approve. And last, be sure you offer them a definite service. It may be in the form of souvenirs, samples, or an invitation to visit your plant, city, or institution. It could be special favors or accommodations to members of the audience, or merely the answering of questions they cared to raise at the conclusion of your remarks. Above all, remember that you are willing to help your audience – you are at their service. (Do not forget to practice this speech aloud before you present it to your audience.)

HOW TO PRESENT A SPEECH TO GAIN GOODWILL

This is a speech in which friendliness, good humor, and modesty count to a high degree. You will be talking about yourself and your organization. Bragging has no place. The information that you present has to be strong and interesting enough to do its own talking. You must be tolerant of your competitors and gracious in your appraisal of them. You must be careful about forcing your material on your audience. If you possess the necessary good feeling and friendliness for your auditors, they will reciprocate these attitudes.

Dress for the occasion, give attention to your posture, be alert and eager to communicate. Talk to be heard and understood. Avoid unnecessary formality. Body language and gesture are in order, as always, if they are used appropriately. Just be friendly and sincere.

SO YOU WOULD LIKE TO BE A DOCTOR
A Speech of Goodwill by Steven Rigby

Many of you will be graduating from high school this May, and enrolling in premedical courses in colleges and universities next September. If I were to ask a few of you just why you think you want to be doctors, I would get many different answers in reply – some good answers, some bad ones. But each of you, for one reason or another, feels that your goal should be medicine. You think that medicine has something to offer you and that you have something to offer medicine. On your list of priorities, medicine is number one.

Many of you see the years of study that lie ahead of you as a mysterious blur. You know, of course, that you will go to college for three to four years. You know that you will then go on to medical school – if you're accepted – for another four years, taking courses in anatomy, physiology and many other courses with long names. And then you will intern in a hospital for a year. You may even decide to specialize and go to school for a few more years. You realize that you have to invest a long period of time and a frightening amount of money, in order to complete your goal of becoming a medical doctor.

But just remember the practice of medicine has always meant something more than just another way to make a living, and that an education in medicine implies something more that the completion of certain science courses and the reading of certain textbooks.

A modern physician can look forward to various rewards for making a contribution to medicine. Most doctors make a good living from their work. I am not going to list average incomes of doctors in their respective specialties as they are listed today because they probably will be quite different by the time you become a doctor. But, by and large, I think you would have to look for quite a while to find a doctor who is starving to death.

Certainly, a physician has a high degree of security. A doctor will never have to worry about finding a job; there has always been a shortage of doctors. A doctor can expect a nice home and a new model automobile. He or she will be able to provide children with a good education.

On the other hand, it would be a mistake to have medicine as your goal because of the tangible rewards that are offered. There are many other occupations in which you can make more money with much less effort, if that is your major concern. Aside from income, there is a multitude of rewards for the physician. A doctor most always enjoys community respect. There is no other profession which is held in as high esteem as the profession of medicine. A doctor is respected for merely being a doctor. A doctor is often regarded as public property and is expected to take part in community progress.

Most important, the physician derives immense satisfaction from doing work that is worthwhile, work which is needed and received with much gratitude. Doctors take pride in doing work which few others can do, and in doing it well.

But at the same time a doctor must assume certain unusual responsibilities. Very often patients forget that doctors are people, as well as being doctors. A doctor must be available when needed. Even if that happens to be at two in the morning, he or she is still expected to accept the call. Most all physicians work hours that would astonish the average person. And they accept this as a way of life.

A doctor's home life is often a very trying situation, especially when first establishing a practice. Doctors may not see their spouses and children regularly. It has been said that any person who marries a doctor is either an idiot or a fool; if this is the truth, I know quite a few very wonderful idiots and fools who are willing to share their spouses with the numerous duties of a medial profession, duties which take the doctor away from home usually half the night and always at meal times.

This demand on a doctor's time is accepted by the profession as part of the game. This is the way a doctor lives, and that's all there is to it. If you don't think you would like this kind of life, you shouldn't be a doctor. There is no one the profession scorns more than the physician who shirks duties, that is, puts personal life above the life dedicated to the profession. The rest of the profession accepts this life – why shouldn't he or she? It is true that many doctors form group practices where they take turns being on call. This does eliminate some of the interruptions a doctor may encounter, but the responsibility still exists.

Who knows, by the time many of you become doctors the single practitioner working twenty hours a day may well be a thing of the past, although, I think the responsibilities will always be there. True, I think it takes a very special person to become a doctor, because the incentive must be there. The opportunities and rewards always outweigh the disappointments. If you have made up your mind to become a doctor, I want to wish you success, because I don't think you will ever regret your decision.

Chapter *16*

THE INTRODUCTION SPEECH

*Question: When I pick a topic do I have to know
everything about it?
Answer: No. You should research it thoroughly so
you may speak with authority and possess a basis
for your views.*

Time limits: 1-2 minutes.
Speaking notes: Key ideas, dates, events, or quotations only.
Sources of information: They may be fictitious or real.
Outline your speech: Prepare a 50-100 word complete sentence outline.

PURPOSE OF THE INTRODUCTION SPEECH

Many untrained speakers are asked to give introduction speeches. Some of the introductions are well done; far too many are haphazard and embarrassing, because the person making the introduction is untrained. This brings criticism upon the person who must present a speaker and it also weakens programs that feature lecturers. Of all the types of speeches you may make in the future, it is probable that one of them will be the introduction of a featured speaker. This assignment will provide an introduction speech experience.

EXPLANATION OF THE INTRODUCTION SPEECH

An introduction speech is one in which a chairperson or other person introduces a speaker to an audience. The purpose is to bring an audience and speaker together in the proper spirit. Several of the requirements are that: the speech should be short; it should make the audience and speaker feel comfortably acquainted; it should interest the audience in the speaker and the subject; it should put the speaker at ease, announce the subject, and give the speaker's name.

The introducer should avoid attempts at being humorous. Never embarrass the speaker either by heaping too much praise upon them or by belittling them. The person introducing a speaker should not call attention to self nor say or do anything to detract from what the speaker plans to say. The person who once said, "Get up, speak up, shut up," probably was thinking of the individual who makes introduction speeches; and the introducer can hardly go wrong if they follow this advice.

Occasions for the introduction speech arise every time a speaker is introduced. They probably number in the millions annually.

HOW TO CHOOSE SUBJECT FOR AN INTRODUCTION SPEECH

You will have to decide for yourself as to the type of imaginary audience and occasion you will use. You will also find it necessary to arrive at some decision concerning the specific person you plan to introduce. Be sure that your speaker is a suitable one for the occasion. Some possible situations include introducing (1) a college president to a high school audience; (2) the mayor to a public gathering; (3) a war hero to a school assembly; (4) a Hollywood celebrity to your school ; or (5) a sports star to an athletic banquet.

HOW TO PREPARE AN INTRODUCTION SPEECH

In preparing this speech you may draw your information from four sources: the speaker, the subject, the audience, or the occasion. Not all of these may be necessary in every speech; however, they are all often suitable if not required sources. You will not need much material, but that which you have must be accurate and pertinent. Know how to pronounce the speaker's name correctly. Discover any background the speaker has that should be known by the audience. This may concern education, special training, travel experience, special honors, membership in organizations, important positions held, books written, or any other notable achievements. Of course, for a famous and well-known person, little need be said, possibly nothing. An example of the latter is the introduction often heard: "Ladies and Gentlemen, the President." However, almost all speakers require more to be said than do the President of the United States, a governor or other high state official. You should know the title of the speaker's subject. As with the name, you must have it right. But you should say nothing about the speech that will tend to "steal the thunder" of the remarks. You should inquire thoroughly into the personnel of your audience so that you may adjust your remarks to them. The occasion of the address should be well-known to you. From the four sources just mentioned and a fifth, yourself, you will construct your introduction speech. Short though this speech is, what you say must really "count." Thus, you must organize and arrange it carefully, selecting those bits of information that are most important.

Before you set your ideas, you should confer with the person you are going to introduce and, in conference, arrive at a definite understanding regarding what you plan to say in your introduction speech. After this point is decided, then rehearse aloud until you are confident that you are thoroughly prepared.

HOW TO PRESENT AN INTRODUCTION SPEECH

When the moment arrives for you to introduce the speaker of the evening, rise calmly, take your place on the platform, pause until the assembly grows quiet, and then deliberately address the audience in your normal voice, yet speak loudly enough for all to hear. Avoid straining or using greater force than is needed. You may say, "Ladies and Gentlemen," or use some other salutation or form of introduction appropriate to the audience and the occasion. Your body language and gestures will be limited. There will likely be no necessity for using either more than moderately. Your voice should be well modulated, the words spoken clearly, and your pronunciation correct – especially that of the speaker's name.

Keep in mind your part of the occasion. People did not come to hear you or see you. You are only a convenient but necessary cog in the events surrounding the speaker. Your poise and confidence and appropriate but brief remarks are all that are expected or wanted from you. You may greet the audience and mention the occasion, extend greetings, and note the fact that there is an exceptionally good audience (if there is). If there is a poor audience, do not remark about it and do not make any apologies.

At the moment you present the speaker, announce the name and subject somewhat as follows: "I am happy to present Dr. A, who will address you (or speak to you) on_____(mention the subject)." Then turn to the speaker with the words, "Dr. A." You may bow slightly or nod and take your chair when the speaker rises and approaches the front of the platform.

If you are chairperson of the assembly, it will be appropriate for you to express publicly the appreciation of the audience to the speaker at the conclusion of the address.

A SPEECH OF INTRODUCTION
by Brent Peterson

Principal Norton, coaches and lettermen of Valley High School. Meeting this evening as a group of athletes we all recall during many basketball games a most unforgettable shot, the "dunk." It is a privilege to have with us such a man who thrilled many spectators. A little six-foot guard through hard work perfected the thrilling shot and became known as "Dunker" to match his own name, Bob Dunkin.

Bob, a three-year basketball letterman at Northside High in Kennington, attended banquets similar to this one. Upon receiving the free throw trophy after making seventy-six percent of his free throws, at the banquet his junior year Bob announced, "Next year I'll shoot ninety percent." The following year persistent Bob made ninety-two percent of his free throws due to his consistent practice during the summer. Coach Dunkin conducts summer basketball camps to develop the abilities of young ball players because he is interested in them.

A competitive college athlete said, "You must always give one hundred percent effort; if you don't, someone, somewhere will, and he will beat you." "Dunker" Dunkin made that statement and has always gone the extra mile in all his life's endeavors and has rarely been beaten. At State U, "Dunker" was all-conference twice, led the conference in free-throw shooting and his team to a berth in the NCAA tournament.

Bob Dunkin's life is the story of persistence, hard work and success. It has been said, "No chance, no destiny, no fate can circumvent or hinder or control the firm resolve of a determined soul." Athletes, I want you to meet and hear this determined man who will speak to you concerning the value of reaching your own potential. Coach Dunkin.

WHAT SHOULD YOU KNOW ABOUT YOUR AUDIENCE

Ask yourself these questions and then find the answers either through actual interviews or if that isn't possible make an educated guess.

1. Who will be in your audience? Classmate? Adults? Children?

2. What are the interests and past experiences of the audience members? How do they relate to your topic?

3. What do they already know about your topic?

4. Will they have any preconceived opinions about your topic?

5. How can you adapt your speech to make it interesting to the majority of your audience?

Chapter **17**

THE SPEECH OF WELCOME

Question: What is meant by "adjusting to the situation?"
Answer: You should make your speech fit the assignment,
the audience, the environment, your own abilities and the
occasion.

Time limits: 2-3 minutes.
Speaking notes: Key ideas only.
Sources of information: None required. They may be real or fictitious.
Outline your speech: Prepare a 50-100 word complete sentence outline.

PURPOSE OF THE SPEECH OF WELCOME

A speech of welcome is of sufficient importance that you should know how it is organized and what it should do. It occupies a high place in speech-making, upon its effectiveness hinges much of the success of public relations among groups that convene daily throughout the country. You may be asked to give a speech of welcome in your own community at any time. It is not enough that you pass the request off lightly or refuse to assist in promoting goodwill because you do not know how to present a speech of welcome. This assignment will provide the experience that will show you how to prepare and present a good speech of welcome. Study it carefully.

EXPLANATION OF THE SPEECH OF WELCOME

A speech of welcome is one made to a single individual or to a group of individuals with the purpose of extending greetings and promoting friendship. The person being welcomed should be made to feel that they are sincerely wanted and that the hosts are delighted to have them. The warmest kind of hospitality should be expressed in the welcoming speech. Its genuineness should be so marked that the hearer enjoys a spirit of gladness as a result of being the guest of a gracious host. The speech is charactered by brevity, simplicity, geniality, and sincerity.

The occasions for the speech of welcome may be extremely varied. The occasion may be a reception for a distinguished visitor, for a native son or daughter returning, or for a total stranger. It may welcome home a citizen from foreign travel, missionary work, diplomatic service, or business enterprise. It could welcome a school official, the new minister, or a county officer. If the occasion is to honor an organization, the welcome may be for a delegation – such as an advertisers' club, a chamber of commerce, a booster club, or a group of county, city, school, or community representatives. In some cases, the welcome may be a special gesture to a conference or convention. But, whatever the occasion, the speech of welcome plays a prominent part.

HOW TO CHOOSE A SPEECH OF WELCOME

Select an occasion that interests you. Decide definitely the organization you will represent and what position you will hold in the organization. Select one that you know something about or one about which you can secure information. Some possible situations include:

1. A native son or daughter returns home.
2. A newly elected school superintendent arrives in your city.
3. A banquet is held for new teachers.
4. The governor visits on state business.
5. A sister city from another country sends a delegation.
6. An organization holds a convention in your city.

HOW TO PREPARE A SPEECH OF WELCOME

First, fix your purpose in mind; you are to make your guests glad to be there. They should admire your hospitality. Next, get your information and set up your speech. Some suggestions follow. You may need to explain the organization which you represent. If so, mention its character, the work it is doing, and points of interest about it, including future plans. Pay a tribute to your guest for their work and tell of advantages gained by their visiting you. Note who the guests are, where they are from, and whom they represent. Explain briefly what their coming means and comment on the common interests your organization holds with them. You should speak of the occasion – its present enjoyment and its future importance. Express anticipated pleasant associations and mutual benefits which are to be derived from the meeting. Invite your guests to feel at home and participate fully in your community. Speak for those whom you represent.

Keep in mind the fact that not all of the above material is always needed in a speech of welcome. Plan to make your remarks brief and to include the appropriate material. Considerable thought and organization will be required. Practice aloud until you have thoroughly mastered your material. Do not memorize the speech word for word.

HOW TO PRESENT A SPEECH OF WELCOME

Let the occasion govern your presentation. If it is formal, act and speak appropriately. If it is informal, adjust yourself and your remarks accordingly. In either case be sincere and genuine. Feel what you say. Give your guests a degree of hospitality and warmth of welcome which they will remember; however, do not overdo it and spoil the effectiveness of the speech. Portray the same gentility and friendliness that is present when you open the door of your home to friends and invite them in.

Speak loudly enough to be heard. Use your normal voice. Speak clearly, pronounce all names distinctly and correctly, and smile pleasantly as is fitting. Let your body language be appropriate to the occasion, the mood, and your remarks. Your spoken language should be simple, vivid, appropriate, and devoid of slang and redundancy. Be brief in time used but complete in your welcome.

WELCOME TO WESTERN AMERICA HIGH
by Setits Raclile

Principal Rogers and delegates to the Seventh Regional Government Conference. It is my pleasure as senior class president to welcome you to our school where we hope you will learn a lot of new information and have a good time doing it. This is the first time you have honored Western America High School by selecting us as your host and I'm glad to tell you we are both proud and happy to have you here today.

Our achievements and our problems are no doubt similar to yours, and they make us either joyous or perplexed, depending on whether we are doing something notable or having trouble. I do believe however, every achievement by schools represented here today should be shared so we may all benefit from each other's successes. And I believe just as strongly we should discuss those problems we all face every year. By doing this we can learn from each other how to improve our individual governments and thus improve our schools in this region.

I told you Western America High is pleased to have you as our guests and to show you we really mean it, our school governing council has arranged free bus tours over Exhibition Scenic Drive during our afternoon recess. Just climb on a bus in the parking lot and you'll get the ride of your life with more hairpin curves and thrilling views than you ever dreamed of. Then tonight at 8 o'clock in this building, there will be a delegates' free dance with an outstanding band, which our students will attend to help make your evening more enjoyable.

Once again I want to tell you how glad we are that you are here. We will do our best to help you have a successful conference and a pleasant visit, thus we will all profit greatly from this wonderful experience. When you leave tomorrow we want you to take our friendship and best wishes with you, but until then have a good time and thank you for joining us.

Chapter *18*

THE RESPONSE TO A SPEECH OF WELCOME

Question: How does one overcome talking fast?
Answer: Give individual words and phrases greater
emphasis. Utilize more pauses. Articulate words dis-
tinctly. Make a conscious effort to speak slower.

Time limits: 1-2 minutes.
Speaking notes: None. This will be impromptu on many occasions. When it is prepared it is so brief that no notes are needed.
Sources of information: None required. They may be real or fictitious.
Outline your speech: If this is a prepared response, construct a 40-75 word complete sentence outline.

PURPOSE OF THE RESPONSE TO A SPEECH OF WELCOME

Many organizations meet on various occasions when visitors are in attendance. Sometimes they just drop in as members of a national fraternal group. At other times they come, representing a similar organization, or they are guests at a convention at which a certain society may be host. On such occasions the visitors are welcomed by a speech. It is of course natural that a response to the welcome be made. Because you may at some time be asked to respond to a welcome speech, it is wise to study a speech of response. The purpose of this assignment is to acquaint you with this type of speech.

EXPLANATION OF THE RESPONSE TO A WELCOME

The speech in response to a welcome is simply a reply to the felicitations expressed by a host. Its purpose is to cement goodwill and friendship, and express these mutual feelings that exist between the groups. It is short, brief, courteous, and friendly. Often, the response is impromptu in nature – which places a burden of doing fast thinking and uttering logical thoughts on the person who presents it. It also demands sincerity and cordiality of manner from the speaker. Naturally, this implies ability and art in the speaking process.

Occasions for this speech occur any time a welcome is given, although a response speech is not always necessary. These occasions may be at conventions, meetings of civic, religious, educational, fraternal, business organizations, and the like.

HOW TO CHOOSE A TOPIC FOR A RESPONSE SPEECH

An obvious place to begin selection of a response for a speech of welcome is to review Chapter 17 and respond to one of the situations suggested there or to a speech given by a classmate to that assignment. Recall situations in which you have heard a speech of welcome and respond. Finally, you can respond to one of these situations:

1. Respond to a civic club welcome.
2. You are a mayor visiting another city. Respond to the mayor's welcome.
3. You are a visiting student. Respond to a student council welcome.
4. You join a new organization. Respond to their welcome.
5. You are a visitor to a foreign country. Respond to a welcome at one of their schools.
6. You are an environmental advocate. Respond to a welcome at a Sierra Club meeting.

HOW TO PREPARE A SPEECH OF RESPONSE

First, keep in mind the purpose of the talk, namely, to express your appreciation of the hospitality extended you and to strengthen mutual feelings of friendship. Second, follow an organization that permits use of good speech construction. Include an introduction and conclusion. Make your entire speech brief.

In general you will make the occasion of the welcome overshadow your own personality. More specifically, your remarks may be developed in the following manner: Address the hosts and those associated with them; acknowledge the greeting of welcome and the hospitality of the organization; and express sincere thanks for their courtesies. Extend greetings from your organization and show how the occasion is mutually advantageous to the hosts and your group. Explain briefly what your organization is, what it stands for. Mention the benefits to be derived from the attitude of mutual helpfulness and enjoyment which are prevalent at this meeting. Predict future pleasant associations with the host organization, showing this acquaintance to be only a beginning of a long-lasting cooperation of friendship. Mention in conclusion that you have been made to feel most welcome and at home. Thank your hosts again for their hospitality, extend best wishes, and then be seated.

This speech may have to be impromptu. Because of the frequent possibility of impromptu speeches of response, you should set up a basic sequence of ideas which you can use in replying to any speech of welcome. Of course, if you are designated ahead of time to present the speech, you should carefully organize and rehearse your speech until you have it well in mind. Under either circumstance, you can be prepared if you give attention to the points presented in the preceding paragraphs.

HOW TO PRESENT A RESPONSE SPEECH

Your attitude and demeanor must be a combination of appreciation and friendliness. Your remarks must have the qualities of sincerity and gratitude. The only way to reach these ends is to demonstrate them through appropriate bodily actions and simple understandable language. There is no call for ostentation, sarcasm, bragging, or for any attempt to show off your personal qualities.

When you are presented by your host, rise politely, smile pleasantly, and begin your response. Maintain your poise by observing an alert posture. Make yourself heard by all, but do not shout or speak overly loud. Adhere to the policy of brevity but do not give the appearance of having nothing to say. When you have finished the speech, sit down. Remember that you are still under observation. Here are a few additional suggestions: (1) Be sure that your speech is appropriate to the audience and the occasion. If the occasion is formal, conduct yourself accordingly; if it is informal, adjust to this situation. (2) Have a few serious thoughts in your speech, even though gaiety fills the air. Do not resort to telling nothing more than a series of stories or anecdotes. (3) Do not apologize or attempt the trite pose of your being surprised. You should know that as a guest you are subject to being called on at any time. Accept your responsibility and meet it as a mature person by having something worthwhile to say.

RESPONSE TO A SPEECH OF WELCOME
by Yenan Noscaasi

Fellow delegates and Principal Rogers. I want to thank Mr. Raclile for his most friendly remarks and tell him we do feel the sincere welcome he speaks of. Already there seems to be present among us a spirit of cooperation and strong desire to exchange information helpful to every school represented at this conference. I truly believe that if each of us can gain only one new idea from our various group meetings and the guest speakers we will all return home with the satisfaction of having attained something worthwhile.

We all trust that our presence here will in a sense express the esteem we hold for Western America High School. It's a privilege to come here to share our experiences and thought with Western's students and delegates in their outstanding facilities. We can all see how much preparation they have made for us and also see they are doing everything possible to make this conference a success.

As representative-at-large from all schools present I want to thank Western America High for arranging our housing and meals; also for the bus tour coming up this afternoon and the big dance tonight. I'm sure everyone will enjoy these events. By having a good time together and exchanging ideas we will have a conference second to none. So to our hosts I want to say on behalf of all of us "thanks for everything."

TOPIC IDEAS

1. Make a list of everything you know more about than other people might. Perhaps you have a hobby or have lived in several different cities. If so, prepare a speech about your hobby or about the special features of a city where you once lived.

2. Interview your parents, grandparents, or an elderly neighbor. Ask about interesting fads or historical events they remember. Use these ideas as a basis for research.

3. What do you want to learn more about? Use a speech as a way to learn it.

4. What do you have strong feelings about? What has someone said lately that you disagreed with? Write a speech and support your viewpoint.

5. What is something that your classmates need to know about: finding a summer job; job opportunities for those not going to college; how to resolve differences without physical violence; how to better understand individuals with different racial, religious, or ethnic backgrounds? Use ideas such as these for informative speeches.

Chapter *19*

PRESENTING A GIFT OR AWARD

Question: How can you lower the tone of your voice?
Answer: This should be undertaken only with the advice and supervision of a trained speech pathologist. Consult such a person.

Time limits: 1-3 minutes.
Speaking notes: Key words, dates, or quotations.
Sources of information: None required. They may be real or fictitious.
Outline your speech: Prepare a 50-75 word complete sentence outline.

PURPOSE OF THE PRESENTATION SPEECH

Many centuries ago, ancient peoples presented gifts and awards. The practice continues today without abatement. Every time the occasion of presenting a gift or award occurs, someone must make the presentation speech. It is not easy to make a public presentation graciously, to handle the situation with ease, and to utter thoughts that symbolize the spirit of the event. Yet, at any time you may be designated to perform this task. When this necessity does arise, you should know something about making a presentation speech. This assignment will tell what to do and say on such an occasion.

EXPLANATION OF THE PRESENTATION SPEECH

A presentation speech is one made in conjunction with the presentation of an award or gift. It is short, sincere, and commendatory of the recipient. It requires tact and good taste because of divided attitudes towards the recipient of the award. Neither too much nor too little should be said about the recipient, because others, no doubt, are just as worthy of the award or gift. Intense rivalry may have been present in seeking the award. Feelings and emotions may have been high. To understand the tenor of the audience, to avoid embarrassing the winner, and to use a language appreciated by all or even a majority requires a simple yet artistic quality of speech.

Occasions for this type of speech vary. One of these occurs when a prize is won in a contest. Here the prize is known beforehand; for this reason there is no surprise relative to what it will be. There will be partisan desire, expectancy, uncertainty, and even divided opinion among the judges regarding the winner. This poses a delicate problem for the speaker who makes the presentation – which may be formal. Emphasis will be placed upon interest, the careful consideration of the judges, and their delicate position.

Another occasion is one in which an object is given to an organization, such as a school, church, city, society, or other group. It is likely that the whole atmosphere will be formal. The procedures, plans, and persons who participate will be known long before the actual donation takes place. There will be no surprise. The speech will be pointed to emphasize the symbolism or utility of the gift.

A third occasion involves awarding a medal or other recognition for service. The surprise element may or may not be present. Depending on the occasion and the type of recognition, much emotion may be present. The ceremony and speech should not make it difficult for the recipient. The deed will obscure the gift, although tribute will be paid the one who is honored. During times of national crisis or emergency, this is a frequent occasion for presentations.

A fourth kind of award is one made in appreciation of service. Surprise is often present. There is no rivalry, but rather good fellowship and possibly a little sadness. Examples of this kind of award are the retirement of a president or other official from a society, a school or civic organization, or the departure of any prominent citizen from community or group service. Here, emphasis is placed on the happy side of joyful fellowship. Some regret for the departure is expressed, but hope for the future is given a prominent place.

HOW TO CHOOSE A TOPIC

You have undoubtedly been present for an award presentation or have observed one on television. In preparing this speech, model your situation after one you have observed. If you have no experiences that immediately come to mind, consider one of the following possibilities:

1. Present a scholarship.
2. Present a cash prize to the winner of a sales contest.
3. Present a medal for a drug free school.
4. Present a medal for outstanding leadership in the community.
5. Present an award to an outstanding teacher.
6. Present an Eagle Scout award.

HOW TO PREPARE A PRESENTATION SPEECH

In preparing this speech, make certain that you are fully aware of the occasion and any particular requirements governing it or the presentation. Keep in mind that it is an honor to present a gift or award, that it is not an opportunity to make a speech on your pet subject. By all means observe proper speech construction.

In preparing your talk, there are several thoughts to bear in mind. First, do not overpraise the individual. Second, it is desirable to pay deserving tribute to the recipient, if wise restraint is exercised. Third, be careful not to over-emphasize the gift or its value. Stress instead the work or merit which the award signifies. Let glory abide in achievement, not in the material object.

Briefly, your specific organization of ideas may fall into the following sequence. Make appropriate remarks to the audience; let these remarks refer to the occasion that brought them together. Relate a short history of the event that is now being fittingly culminated. Give the immediate reasons for the award and show that, regardless of its value, the award is only a token of the real appreciation for the service rendered or the esteem felt for the recipient of the award.

Recount the recipient's personal worth and tell how this worth was recognized or discovered. If you personally know the honoree, mention the fact that you are intimately aware of the person's service or merit.

Next, explain the character and purpose of the gift or award. Should the object be a picture or statue, the custom is to have it veiled until the speech is concluded or nearly concluded. At the proper moment, withdraw the veil. If the gift or award is to be presented to an organization, the ceremony will go more smoothly if someone is informed ahead of time to represent the group in receiving the gift.

Prepare your ideas by rehearsing aloud until you have them thoroughly in mind. Do not memorize your speech but be sure to know what you are going to say.

HOW TO PRESENT A PRESENTATION SPEECH
Your attitude and manner must convey the sincerity behind the entire occasion. There must be no ostentation, show, or flamboyancy in your speech or actions. Be sure that the award or gift is available and ready to be presented.

When the moment arrives for you to transfer the award or gift to the donee, call them to the platform. If they are already there, address them by name so that they may rise in response. Then, in a few words properly chosen, present the gift by summarizing the reasons for the presentation. Mention the appropriateness of the award and offer the recipient good wishes for the future. After the recipient has accepted the object, allow the opportunity to thank you or make other remarks to you or to the people gathered around. An acceptance speech will be in order.

A few technicalities to observe are these: Be sure you stand so that the audience can see and hear you. Do not stand in front of the gift. Let the audience see it. Near the conclusion of your speech, when you are ready to make the presentation, pick up the gift or award, being particular to hold it so that it is clearly visible to everyone. Stand at an angle with your side slightly toward the audience. Hand the gift to the recipient by using the hand nearest to them (the upstage hand). They will in turn accept it with their upstage hand. If it is a medal you wish to pin to their coat, stand with your side to the audience while pinning it on. Should the object be a picture, statue, or other material which cannot be transferred from hand to hand, it will of course be unveiled or shown at the moment of presentation. Be sure you speak loudly enough to be heard by all, especially when you are turned partially away from the audience.

SPEECH PRESENTING A GIFT OR AWARD
by Valerie Ritter

Fellow Parents and Athletes: This awards banquet has been an annual event for several years. Some of you here tonight will look forward to many more banquets such as this, while others will reminisce of the banquets past. These are special nights for athletes and parents, for it is because of you that these banquets are held. As President of the Scholarship Selection Committee it is with great pleasure that I am able to present this award.

This evening there is a student present who has earned recognition by means of his outstanding performance as an athlete. This recognition presented by the University is an annual event arranged to provide financial assistance for students with athletic ability.

The recipient is a transfer student from the College of DuPage located in Glen Ellen, Illinois. He has been active as an athlete throughout his school years. Tonight I wish to present Mr. Rich Kielczewski with a scholarship recognizing his ability in the game of tennis.

Rich is honest and hard-working and is dedicated to the sport of tennis. He always seems to put forth more effort than is originally necessary. He is also a qualified and very competent tennis instructor.

Rich has entered many amateur tournaments. Among those in which he has captured the crown are the Chicago District Tournament and six consecutive conference titles. He has also received recognition of the people of Illinois by being ranked sixteenth in the state.

I have known Rich for a long time and have many times witnessed his stunning ability to overcome his opponent. I personally know of no other person more deserving of this tennis scholarship. In view of these outstanding qualities and accomplishments, I am very pleased to present Rich Kielczewski with this scholarship on behalf of Northwest Missouri State University.

Chapter *20*

ACCEPTING A GIFT OR AWARD

Question: Should pitch vary much during a speech?
Answer: Yes. It will add variety.

Time limits: 1-2 minutes.
Speaking notes: None. Your remarks will be impromptu or, if not, then very brief.
Sources of information: None required. They may be real or fictitious.
Outline your speech: If this is not impromptu, prepare a 50-75 word complete sentence outline.

PURPOSE OF THE SPEECH OF ACCEPTANCE OF A GIFT OR AWARD

Because untold numbers of presentation speeches for gifts and awards are made every year, we are justified in assuming that almost as many acceptance speeches are made by the individuals who are honored with the awards. The custom is as old as the centuries. Recipients are not always told in advance that they will be honored by a gift or award; hence they can be embarrassed if they do not know how to accept the honor with simple sincerity. This speech experience will provide you a definite background for such an event; for this reason it is important.

EXPLANATION OF THE ACCEPTANCE SPEECH

A speech made by the recipient of a gift or award is a sincere expression of appreciation of the honor accorded. It should establish the person as a friendly, modest, and worthwhile individual to whom the people may rightfully pay tribute for merit and achievement. Its purpose should be to impress the donors with the worthiness of the receiver and to make them happy in their choice. To do this will demand a gentility and nobleness that springs naturally from the heart of the receiver. There can be no artificial or hollow remarks uttered by a shallow mind.

It should be noted that in some instances no speech is necessary, the only essential propriety being a pleasant "thank you," accompanied by an appreciative smile. To do more than this when it is not appropriate to do so is awkward. However, when a speech is in order, it must be propitious. The recipient must decide on each occasion whether or not a speech is wanted or needed.

Occasions for acceptance speeches arise, potentially, every time an award or gift is presented. They occur in schools, clubs, societies, civic and religious organizations, business houses, or government offices. Any of these groups may wish to honor a member of their organization, another organization, or someone else for service, merit, achievement or winning a prize. Possibilities for presentations and their accompanying speeches are unlimited.

HOW TO CHOOSE A TOPIC FOR AN ACCEPTANCE SPEECH

If you have ever received an award, give your acceptance speech again for this assignment. If you haven't, respond to one of the situations given in Chapter 19. A final source of topics is the list given below. Your main goal in selecting a topic is to choose a situation in which you would like to find yourself.

1. Accept a scholarship.
2. Accept a prize for writing poetry.
3. Accept a donation of funds for the new ball park.
4. Accept a top environmental award.
5. Accept a medal for outstanding community service.
6. Accept an award for outstanding performance of duty.
7. As captain of your basketball team accept a championship award.

HOW TO PREPARE AN ACCEPTANCE SPEECH

This speech will necessarily be impromptu on some occasions; hence little preparation can be made other than by formulating a basic pattern of ideas about which you will speak. If you are warned or informed early that you will receive a gift or award, then, of course, you should certainly prepare a speech. In this case all the principles of good speech construction and organization would be followed. However, in either case, there are several important points to be noted. First, utilize simple language. Second, express in your initial remarks a true sense of gratitude and appreciation for the gift. If you are really surprised, you may say so; however, the surprise must be genuine. If you are not surprised, omit any reference to your feeling. No one will be moved by an attempt at naiveté. Next, you should modestly disclaim total credit for winning the award. Give credit to those who assisted you in any way, for without them you could not have achieved your success. Praise their cooperation and support. Do not apologize for winning. Do not disclaim your worthiness. Inasmuch as you were selected to receive a tribute, be big enough to accept it modestly and graciously. Your next point may be the expression of appreciation for the beauty and significance of the gift. Its nature will determine what you say. Do not overpraise it or over value it. Observe suitable restraint. In no manner should you express disappointment. Conclude your remarks by speaking of your plans or intentions for the future, especially as they may be connected with the award or gift or work associated with it. As a final word you may repeat your thanks for the object or recognition.

HOW TO PRESENT AN ACCEPTANCE SPEECH

Your attitude must be one of sincerity, friendliness, appreciation, modesty, and warm enthusiasm. Conceit and ego must be entirely lacking. You should be personal, if the award is for you. If you represent a group, use the pronoun "we" instead of "I."

When the donor speaks to you, either come to the platform or rise and step toward the speaker if you are already there. Should you approach from the audience, move forward politely and alertly. Neither hurry nor loiter. Let your bearing be one of appreciation for what is to come. Arriving on the platform, stand near the donor but avoid viewing the award anxiously or reaching for it before it is extended to you. Do not stand in front of it. In accepting the award stand slightly sideways toward the audience, reach for and receive the object in the hand nearest the other person (this will be the upstage hand); in this way you avoid reaching in front of yourself or turning your body away from the audience. After receiving the object, hold it so it remains in full view of the audience. If it is too large to hold, place it in an appropriate spot on stage, step to one side and begin your speech; that is, if a speech is in accord with the proceedings and occasion. If you return to a seat in the audience, carry the gift in your hand, do not stuff it into a pocket if it is a small object.

As to the speech itself, observe all the elements of acceptable stage presence. Be dressed appropriately, maintain an alert and polite posture, speak clearly and distinctly and loudly enough to be heard by all. If your speech is impromptu, you will not be expected to possess the fluency of one who was forewarned of the occasion. Insofar as is possible, let your manner express an undeniable friendliness and appreciation for the honor being accorded you. This sincerity is the most important part of your speech. It will have to be evident in your voice, your bodily actions, your gestures, the look on your face, everything about you. Be sure to express no shame. Do not be afraid of a little emotion; just control it so that you are not overcome by it. Make no apologies for your speaking. Avoid awkward positions that are indicative of too much self-consciousness. Do these things and your acceptance will be genuine and applauded by all who see and hear you.

SPEECH ACCEPTING A GIFT OR AWARD
by Sherri Dunker

Three years ago if anyone had told me I would someday join a sorority, I would have laughed in her face -- there was just no way I was going to become a part of those, quote "cliquey snobs." But to this day I bless the friend who persuaded me to find out what sororities were really about. They weren't snobs at all but beautiful people with the same fears, frustrations, and hopes many women have.

Now I am very proud to say that I too am a sorority woman, and with honor I accept this "Most Spirited Kappa Delta Award." This sorority has taught me more than any text or instructor, and it's given me my "people" degree in college.

Kappa Delta has shown me the importance of budgeting time wisely, accepting and utilizing criticism, respecting and listening to others' ideas, social etiquette, and especially leadership experience. Incalculable are KD's gifts, but I'll never forget the most precious of all – my vast circle of sisters who genuinely care. You accepted me for what I am and have helped me build my self-confidence. Thanks for standing by me through my moments of despair and making college life a pleasant life.

I truly believe in you, Kappa Delta, and all for which you stand – the most "honorable, beautiful and highest!" (Open Motto of Kappa Delta) I shall treasure this award and when I glance upon it long after I have graduated, I shall remember all the glorious memories and sisters of Kappa Delta. Thank you.

SPEECH ACCEPTING A GIFT OR AWARD
by Ed Ashcraft

(The recipient was completely surprised to receive this award.)

Thank you Dr. Ellis, thank you Ladies and Gentlemen. I really don't know what to say, I am at a complete loss for words.

My principal called me this evening to the phone and told me he would be at the school board meeting this evening, to give the board some input on our needs in the Science Department. He asked if I could be there in case he needed some off-hand information about our department. Of course, I said I would be happy to attend, since we had discussed these needs many times.

As you have heard, Mr. Soderquist gave us quite an in-depth list of our needs, plus some methods for improving our department. When he finished his presentation, I assumed he managed to get through it without my help. But I felt good about being there, just in case I was needed.

But I certainly did not expect this. The Golden Apple Award for the most outstanding teacher? Me?

I've held so many differing types of job in my life, but I knew the first day I walked into a classroom that this would be where I would spend the rest of my life. I look forward to Monday morning, getting back to my kids. To receive such a prestigious award for something I enjoy doing so much, well. As my students would say, "This is too much, man.!"

I certainly want to thank my principal for recommending me for this award. Also, all of my fellow teachers, who voted for me. I can't thank the school board enough for this great honor.

I will keep my Golden Apple on my desk. Each morning I will take a minute to remind myself of the great trust that's been placed in me. I will do the best that I can to honor that trust. Thank you again.

Chapter *21*

THE FAREWELL SPEECH

Question: How fast should you talk when giving a speech? Answer: The rate varies with the ability to talk distinctly – 125 to 150 words per minute is about average; however, these figures vary considerably.

Time limits: 4-5 minutes.
Speaking notes: Do not use any for this speech.
Sources of information: None required. They may be real or fictitious.
Outline your speech: Prepare a 75-100 word complete sentence outline.

PURPOSE OF THE FAREWELL SPEECH

Many times a person is the guest of honor at a farewell party. The guest of honor is invariably asked to say a few words as a last expression before leaving. Too often, what is said may be only a mumbling of incoherent remarks, because the guest has never had a previous experience of this kind and does not know what is appropriate at such a time. This speech assignment will give you an experience that will point the way when you are called upon to make a farewell speech.

EXPLANATION OF THE FAREWELL SPEECH

A farewell speech is one in which a person publicly says goodbye to a group of acquaintances. It should express the speaker's appreciation for what acquaintances have helped them accomplish and for the happiness they have brought them. It may be given at a formal or informal gathering, a luncheon or a dinner. Frequently, on this occasion, the guest of honor will receive a gift from the group. A common informal party occurs when "the boss," a superior, or some other leader calls an informal meeting following the day's work, at which time the person who is leaving will receive commendation, favorable testimonials, and possibly a gift. They, too, will be expected to "say something." The formal occasion is, of course, much more elaborate and is surrounded by formalities from start to finish.

Occasions for the farewell speech are of one general kind – leave taking. Situations may vary greatly; however, a few of the usual ones are the following: retirement after years of service in a certain employment; taking a new job; promotion to a different type of work that demands a change in location; concluding service in a civic or religious organization; leaving school; or moving to another community for any reason whatsoever. The occasion, whatever its nature, should not be treated with too much sadness. It should be approached with true sincerity and honesty. Feelings of deep emotion may be present, and if so, they should be expressed in a manner in keeping with the occasion and all persons present.

HOW TO CHOOSE A TOPIC FOR A FAREWELL SPEECH

Think about the situations outlined in the previous section. Do any of these appeal to you? Have you ever moved from one community or school to another? Was there something you wanted to say to someone you were leaving behind? Select a situation that is realistic for you as a result of your experiences or observations. If you are having difficulty formulating your own topic, consider the following:

1. Going home from a foreign country.
2. Moving to a new location – any reason.
3. Going back home after completing a year's job.
4. Leaving for South America to study rain forests.
5. Going to New York to become an actor.
6. Leaving for college on an athletic scholarship.

HOW TO PREPARE A FAREWELL SPEECH

Remember that this is a special occasion and that old friends are honoring you. Remember, too, that there may be an atmosphere of considerable sentiment and emotion, or there may be one merely of friendly gaiety. This means you must carefully analyze your audience, their probable mood, and the general atmosphere. If you are likely to be presented a gift, plan your remarks so that you may accept it graciously. Sincerity must dominate your utterances whatever they may be.

Farewell speeches usually follow a well-defined pattern with appropriate variations which the speaker deems necessary. It is advisable to begin your talk by referring to the past, the time when you first arrived and why you came to the community. A bit of humor of some interesting anecdotes may be in good taste. The way you were made welcome or to feel at home might be an excellent recollection. Continue your thoughts by pointing out how your ideals and those of the audience, though not completely attained, inspired you to do what you did, that work remains still to be done.

Express appreciation for their support of your efforts which made your achievements possible. Commend the harmony and the cooperation that prevailed. Tell them that you will always remember your associations with this group as one of the outstanding events in your life. Speak next of your future work briefly but sincerely. Explain why you are leaving, and what compelled you to go into a new field or location. Show that your work just completed will act as a background and inspiration to that which lies ahead. Continue by encouraging those who remain, predict greater achievements for them, praise your successor if you know who he is, and conclude with a genuine expression of your appreciation for them and a continued interest in their future. Remember, if you received a gift, to give a final word of thanks for it.

In your speech omit any and all references or illusions to unpleasantries or friction that may have existed. Do not make the occasion bitter or sad. Be happy and leave others with the same feeling. Smile. Make sure that a good impression will follow you.

HOW TO PRESENT A FAREWELL SPEECH

In this speech fit your manner to the mood of the occasion and audience. Do not go overboard in solemnity, emotion, or gaiety. Be appropriate. Use a friendly and sincere approach throughout. Adjust your introductory remarks to the prevailing mood; then move into your speech. Speak loudly enough to be heard by all. Use bodily action suitable to the audience, the occasion, the speech, the environment, and yourself.

Be sure that your language is appropriate to the five requirements just given. Avoid ponderous phrases, over-emotionalized words and tones, redundancy, and flowery or florid attempts at oratory. Let everything you do and say, coupled with a good appearance and alert posture, be the evidence that you are genuinely and sincerely mindful of their appreciation of you at your departure.

FAREWELL SPEECH
by Reed Adams

Fellow faculty members, students, parents, and guests. I am greatly honored by your presence tonight. I have always had a rule to live by when leaving a place to move on in the world, that is to just leave and try to forget the people left behind as soon as possible. However, that will not be possible for me to do with you.

For the last eight years you have shared in my joys and my sorrows; we have shared in change but have learned that change just for change does not work. You people as the community have brought my family and myself from vagabonds of the educational system to actual professionals in that field. I am certain it is your ideals and your school that have made this change in me. Without this change I would not have the opportunity that has now availed itself to me.

I remember my first day at this school just like it was yesterday. I had such high hopes of how I was going to change the whole education system, but my first day at school changed that. The students entered the room and took their seats, but it seemed my techniques of teaching would not work. It seemed that the harder I tried the more the students seemed to resent me and what I was trying to teach them. Then one of the students came up to me at the end of the day and said that he really would have enjoyed my class if he had not had so much on his mind.

I asked him if it was something I could help him with and he said he wished that I could, but I was a little bit too old to be on the football team. I had been so wrapped up in changing the system that I had forgotten to listen and learn what was happening in the school. The biggest game of the season was the first one with us playing Western High. The whole student body was more interested in that than what I was trying to teach, so that's how we got our ten minute rap sessions at the first of every class.

We have had good times, bad times, broken hearts, and romance, but the most important thing we have learned is that we are people and we all make mistakes. That is why we accept other people and their mistakes, as well as our imperfect selves. I am indebted to you all for the wonderful example you have set for me and my family in this area.

Next fall you will continue in your education. Some of you to become doctors and lawyers and others to find jobs out of high school, but whatever you do, I hope you will remember, as I will, the wonderful experiences and academic achievements as well as the sports of Highland High School.

The new house we have purchased in Mississippi has a large mantel in the center of the room and this plaque you have given me tonight will go there beautifully. We had been wondering what we where going to put there. Thank you very much and may whatever you believe in bless and keep you happy.

Chapter *22*

THE EULOGY

Question: What is a pleasant voice – high, low, medium?
Answer: A well-controlled voice of any pitch which is not
extremely high or low may be "pleasant." It is not so
much the pitch as how it is used.

Time limits: 5-6 minutes.
Speaking notes: 10-word maximum.
Sources of information: Two are required, preferably three. For each source give the specific magazine or book it was taken from title of the article, author's full name, date of publication, and the chapter or pages telling where the material was found. If a source is a person, identify the source completely by title, position, occupation, etc. List these on the outline form.
Outline your speech: Prepare a 75-150 word complete sentence outline.

PURPOSE OF THE EULOGY

The speech is assigned so that you may learn by doing and thus become familiar with the speech of eulogy. Frequently a person is called upon to eulogize or praise someone. There are several ways to do this. Of course, the type of eulogy you may be asked to present will depend on different aspects of the speech situation. But whatever that requirement may be, you will be better prepared to do a creditable job if you have had previous experience. This assignment will provide that experience.

EXPLANATION OF THE EULOGY

The eulogy is a speech of praise that is delivered in honor or commemoration of someone living or dead. Sometimes eulogies are presented for animals, particularly dogs, horses, and others. A more fanciful and imaginative eulogy would be one to inanimate objects, such as the sea or the mountains. Some eulogies are written to trees and flowers, but these, too, are abstract and fanciful in nature.

The purpose of a eulogy is to praise and evaluate favorably that which is eulogized; it commends and lifts up the finer qualities and characteristics of the subject eulogized. It stresses the personality of the person (or thing) that it concerns; it tells of their greatness and achievements, their benefits to society, and their influence upon people. It is not merely a simple biographical sketch of someone. To illustrate the point, imagine a eulogy of a great oak, in which the speaker tells the date on which the acorn sprouted, and a later date when the tiny plant emerged from the soil; next the number in inches it grew each year thereafter; and finally the number of leaves it developed in forty years. Compare this with the eulogy of a person, and you can see why a biographical sketch is not a eulogy. Actually, it sounds like a scientific report on a person (or tree).

Occasions for eulogies are many. For persons who are living, the speech may be given on a birthday, at a dinner in honor of an individual, at the dedication of a project someone has created and/or donated. Eulogies often appear at the formal announcement of a political candidate or at an inauguration. For persons who are dead, not considering funeral tributes, eulogies are offered on birthday anniversaries or in connection with notable events or achievements in individuals' lives. Sometimes eulogies in the form of character studies are presented as evidences of good living. They become lessons of life.

HOW TO SELECT A PERSON TO EULOGIZE

First, it is essential that you eulogize someone whom you greatly admire and who, in your opinion, is living or has lived a commendable life. This is necessary, for your eulogy to be completely sincere. Second, select someone about whom you can secure adequate information. Finally, think twice before deciding to eulogize a tree, the sea, the mountains, or an animal, as these are probably more difficult to eulogize than a person. It is wiser to select a person as a subject to eulogize. Suggestions are given in Appendix A.

HOW TO PREPARE A EULOGY

The purpose of eulogy is a set objective, regardless of the time, place or occasion. Since eulogies are intended to stimulate an audience favorably toward the subject and to inspire them to nobler heights by virtue of the examples set by the person being praised, the speaker is not required to determine a purpose in preparing a eulogy.

Having selected the person to be eulogized, you should decide upon the method which you will use in developing the eulogy. Your method and whether or not the individual is living will determine the material that is necessary. Let us examine several different methods of constructing a eulogy.

First, you may follow a chronological order, that is, you will take up events in the order of their development. This will permit a study of their growth and orderly evolution of character in the subject. As you touch upon these broad and influential events in the subject's life, you will point to them as evidences of (1) what the person has accomplished, (2) what they stood for, (3) the nature of their influence upon society, and (4) their probable place in history. In building your speech chronologically do not end by composing a simple biographical sketch. If you do, you will have an informative speech but not a eulogy. It is not enough to list the significant happenings in a person's life chronologically and consider that you have built a eulogy. You must state how they reacted to the events in their life and what happened as a result of them.

For example, if you were eulogizing Franklin D. Roosevelt (chronologically), you would recount, as one event, how he was stricken with infantile paralysis when a grown man, but you would not merely make a statement regarding the tragedy that befell him and then pass on. Rather, you would show how his illness became a challenge to him, how he resolved to live a great life despite a pair of useless legs, how he did overcome his handicap. You would show that, as a result of his illness, he became more resolute, more determined, more kindly. Other incidents should be given similar treatment.

A second method of developing a eulogy might well be labeled the period method. It is the one which covers the growth of an individual by treating different periods in his or her life. It is very broad and makes no attempt to enumerate the many events of their life with their attached significance. Instead of this, using Franklin D. Roosevelt again as an example, you could speak of him as he grew through: (1) boyhood, (2) college life, (3) early political life, (4) late political life.

In following this method you would attempt to bring out the same basic points mentioned above – namely, (1) what they accomplished, (2) what they stood for, (3) their influence upon society, (4) their likely place in history. Although this treatment is broad, it is quite effective.

It should be emphasized at this point that, regardless of which method you use, there are certain necessary points to be observed. A discussion of these follows. First, omit the unimportant events, the small things, and the insignificant details. Second, in developing your speech, point out the struggles which they met in order to achieve their aims. Avoid overemphasis and exaggeration when you are doing this. Third, show the development of ideas and ideals. Fourth, describe relations and services to others and indicate their significance.

It is not necessary to cover up for an individual but rather to admit the human element in them. In doing this, mentioning the human element is enough. It need not be dwelt on nor apologized for. It can be shown that despite weaknesses or shortcomings a person was great. It can be shown that a person lived above these frailties of human nature. But whatever the qualities of your subject, be honest in your treatment. It is only fair to assume that the good outweighed the bad by far, or you would not have elected to eulogize them.

In constructing your speech, be sure you pay careful attention to your introduction and conclusion. Aside from these, do not neglect the logical organization and arrangement of the remainder of your talk. Actually, a eulogy is a difficult speech to prepare. However, if you go about it knowing what you wish to put into it, you should have no particular trouble. When you have the eulogizing speech ready for rehearsal, it will be advisable to practice it aloud until you have thoroughly mastered the sequence of ideas. Do not memorize the speech word for word.

Materials for eulogies may be found in Who's Who, histories, biographies, autobiographies, encyclopedias, newspapers, magazines, and similar sources. Consult your librarian for assistance.

HOW TO PRESENT A EULOGY

Your overall attitude must be one of undoubted sincerity. Be a true believer in the person about whom you speak. Aside from your attitude, you will, of course, observe all the requirements of good speech. There should be no showiness or gaudiness in your presentation that will call attention to you instead of your ideas about the subject of your speech.

You will need to be fully aware of the occasion and atmosphere into which you will step when you deliver the eulogy. It is your responsibility to know what will be required of you in the way of carrying out rituals or ceremonies if they are a part of the program. Since you will be in the limelight, you should fit easily into the situation without awkwardness. Naturally you must adjust your bodily actions and gestures to your environment – and your audience. Your voice should reach the ears of all present. If you are sincere, well prepared, and mean what you say, the eulogy you present should be inspirational to all who hear it.

THEY LABOR UNTIL TOMORROW
A Eulogy to the Living
by Clark S. Carlile

My parents are walking with slowed steps into the last sunset of a long evening. Together they have watched and waited sunsets more than half a century and now the sun hangs low. The night, when it comes, will be lighted by uncounted stars, each recalling days of doing, days of deeds, and love of life and living. The moon will shine through the mists of eternity as the glow of memory lingers after. It will be soft and warm and will light my way.

Our parents can give us life and they can love us. They can teach us truth and train us to be honest and humble. They can guide us to be self-sufficient and enterprising. They can imbue us with courage to do right, to abhor evil, and to so live that the life we leave behind will be exemplary. All this they did, and they were exemplary.

Courage and brave living were and are the moral fiber of my parents' lives. In the debacle of the great depression when financial failure, unemployment, sickness and the hand of defeat hovered over them they were never fugitives of fear. They knew it not. When land they lived on swirled in black clouds above them and when drought laid the land naked of crops and vegetation and cracked it open they did not flee from it nor did they abandon hope. When the years before them were bleak and barren and dry winds seemed interminable they looked each night to the west for the sign of rain.

I saw my father refuse money and aid when he was broken to disaster by blowing dust and the debts of others. I saw him in middle age assume an unbelievable burden helpless debtors placed on his shoulders to free their own. And in this same hour of horror death haunted his only daughter week after week from spring to summer. By his side in those days of doubt and torment my mother was his helpful, steady companion. Together they conquered uncertainty, calmly they waited, and with courage God gives only to kings and queens they saw life reappear in a wasted body and new hope whisper with each dawn.

Years passed as the family necessities were provided. Hands grew tired and calloused by labor, and unending work left its sign on their faces. In those tines of distress there was never defeat. If it ever raised its voice my parents never let it show its form. The five children growing to adulthood knew no words touching despair nor did they hear them. "Things will be better next year," "We must work hard," "We'll wait a little while," "We'll do it later." These were the words. These were the courage. Never the admission that anything was wrong. And now since the years have hurried to yesterday I see their hope, I see their faith, and I know the sacrifice. I know their love and I shall never cease thanking God for them.

Man's religions teach him great principles of the ages and they teach him how to live with his fellow men. My parents have never attended church often. They know well the charities of each day and those on Sunday only. They live every day like Sunday and in their souls is peace of mind known only to those who live well. If God is righteousness, they are Godlike. If God is love, they are Godlike. If God is charity and hope, they are Godlike.

My parents have no wish for fame nor do they seek its fascination. They are not ostentatious. They are in their later years extremely busy. Almost a generation past the age when men retire, my parents are working each day giving to the world a new dignity to labor and hope eternal. And their children, impressed by the lifetime habit of work, attempt to emulate their example of more than half a century.

The sun is sinking low and soon twilight must mingle light and shadows into the darkness of eternity. My parents approach the horizon with uplifted faces and the light of a new day shines on them. They will pass the setting sun leaving only their labors behind. Two people will have lived for their children and for the world. No parents could do more and no parents will have lived better.

EULOGY TO THE CHALLENGER ASTRONAUTS
by President Ronald Reagan
Address to the Nation, January 28, 1986

Ladies and gentlemen, I'd planned to speak to you tonight to report on the state of the Union, but the events of earlier today have led me to change those plans. Today is a day for mourning and remembering.

Nancy and I are pained to the core by the tragedy of the shuttle *Challenger*. We know we share this pain with all of the people of our country. This is truly a national loss.

Nineteen years ago, almost to the day, we lost three astronauts in a terrible accident on the ground. But we've never lost an astronaut in flight; we've never had a tragedy like this. And perhaps we've forgotten the courage it took for the crew of the shuttle; but they, the *Challenger* Seven, were aware of the dangers, but overcame them and did their jobs brilliantly. We mourn seven heroes: Michael Smith, Dick Scobee, Judith Resnik, Ronald McNair, Ellison Onizuka, Gregory Jarvis, and Christa McAuliffe. We mourn their loss as a nation together.

For the families of the seven, we cannot bear, as you do, the full impact of this tragedy. But we feel the loss, and we're thinking about you so very much. Your loved ones were daring and brave, and they had that special grace, that special spirit that says, "Give me a challenge and I'll meet it with joy." They had a hunger to explore the universe and discover its truths. They wished to serve, and they did. They served all of us.

We've grown used to wonders in this century. It's hard to dazzle us. But for 25 years the United States space program has been doing just that. We've grown used to the idea of space, and perhaps we forget that we've only just begun. We're still pioneers. They, the members of the *Challenger* crew, were pioneers.

And I want to say something to the schoolchildren of America who were watching the live coverage of the shuttle's takeoff. I know it is hard to understand, but sometimes painful things like this happen. It's all part of the process of exploration and discovery. It's all part of taking a chance and expanding man's horizons. The future doesn't belong to the fainthearted; it belongs to the brave. The *Challenger* crew was pulling us into the future, and we'll continue to follow them.

I've always had great faith in and respect for our space program, and what happened today does nothing to diminish it. We don't hide our space program. We don't keep secrets and cover things up. We do it all up front and in public . That's the way freedom is, and we wouldn't change it for a minute.

We'll continue our quest in space. There will be more shuttle flights and more shuttle crews and, yes, more volunteers, more civilians, more teachers in space. Nothing ends here; our hopes and our journeys continue.

I want to add that I wish I could talk to every man and woman who works for NASA or who worked on this mission and tell them: "Your dedication and professionalism have moved and impressed us for decades. And we know of your anguish. We share it."

There's a coincidence today. On this day 390 years ago, the great explorer Sir Francis Drake died aboard a ship off the coast of Panama. In his lifetime the great frontiers were the oceans, and an historian later said,"He lived by the sea, died on it, and was buried in it." Well, today we can say of the *Challenger* crew: Their dedication was, like Drake's complete.

The crew of the space shuttle *Challenger* honored us by the manner in which they lived their lives. We will never forget them, nor the last time we saw them, this morning, as they prepared for their journey and waved goodbye and "slipped the surly bonds of earth" to "touch the face of God."

Chapter *23*

THE DEDICATION SPEECH

Question: What is fluency?
Answer: It is the readiness and ease with which words are spoken.

Time limits: 3-4 minutes.
Speaking notes: This is a short speech – you do not need any.
Sources of information: Two are required, preferably three. For each source give the specific magazine or book it was taken from, title of the article, author's full name, date of publication, and the chapter or pages telling where the material was found. If a source is a person, identify the source completely by title, position, occupation, etc. List these on the outline form.
Outline your speech: Prepare a 75-150 word complete sentence outline.

PURPOSE OF THE DEDICATION SPEECH

You may not give a speech at dedication ceremonies for a long time, then again the occasion for a speech of this kind may arise sooner than you had thought possible. But regardless of when you are called on for this type of speech, one thing is sure, and that is that you must know its requirements. The dedication speech occurs on an occasion and in an atmosphere that requires very strict observance of certain aspects of speechmaking. This speech assignment is designed to give an experience like the "real thing," so that you give a creditable performance when the opportunity presents itself.

EXPLANATION OF THE DEDICATION SPEECH

The dedication speech is one presented on commemorative occasions. It is generally brief and carries a serious tone. It employs excellent language, demands careful construction, fine wording, and polished delivery. Its purpose should be to commemorate, to honor an occasion, and to praise the spirt of endeavor and progress that the dedication symbolizes. The speech should thrill the audience with pride regarding their community, ideals, and progress. Occasions for the dedication speech usually involve a group enterprise. Common among these are occasions such as: erecting monuments, completing buildings, stadiums, and baseball parks, or laying corner stones and opening institutions. Similar events considered as marks of progress are also occasions for dedication speeches. Lincoln's Gettysburg Address is one of the finest dedication speeches ever made.

HOW TO CHOOSE A TOPIC FOR A DEDICATION SPEECH

This will involve a bit of imagination on your part; however, choose an occasion that you wish were actually true, really being enacted. For instance, think about someone you consider to be a hero or heroine and dedicate a statue to that person. Would you like to have a new community center in your neighborhood where you could play games with your friends? Then, create a ceremony to break ground, lay a cornerstone, or dedicate a completed building. If you are having trouble developing a topic, consult your teacher for additional suggestions.

HOW TO PREPARE A DEDICATION SPEECH

First, know your purpose. It must dominate this speech the same as the purpose dominates every speech. This means that you are to compliment the ideals and achievements which the dedicated structure symbolizes, thus setting it apart for a certain purpose.

These are the points to cover in the speech. Give a brief history of events leading up to the present time. Mention the sacrifice, the work, the ideals, and the service that lie behind the project. Next, explain the future use or work, the influence or significance that will be associated with the structure being dedicated. Place the emphasis upon what the object dedicated stands for (ideals, progress, loyalty) rather than upon the object itself.

The above thoughts will constitute your material. Now, organize your speech carefully. Pay particular attention to the introduction, the conclusion – yes, everything in your speech. It must have order. To accomplish the organization of the speech you will first outline it. Wording it follows. Do this meticulously. Be understandable and simple in language. The speech is serious, not frivolous. Leave your humor at home.

You are now ready to practice. Do this orally. Rehearse aloud until you have definitely fixed the order of the speech in your mind. Avoid complete word for word memorization. You may memorize certain words and phrases, but you should not memorize the entire speech. When you have mastered an effective presentation, you will be ready to speak. Remember to include appropriate bodily action, gestures, and voice in your practice.

HOW TO PRESENT A DEDICATION SPEECH

The attitude of the speaker should be one of appropriate dignity. Emotion and sentiment should be properly blended to fit the noble sentiments that will be present. The adequacy and poise of the speaker would be obvious from appearance, bearing, and self-confidence.

Body language must be keyed to the tone of the speech. The environment surrounding the speaker may permit much action or limit it severely. If a public address system is used, the speaker cannot move from the microphone. The speaker can and should utilize gestures.

Whether speaking with the aid of a microphone or not, the voice should be full and resonant and easily heard. If the crowd is large, a slower speaking rate should be used. Articulation must be carefully attended, yet not so much so that it becomes ponderous and labored. Voice and action must be in tune, neither one overbalancing the other. The speaker must be animated, alive to the purpose, desirous of communicating, and capable of presenting a polished speech.

DEDICATION OF THE MINI DOME
by Philip Jones

Faculty, students and guests. Some time ago an idea began in the heads of "Dubby" Holt, ISU's athletic director, and Ralph Clark, a construction engineer from Washington, D.C., whose son, Joe Clark, had been a football player at Idaho State University. The idea grew to include "Bud" Davis, ISU's president, who would be instrumental in carrying the idea to students, faculty, and the state board.

Four years ago, when ISU played the University of New Mexico at Albuquerque, Bud Davis, Dubby Holt, Ralph Clark, ISU's financial vice-president William Bartz, and Pocatello architect Cedric Allen went to see and inspect that university's basketball arena. The arena was too small for ISU's football needs, but the trip strengthened the idea, and resolved that ISU could have its own indoor sports arena.

In December of that year the cost and program were submitted to the student body for approval. In January, by popular vote the student body accepted the project and the necessary student revenue bonds.

From this point on we are indebted to the fine efforts of the design team who carried the project through. Many thanks and congratulations must go to those men who spent thousands of hours working on this project. The coordination, cooperation, and communication among the architect, engineers, contractors, sub-contractors, and university are commendable.

Special thanks must go to Cedric Allen – Architect, Ballif and Associates – Structural Engineers, Bridgers and Paxton – Consulting Engineers, Arthur Nelson, Jr. – Electrical Engineer, and John Korbis – ISU's Physical Plant Director for coordinating the design team's efforts.

The significance of the Mini Dome will be measured only by time. It is a structure with a multiplicity of uses. It brings to Idaho the first enclosed collegiate football stadium. This structure will be used for sports at ISU, football, basketball, and track, along with being used by the student body for intramurals and physical education.

The Mini Dome also provides for the community of Pocatello and to Southeast Idaho a large area for the presentation of cultural and civic events that would not otherwise be possible.

The Mini Dome stands for new ideas, vision, and progress. Progress we can be proud of in Pocatello, Idaho. And so by the authority vested in me by the Idaho State Board of Education, I hereby dedicate the Mini Dome to Idaho State University students – past, present, and future.

THE GETTYSBURG ADDRESS
by Abraham Lincoln

Four score and seven years ago our fathers brought forth upon this continent a new nation, conceived in liberty, and dedicated to the proposition that all men are created equal.

Now we are engaged in a great civil war, testing whether that nation so conceived, and so dedicated, can long endure. We are met on a great battlefield of that war. We have come to dedicate a portion of that field as a final resting-place for those who here gave their lives that that nation might live. It is altogether fitting and proper that we should do this.

But in a larger sense, we cannot dedicate – we cannot consecrate – we cannot hallow this ground. The brave men, living and dead, who struggled here, have consecrated it far above our poor power to add or detract. The world will little note, nor long remember, what we say here, but it can never forget what they did here. It is for us, the living, rather, to be dedicated here to the unfinished work which they who fought here have thus far so nobly advanced. It is rather for us to be here dedicated to the great task remaining before us – that from these honored dead we take increased devotion to that cause for which they gave the last full measure of devotion – that we here highly resolve that these dead shall not have died in vain - that this nation, under God, shall have a new birth of freedom and that government of the people, by the people, and for the people, shall not perish from the earth.

Delivered at the dedication of the cemetery in Gettysburg, November 19, 1863, after Edward Everett had made the formal speech of the day.

Chapter *24*

THE ANNIVERSARY SPEECH

Question: How do you speak fluently?
Answer: Fluency varies greatly. Whatever your fluency
is you will be wise to accept it. Thorough preparation,
much oral rehearsal, and experience will help.

Time limits: 5-6 minutes.
Speaking notes: It is advisable to use none. Try it.
Sources of information: Two are required, preferably three. For each source give the specific magazine or book it was taken from, title of the article, author's full name, date of publication, and the chapter or pages telling where the material was found. If a source is a person, identify the source completely by title, position, occupation, etc. List these on the outline form.
Outline your speech: prepare a 75-100 word complete sentence outline.

PURPOSE OF THE ANNIVERSARY SPEECH

The experience of presenting an anniversary speech now will prove helpful to you at some later time when you meet the real situation requiring knowledge of its structure and presentation. A speaker is often disturbed, nervous, and ill at ease when speaking on an occasion that they have never previously experienced. Feelings of uncertainty probably spring from lack of familiarity with the environment. In your case, having known what it is to give an anniversary talk at least once, you should find future performances considerably easier and perhaps enjoyable.

EXPLANATION OF THE ANNIVERSAY SPEECH

The anniversary speech is one presented in commemoration of an event, a person, or occasion of the past. Its purpose is to recall and remember the past so that we may more adequately serve the present and courageously prepare for the future. It will weigh the past, observe the blessings of the present, and look to the future optimistically. Elements of loyalty and patriotism usually are contained in the remarks.

Because this talk is similar to the dedication speech, its requirements of the speaker do not vary noticeably from those for the dedication speech. The speaker should be a good person, both in character and ability. They should be fully acquainted with the history, the present status of the anniversary, and future plans as they pertain to it. You might think of the anniversary as a birthday celebration and incorporate all the ideals and ideas associated with such a day.

Occasions for anniversary speeches arise whenever the passing of time is marked by a pause in which people lay aside their work long enough to note what has been accomplished. The remembrance of Independence Day, landing of the Pilgrims, Armistice, Thanksgiving, Christmas, Labor Day, birthday of a national, state or local figure, are all examples of such occasions. Observance of the progress during a certain number of years of a business firm, a school, a church, a city, state or nation, or any organization, may form the basis of an anniversary speech. During recent years, state centennials marked by regional and state fairs have proved themselves worthwhile as anniversaries. Every day is the birthday of somebody or something; hence every day is a potential anniversary, whether it is observed or not.

HOW TO CHOOSE A TOPIC FOR AN ANNIVERSARY SPEECH

If you have a particular loyalty or devotion, it would be advisable to construct your speech around it at an imaginary or real anniversary. National holidays are natural events for anniversary speeches. They recognize historical events or individuals. Use this assignment as a way to learn something about the history of your school or community. For other suggestions, consult your teacher. Be sure you are interested in the topic you select for your speech.

HOW TO PREPARE AN ANNIVERSARY SPEECH

Remember that your purpose is to commemorate. Keep this purpose in mind constantly. Your thoughts must be constructed to achieve this end. Second, the organization of your speech is important. Here you must observe all the characteristics of adequate speech composition. You should include the following points: Tell why you are especially interested in this anniversary. Show historically that the people and their ideals are responsible for the organization's celebration. Trace the development of these ideals.

Anecdotes, stories, incidents, and humor are appropriate and impressive if properly used. The past should vividly live again for your audience. Turn next to the present; compare it with the past. Avoid references to or implications of partisan or class views. Speak broadly for all the people by utilizing a spirit of friendliness and goodwill. Bend your energies toward unity and interest for the common good. Speak next of the future. By virtue of a splendid past and a significant present, the future holds promises of greater things to be. Speak confidently on this thesis. Indicate that the cooperation of all persons directed toward a determined effort for a greater service to mankind is the goal all are seeking. Show the relationship of this anniversary to the welfare of the state and nation.

After having constructed the speech, be sure to rehearse it aloud until you have fixed the order of points in your mind. Do not memorize it. Practice body language and gestures while rehearsing, but be sure to avoid mechanical movements.

HOW TO PRESENT AN ANNIVERSARY SPEECH

Speak sincerely. If you cannot and do not mean what you say, you should not speak. Your body language and your voice, should evoke sincerity. Maintain good eye contact with your audience. You should be easily heard by all and be completely in their view. Your dress should be appropriate to the occasion. Observe time limits.

REMEMBERING DR. MARTIN LUTHER KING, JR.
by Kansas Governor John Carlin, January 15, 1986

It is a pleasure to be with you once again as we celebrate the birthday of Dr. Martin Luther King, Jr. And I look forward to the first national holiday next Monday. We, in Kansas, can take pride in the fact that we began our recognition one year before the nation. And as we prepare to celebrate our second official holiday, I want to share a few thoughts with you about this celebration, Dr. King, and what his work means to all of us.

National holidays serve as a means of uniting us into a common purpose or reason for celebration. Dr. King's birthday should do both for all Americans. For the one thing we should never forget is that the dream Dr. King had was the American dream — freedom, justice, and opportunity for all. And pursuit of that dream is what all Americans hold in common. Dr. King's life was committed to pursuing and preserving all that America stands for.

And while Dr. King is associated first with his crusade for racial equality, we should all note that he was concerned with the human condition of people throughout the world. So today as we remember Dr. King, we should think about what it means to be "Living the Dream." And we are indeed living the dream when the first woman, Black, or Hispanic astronaut boards the space shuttle.

We are living the dream when a Black Lt. Governor is sworn into office in Virginia. We are living the dream when millions of Americans donate dollars to aid the starving throughout the world. And we are living the dream when a Kansan becomes the first woman on the Globetrotters. In fact, we are living the dream when anyone – Black, White, Brown, or Yellow, male or female – achieves his or her potential. Whenever there is a first, or even a second or twentieth notable achievement by one who previously would not have been allowed to achieve, we all share in the dream. Through such successes, we come one step closer to achieving equal opportunity for all of us.

Dr. King's work has had a tremendous impact on this country and on the world. And not just socially, but economically as well. There are many in our society who are now productive, contributing members who previously would have been denied access. We are long past the days in this country when it took the National Guard to integrate schools, or when fire hoses and police dogs were turned on those pursuing nonviolent means of bringing about racial equality. However, we still have work to do before we can truly say that we have made the dream real for people throughout the world.

Holidays such as this one are an affirmation of our faith, of our belief in what this country stands for. Dr. King believed in this country. And if he were with us today, he would still be working on his dream. So if we live the dream through our actions, through our faith, and through our celebrations of the memory of those who dream, we will make it possible for this generation and future ones to truly be living the dream.

HOW CAN AN INTRODUCTION
GET THE ATTENTION OF THE AUDIENCE?

1. Use a quotation. Sometimes a familiar quotation or a quotation from a familiar person can help the audience get involved with your presentation.

2. Use an important fact or statistic. Find a striking fact or statistic that will immediately catch the interest of the audience so they will say, "I didn't know that."

3. Tell a story or a joke. This will sometimes help break the ice and grab the attention of the audience.

4. Use an action. Actually do something that will attract the attention of the audience.

5. Ask a question. This will often get the audience to think about your topic and draw them in so they want to hear more.

6. Combine any of the methods. Use an action and a story, or ask a question and present a fact. Try your own combinations.

Chapter *25*

THE NOMINATING SPEECH

Question: If your remarks draw applause what should you do?
Answer: Be very happy, wait until it subsides, then go on.

Time limits: 2-4 minutes. Keep your speech within the allotted time.
Speaking notes: Nobody wants to watch you use notes so you will remember how good the candidate is. Do not use notes.
Source of information: None required, however, you should be accurate in your statements regarding qualifications of your nominee and the office they will fill.
Outline your speech: Prepare a 75-150 word complete sentence outline.

PURPOSE OF THE NOMINATING SPEECH

How many times have you heard the remark, "I wish I had nominated Mary for president last night; I almost did. She'd be better than Bill." but, the sad fact remains that Mary, well qualified and capable, was not nominated. Why? Probably because the person who wanted to nominate her lacked the courage to get up and also lacked the knowledge of what to say in order to nominate her effectively. It is hoped that should you ever wish to nominate a capable leader, you will have the courage to rise and speak with the knowledge to utter appropriate thoughts. This experience should show you what to do and how to present an effective nominating speech should the occasion for one arise.

EXPLANATION OF THE NOMINATING SPEECH

A nominating speech is one in which a speaker places the name of another person before an assembly as a candidate for office. The speech is usually not long, most often lasting only a few minutes. There are exceptions, of course. In presenting the candidate to the audience, the speaker tells why the candidate is especially fitted for the office in question. All remarks made by the nominator should be expressed in such a way that they set forth, in an orderly manner, the reasons why the candidate should be elected.

Before a speaker can make a nomination, the chairperson of the assembly must announce that nominations for the _____ office are in order. The speaker must be recognized by the chairperson. This is accomplished when the speaker rises and addresses the chair by saying, "Mr./Madam Chairperson." At the time, the presiding officer will give the speaker permission to speak either by calling the person's name, by nodding, or by some other word or sign. Only then will the nominating speech be in order.

Occasions for nominating speeches arise most often when officers for a society of any kind are elected by a group of people. Many common occasions occur at meetings of political delegates, church representatives, fraternity and sorority members, civic organizations, councils, charitable groups, business leaders, labor unions, school meetings, and many other assemblages or congregations.

HOW TO CHOOSE A CANDIDATE FOR A NOMINATING SPEECH

First, you must have confidence in the ability of the person whom you nominate. Second, be sure that the person is acceptable as a candidate. Choose someone reasonably well-known with a good record. Make certain that if elected the person will do their work competently. For this assignment, think about organizations to which you belong and nominate an officer. Another possible choice for this assignment is to nominate a person for a political office. You can research campaign literature to help you.

HOW TO PREPARE THE NOMINATING SPEECH

The purpose of this speech is obvious. It is equally obvious that all of the elements of the speech should point in one direction: Elect This Candidate! A careful organization should be worked out in which you utilize an arrangement somewhat as follows: Name the office, set forth its specific requirements and indicate what its needs are. Once these points are established, show that your candidate has exceptional fitness to satisfy all the needs and demands of the office. Be specific. Mention training, experience, abilities (especially those of leadership and cooperation with people), outstanding qualities of personality and character, and clinch your point with a statement to the effect that he/she is undoubtedly the person best suited for the office.

If the candidate is well-known, you may present their name at the conclusion of the speech. If they are not well-known, it is advisable to offer the name earlier in the speech, and to mention it once or twice more at appropriate points as well as concluding with it. Gather all information, organize and arrange it as indicated; then practice until you have it well enough in mind to make an effective extemporaneous delivery.

HOW TO PRESENT THE NOMINATING SPEECH

You must have confidence in yourself. The audience can and will sense this. The speaker may achieve the appearance of self-confidence by observing an alert, polite and erect (not stiff) posture. The use of appropriate body language and gestures will be evidence of poise and confidence.

The words of the speech must be vivid, descriptive, and meaningful. They must be carried to your listeners in a voice that is heard clearly and distinctly without traces of straining. There must be a fluency and readiness of speech that fairly shout to the audience that you know what you are talking about and that you want them to understand how important it is that the right person (your candidate) is elected for office.

Your emphasis, spontaneity, and sincerity must be manifested by your entire body. This will be shown by what you do, the way you look, and how you sound. You should avoid giving the appearance of being overconfident, overbearing, or conceited. Have a lively, energetic, unhesitant manner, as well as a pleasant, confident voice, an appropriate appearance, and a sincere desire to communicate. Then you will make a good speech.

NOMINATING SPEECH
by John R. Knorr

In the past years, the Medical Practice Board of Missouri has made many innovative moves, a few of which have been nationwide firsts. These moves have often been spearheaded by a single person. Tonight I am proud to put before the Board such a person for nomination to be chairperson of the Allied Health Advisory Committee, Nell Healy, R.N. Ms. Healy through her work as Head of Nursing at Washington University Hospital has seen the health care field from many sides. She not only has the foresight the chairmanship demands, but also the experience to convert the future into the present. Ms. Healy was at the head of the lobby for the Nurse Training Act that was adopted by the Missouri Legislature last month.

Ms. Healy has shown the Board that there is more to the health care field than patient care in understaffed hospitals. There are dedicated people today who would go into the nursing field if only given the chance. This is because the most vital programs of Nursing Education can't presently give them that chance.

As chairman of the Allied Health Advisory Committee, Ms. Healy will be an advisor to the Missouri Legislature on health care matters. She will be at the head of a branch of the Medical Practice Board that everyone will be proud to represent.

Ms. Healy has shown through her expressed views that the patient and the patient's health are our highest priorities. This post needs a chair with this outlook. For these reasons I am proud to put before the Board Ms. Nell Healy for nomination to be chairperson of the Allied Health Advisory Committee.

CONCLUSIONS

The conclusion is an extremely important part of a speech. It is important to leave the audience with a strong, straightforward impression.

1. Summaries are the most common type of conclusion. If using a summary conclusion, be brief and recap only the main points.

2. Attention-getting materials or anecdotes also make effective conclusions.

3. Review the introduction and see if there is a way to tie the conclusion to it. For instance, if you quote a famous person in the introduction, refer back to the quotation to summarize or quote a similar thought from the same or a different person.

4. Always keep in mind the purpose of the speech and develop an appropriate conclusion. If the purpose is to persuade, an appeal at the end may be effective. If the purpose is to entertain, an amusing story may be the most effective. An appropriate quotation can also be a good way to end a speech.

Chapter **26**

ACCEPTING A NOMINATION OR OFFICE

Question: Should a person try to speak like someone he or she admires?
Answer: No. Develop your own effective speaker style and personality.

Time limits: 1-3 minutes.
Speaking notes: None.
Sources of information: Yourself.
Outline your speech: Prepare a 50-75 word complete sentence outline.

PURPOSE OF ACCEPTANCE SPEECH

Right now you may consider that you are the last person in the world who will ever be nominated for an office or elected to one. Because fate alters circumstances and changes our minds, you may be among those to achieve the distinction of being asked to perform public service. On the other hand, you may openly seek nomination for public duty. Whatever the events that may place you on the rostrum at some future date, you should know beforehand something about accepting a nomination or an office. This speech experience will provide much useful information for you if you are ever to make a speech to accept a nomination or an office.

EXPLANATION OF ACCEPTANCE SPEECH

A speech in which you accept a nomination or an office is one in which you publicly recognize your own nomination or your election to an office. The speech is much the same for either occasion; hence it is unnecessary to make a distinction between the two as far as this discussion is concerned.

Your speech should firmly establish you as a person of ability, courage, and modesty. It should create confidence in you in the minds of the audience. Your purpose is to establish this confidence. An occasion of this sort is potentially important. Anything you say may be used for you or against you. Hence it is essential to say the right thing. It is possible although a bit improbable that you could be nominated or elected and the situation would be a total surprise to you. If this surprise should ever occur, you might be wise not to speak because of unpreparedness, for you could easily say the wrong thing. In such a situation, your own judgment will have to tell you what to do.

Occasions for accepting a nomination or an office may arise any time that candidates are selected or elections held. The selection of officers for private clubs, social and civic organizations, political parties, schools, churches, fraternal groups, and others offer occasions for the acceptance speech.

HOW TO CHOOSE A SUBJECT FOR ACCEPTANCE SPEECH

Base your decision on your own interest in the topic and in the suitability to your audience. Think about the clubs and organizations to which you and your classmates belong. If you hold an office or have held or run for one, recreate that situation.

HOW TO PREPARE ACCEPTANCE SPEECH

First of all, be sure to adhere closely to the rules for preparing and constructing any speech. Assuming that you know these, the next point to consider is the purpose of the speech. The purpose is to establish yourself as a leader and to impress upon people the fact that you are a capable leader. The next logical step is to discover how to accomplish this end. To do this, you will generally speak in appropriate and well-chosen words your appreciation and thanks for the honor conferred upon you. (Do not talk about yourself.) Speak of the organization and its importance. Commend its history, its achievements, and its principles. Explain how these have made it grow and how they will continue to operate in the future. You may refer to the names of great people of past fame in the organization and pay them tribute. You should promise to uphold their ideals. Finally, pledge your loyalty and support to the principles of the organization. State frankly that you accept the nomination or office with a complete realization of its responsibilities and that you intend to carry them out. It will be appropriate as a last remark to express again your appreciation of the honor conferred upon you.

A few points to keep in mind are these: Do not belittle yourself or express doubt regarding your fitness. This would be a perfect opening for your opponent and it would not build confidence among your supporters. Do not express surprise at your nomination or election; this is an old trick worn out long ago and it has little truth or sincerity in it anyway. In no way should you "let the people down" by causing them to feel that they have made a mistake. Rehearse your speech aloud until you have the sequence of ideas well in mind. Give particular attention to the introduction and conclusion.

HOW TO PRESENT ACCEPTANCE SPEECH

Your attitude should be one of dignity, friendliness, sincerity, and enthusiasm. Your manner, your voice, your nonverbal language should all reflect your attitude. Attention should be paid to your dress so that it is appropriate to the occasion, the audience, and yourself.

When you rise to speak, it is likely that there will be applause. Wait until the applause subsides before you begin to speak. If the applause continues long, raise your hand to ask for silence and a chance to speak. Talk loudly enough to be heard by all, speak clearly and distinctly, and do not talk either too fast or too slowly. If your voice echoes, slow down. Try to make your ideas understandable, and you will be likely to present a good speech.

ACCEPTING A NOMINATION
by Tom J. Mayer

Mr. President, officers, and fellow members of F.F.A., all of you are dedicated to a purpose which can be realized: The purpose of strengthening the agricultural backbone of our country and restoring the farm family to its rightful position. We have seen our parents and grandparents toil long hours to nurture life in once fallow tracts of land. The recognition they deserve still lies fallow, but the Future Farmers of America are seeing more than the vision of our parents – we are seeking the culmination of world events that must place the fruits of our labor in utmost demand.

The heritage of the farmer in this country is rich. Cities, towns, even countries have been fed, and they receive the fruit of our greatest office, that of provider. Each one of us stands in the gap as provider for the world. Let us stand boldly in recognition of the office handed us by our parents, and make them as proud to be called our parents as we are to be called their children.

The nomination to the office of national president of Future Farmers of America is a special privilege, and one I accept with much pride and appreciation. The challenge demanded by this position is great, not only because of the decisions concerning future operations, but because of the standards realized by all of you. I accept this nomination with confidence in the foundation of our heritage and the progressive attitude of our membership.

ACCEPTING AN OFFICE
by Mary-Alice Shaw

President Ugaki, members of the Board, and delegates: Three years ago I was attracted to the Intermountain Hospice Support Group for personal reasons. I admired the unique combination of compassion and professionalism evident within the organization, and I appreciated the fact that your support existed for those of us left to deal with terminal illness at some level in our lives.

As I look around at those of you here today, I see the past three years reflected back at me. I see the tears shared, the small joys experienced, and the patience and understanding given so readily and so often. I see a concept which has grown and flourished and gained validity and worldwide recognition.

I have endeavored to contribute as much of my abilities and talents and time as I could toward our common goals, and I have been proud to be a part of the whole. The challenges have been difficult, the failures few but palpable and the satisfactions many, but the people involved have impressed me the most.

I've come to respect each of you with whom I've worked for your cooperative spirit and extensive knowledge and extreme caring. Your willingness to teach me what you could was gratifying. Your criticisms were valid and offered in a constructive manner. You supported my ideas and projects, and you gave me that important pat on the back for encouragement when most needed. This has all provided me with one of the most positive work environments imaginable, and I thank you for that.

Just when I thought I had the best of situations, you topped it by asking me to accept the position of Regional Coordinator. I'm pleased and humbled by the realization that you know I can do this most important job for you and do it well.

We have difficult decisions ahead of us. There are many questions on controversial subjects to be answered. There are sensitive ethical and moral realities to be faced. I appreciate your confidence in my ability to make those decisions wisely.

I willingly accept that challenge. I am excited by the responsibilities which await us, and I know that together we can accomplish so much in the field of terminal care giving. I am honored to be able to represent you as your Regional Coordinator. Thank you.

Chapter **27**

THE COMMENCEMENT SPEECH

> *Question: How important is the speech introduction?*
> *Answer: Very important! It is the audience's first impression*
> *of you as a speaker.*

Time limits: 5-7 minutes.
Speaking notes: 10-word maximum limit.
Sources of information: Two are required, preferably three. For each source give the specific magazine or book it was taken from, title of the article, author's full name, date of publication, and the chapter or pages telling where the material was found. If a source is a person, identify the source completely by title, position, occupation, etc. List these on the outline form.
Outline your speech: Prepare a 75-100 word complete sentence outline.

PURPOSE OF THE COMMENCEMENT SPEECH

How many times have you been to a graduation of a friend or relative only to hope that the speeches are short so you can get on with the ceremony? Unfortunately, this is the way many people feel about the speeches presented at graduation ceremonies. The speaker is not really the highlight of the ceremony. But the commencement speech need not be boring for the audience. A well executed commencement address will cause the audience to reflect on the past and inspire them to action in the future. This speech has its own unique difficulties. The speaker must be able to adapt to a dual audience of parents and relatives along with the students. The ability to adapt to both audiences and present an interesting, stimulating speech is the focus of this assignment.

EXPLANATION OF THE COMMENCEMENT SPEECH

Occasions for commencement speeches are not as numerous as are those for other types of speeches. Commencement ceremonies usually limit their speakers to a special guest, the senior class president, the valedictorian or salutatorian. But they are nonetheless a very important part of the whole ceremony. There are several objectives for the commencement speech. The speech should congratulate the students and family members on their accomplishments which led to graduation. The importance here is to not neglect parents and relatives in the audience who had a part in the student's education. It is important to emphasize both groups' accomplishments. A similar objective is to pay tribute to the teachers and administrators who helped the students through the education system. Another objective is to reflect on past memories and traditions.

This part of the speech is one most appreciated by the students in the audience. Stories about the things that have happened over the years and special memories are reflected by the speaker. The caution here is not to present stories that are too "inside" for the rest of the audience to understand. The speech should have a serious overtone, but humorous anecdotes and stories can help liven up the presentation. A third objective is to issue a challenge to the graduates for the future. The speaker must inspire the audience to do great things as they embark on a new chapter in their lives.

SUGGESTED TOPICS FOR A COMMENCEMENT SPEECH
The occasion of a commencement speech generally dictates the topics that are included in the presentation. Therefore, the speaker needs to find appropriate examples and inspiring stories to include in the speech. A future challenge should also be one of the topics that the speaker should cover.

HOW TO CHOOSE A TOPIC FOR YOUR COMMENCEMENT SPEECH
One of the most important things to remember about choosing a topic is that it needs to be adaptable to the variety of audience members. The speaker will be dealing with the students who are anxious to graduate, along with the different generations of parents, grandparents and friends. Many of these people have attended these types of ceremonies before and have certain expectations of commencement speeches. The student speakers should remember that "inside" stories of past experiences may not be of interest, or make much sense, to anyone other than their classmates.

HOW TO PREPARE YOUR COMMENCEMENT SPEECH
As with any speech presentation, careful attention should be paid to organization and supporting material. The speaker should prepare examples and stories which support the themes of the presentation. The examples should be vivid, interesting and make the principles of the speech come alive. Quotations from philosophers or other respected individuals may be utilized. Use of contrast may be helpful as the speaker issues challenges for the students' new endeavors. Commencement is a beginning along with an ending and may be contrasted with other beginnings. The speech must leave the audience with a sense of accomplishment and an eagerness to move into the future. Therefore, organization of the presentation must build to these points.

A guest speaker should attempt to impart some personal wisdom, which comes with age, to the audience. The audience is being prepared for something the speaker will have already been through, and for the problems that will be faced by the students. The speaker becomes the expert, leading the younger generation into their new world. A senior class president, valedictorian or salutatorian becomes the representative of the student body at the commencement ceremony. Their presentations should reflect the themes that are important to their classmates. They should bring back memories of happy times, sad times and important times in their lives. The examples and stories need to relate well to both the studentsinf the audience and the parents and relatives who are in attendance.

HOW TO PRESENT THE COMMENCEMENT SPEECH
Since the commencement speaker is not the real highlight of the ceremony, the speaker needs to grab and hold onto the attention of the audience. The speaker must be dynamic and enthusiastic. But at the same time the speaker must be sincere and earnest.

Many times the student speaker must deal with the emotions that are present during this time. Practice is essential. Practice in front of people should be a requirement. The parts of the speech that need to be inspiring should be delivered in that enthusiastic, dynamic tone. Other parts of the speech which call for earnest reflection, and sincere gratitude also need to be delivered in the appropriate tone. The speech should also be long enough to get the message across but not too long so that the audience feels trapped or begins to feel bored. The speaker must remember that there are other parts to the ceremony. A long commencement speech is generally not well received by the audience.

All other presentational skills for speaking to large audiences should be observed. Speakers may wish to review the chapter dealing with speaking from a microphone prior to presenting this speech. Also prior to presenting, a review of the chapters which cover speeches to persuade and convince might be helpful.

CHOICES AND CHANGE: YOUR SUCCESS AS A FAMILY
by Barbara Bush, First Lady of the United States

Thank you President Keohane, Mrs. Gorbachev, trustees, faculty, parents, Julie Porer, Christine Bicknell and the Class of 1990. I am thrilled to be with you today, and very excited, as I know you must all be, that Mrs. Gorbachev could join us.

More than ten years ago when I was invited here to talk about our experiences in the People's Republic of China, I was struck by both the natural beauty of your campus and the spirit of this place.

Wellesley, you see, is not just a place, but an idea, an experiment in excellence in which diversity is not just tolerated, but is embraced.

The essence of this spirit was captured in a moving speech about tolerance given last year by the student body president of one of your sister colleges. She related the story by Robert Fulghum about a young pastor who, finding himself in charge of some very energetic children, hit upon a game called "Giants, Wizards and Dwarfs." "You have to decide now," the pastor instructed the children, "Which are are. . . a giant, a wizard or a dwarf?" At that, a small girl tugging on his pants leg, asked, "But where do the mermaids stand?"

The pastor told her there are *no* mermaids. "Oh yes there are," she said. "I am a mermaid."

This little girl knew what she was and she was not about to give up on either her identity *or* the game. She intended to take her place wherever mermaids fit into the scheme of things. Where *do* the mermaids stand...all those who are different, those who do not fit the boxes and the pigeonholes? "Answer that question," wrote Fulghum, "And you can build a school, a nation, or a whole world on it."

As that very wise young woman said..."Diversity, like anything worth having requires *effort.*" Effort to learn about and respect difference, to be compassionate with one another, and to cherish our own identity, and to accept unconditionally the same in all others.

You should all be very proud that this is the Wellesley spirit. Now I know your first choice for today was Alice Walker, known for the *The Color Purple.* Instead you got me – known for the color of my hair! Of course, Alice Walker's book has a special color, and for four years the class of '90 has worn the color purple. Today you meet on Severance Green to say goodbye to all that, to begin a new and very personal journey, a search for your own true colors.

In the world that awaits you beyond the shores of Lake Waban, no one can say what your true colors will be. But this I know: You have a first class education from a first class school. And so you need not, probably cannot, live a "paint-by-numbers" life. Decisions are not irrevocable. Choices do come back. As you set off from Wellesley, I hope that many of you will consider making three very special choices.

The first is to believe in something larger than yourself, to get involved in some of the big ideas of your time. I chose literacy because I honestly believe that if more people could read, write and comprehend, we would be that much closer to solving so many of the problems plaguing our society.

Early on I made another choice which I hope you will make as well. Whether you are talking about education, career or service, you are talking about life, and life must have joy. It's supposed to be fun!

One of the reasons I made the most important decision of my life, to marry George Bush, is because he made me laugh. It's true, sometimes we've laughed through our tears, but that shared laughter has been one of our strongest bonds. Finds the joy in life, because as Ferris Bueller said on his day off:

"Life moves pretty fast. Ya don't stop and look around once in a while, ya gonna miss it!"

The third choice that must not be missed is to cherish your human connections: your relationships with friends and family. For several years, you've had impressed upon you the importance to your career of dedication and hard work. This is true, but as important as your obligations as a doctor, lawyer or business leader will be, you are a human being first and those human connections, with spouses, with children, with friends, are the most important investments you will ever make.

At the end of your life, you will never regret not having passed one more test, not winning one more verdict or not closing one more deal. You will regret time not spent with a husband, a friend, a child or a parent.

We are in a transitional period right now, fascinating and exhilarating times, learning to adjust to the changes and the choices we, men and women, are facing. I remember what a friend said, on hearing her husband lament to his buddies that he had to baby-sit. Quickly setting him straight, my friend told her husband that when it's your own kids, it's not called babysitting!

Maybe we should adjust faster, maybe slower. But whatever the era, whatever the times, one thing will never change: fathers and mothers, if you have children, they must come first. Your success as a family, our success as a society, depends not on what happens at the White House, but on what happens inside your house.

For over 50 years, it was said that the winner of Wellesley's annual hoop race would be the first to get married. Now they say the winner will be the first to become a C.E.O. Both of these stereotypes show too little tolerance for those who want to know where the mermaids stand. So I offer you today a new legend: the winner of the hoop race will be the first to realize her dream, not society's dream, her own personal dream. And who knows: Somewhere out in this audience may even be someone who will one day follow in my footsteps, and preside over the White House as the president's spouse. I wish him well!

The controversy ends here. But our conversation is only beginning. And a worthwhile conversation it is. So as you leave Wellesley today, take with you deep thanks for the courtesy and honor you have shared with Mrs. Gorbachev and me. Thank you. God bless you. And may your future be worthy of your dreams.

Delivered at Severance Green, Wellesley College, Wellesley, Massachusetts
June 1, 1990

Reprinted with permission from *Vital Speeches of the Day,* July 1, 1990, p. 549

Chapter 28

MAKING AN ANNOUNCEMENT

Question: What can be done if your throat becomes dry while speaking?
Answer: Not much when it happens. Don't panic. Experience before an audience
usually causes this dryness to disappear. Take precautions by drinking tap water
before you speak and having a glass at the podium.

Time limits: 2-4 minutes. (This means the total time to be used for all of your announcements combined.)
Speaking notes: Yes. Be sure you have exact information.
Special note to student: Prepare at least two or three announcements for his assignment.
Sources of information: If the announcements are real, state your sources of information on the outline form.
Outline your speech: Prepare a 20-40 word complete sentence outline for each announcement.

PURPOSE OF MAKING AN ANNOUNCEMENT

Each year many millions of announcements are made. Each year many people who hear these announcements are left in a confused state of mind because the information presented was poorly organized, obscure, incomplete, or could not be heard. Often, as a result, attendance at clubs, schools, churches, and other organizations has been disappointing. It is true that you cannot force people to attend a gathering, but it is just as true that you can increase attendance by making absolutely certain that everyone within hearing distance of your voice is completely informed of and aware of the event that you are announcing. Because announcements are so very important, this speech experience is assigned to you.

EXPLANATION OF AN ANNOUNCEMENT

An announcement is a presentation of information. It is brief, concise, to the point, and pertinent. It tells specifically about something in the past (who won a prize), about immediate events to occur (the governor will appear in one minute, or, there will be an important business meeting following adjournment), or about events in the near future (a dance to be sponsored next month). An announcement should be crystal-clear in meaning, contain all necessary and helpful data, be stated in easily understandable terms, and be heard by everyone present. Occasions for its use arise at practically every kind of meeting where people convene.

HOW TO CHOOSE AN ANNOUNCEMENT

Think about your activities. What events are connected with them? What events have you attended that were sponsored by a group of which you are not a member? Use those real experiences as the basis for your announcement. Consider some of the following as well: a school dance, a picnic, a special sale, a visit by a yearbook salesperson. Check the community events calendar in your local newspaper or ask your instructor for other ideas.

HOW TO PREPARE AN ANNOUNCEMENT

The chief purpose of an announcement is to inform. Keep this in mind as you prepare your material. Organize your information in the manner that you would organize any good speech. Have an interesting introduction and a strong conclusion, as well as good organization of the other necessary parts of a speech.

Your first job will be to gather information. Be sure you secure this from authentic and authoritative sources. Do not rely on hearsay. Be absolutely certain that your data are accurate and correct to the last detail. If there is any doubt at all, recheck the material before presenting your announcement. It is your responsibility to have in your possession any and all last minute information available. Ascertain whether any changes have occurred since you first received your information.

The organization of your announcement is important. You must determine the order in which you will present your information so that it will be in logical sequence. It is considered advisable according to some research to place your most important point first to achieve greatest effectiveness.

Generally, your announcement would follow an order of items for presentation similar to the following. Show that the event is timely and opportune. If there are known or probable objections, refute them impersonally; however, avoid going into defensive debate or offering a long list of excuses for the action your announcement proposes. (Show its value and appropriateness as related to the audience.)

Second, name the exact place of meeting and its location. Tell how to get there, if this is advisable. If it is necessary, indicate the advantage of the place. State the time. Give the date, the day, and the exact hour. If there is an admission charge, give the price or prices. If desirable, tell about the reasonableness of the charges, and where the money will go, especially when the project is a worthy one. If there are tickets, tell where, when, and how they may be secured. If reserved seats are available, explain any special conditions concerning them. Finally, summarize by restating the occasion, the place, the time, and the admission. Omit "I thank you" when you finish.

Not all of the above points are included in every announcement. Your own judgment will tell you what should be omitted or added.

Prepare notes to be used in making your announcements so that nothing essential is omitted. Use cards at least three inches by five inches in size. Make your notes brief, orderly, and legible. Rehearse them until you have everything well in mind.

HOW TO PRESENT AN ANNOUNCEMENT

Your attitude will be one of alertness and politeness. There will be no great need for bodily action other than that which naturally accompanies what you have to say. You must speak clearly and distinctly. All places, dates, days, and times must be articulated so that no misunderstanding prevails when the announcement is given.

Your place should be before the audience where all can see and hear you, not back in an obscure corner or elsewhere among the crowd. Go to the front and stand near the center of the platform. Observe good posture. Pause until you have gained the attention of the audience. Your first words should be heard by everyone. In some cases you may need to raise your hand or rap on a table to get attention. However, do not attempt to talk above crowd noises if the audience is slow to respond. When referring to your notes, hold them up so that you can keep your eyes on the assembly and avoid talking to the floor. When you finish, simply resume your former position in the audience or gathering.

ANNOUNCEMENT
by Sue Watson

Attention	ATTENTION, all middle-school students!
Who	All sixth, seventh, and eighth grade students are invited and encouraged to participate in Mueller Middle School's Annual Earth Day Celebration.
When	On Monday, April 24, Mueller will recognize Earth Day by sponsoring a
What	Neighborhood Cleanup, Recycling and Graffiti Removal Day.
Where	Students should report to the Commons Area after Second Hour.
Details	Wear jeans, long-sleeved shirts, soft-soled shoes and bring gloves from home if possible.
Summary	All who participate will receive extra-credit and a sense of pride in our community. Remember to participate in this worthwhile event. Help protect our fragile planet! See Ms. Watson for more information or questions.

TRANSITIONS:
HOW TO HOLD YOUR SPEECH TOGETHER

Transitions are a very important part of a speech. Transitions act as the glue that holds a speech together. Effective transitions create coherency and flow.

Where are transitions needed? Transitions are needed throughout the speech between the major parts such as the introduction to the body or body to conclusion. Transitions are also needed to tie supporting materials to main points or to move from one example or main point in the body to another. Pay close attention to transitions. Let transitions guide your audience through your speech.

Examples:

This leads us to the conclusion . . .
The next topic . . .
In review . . .
What point can be drawn from these statistics?
In summary . . .
This story illustrates . . .
First of all . . .
Another . . .
However . . .

Chapter **29**

THE INTERVIEW

Question: Is loud and boisterous speech effective?
Answer: No. It may interfere with what you are saying.

Time limits: 4-6 minutes for report of an interview.
1/2 -2 minutes for role-played telephone appointment.
5-10 minutes for a role-played interview.
Speaking notes: 25-50 words for interview report.
Sources of information: List the person interviewed.
Outline your speech: Prepare 75-100 word complete sentence outline.

PURPOSE OF THE INTERVIEW EXPERIENCE

The interview, in some form or another, will be a probable event in your life. Perhaps you have already interviewed for a job or are planning to do so. Unless you are that one person in a million you will be interviewed (briefly or extensively) before you are employed and whether or not you get the job, or any other favorable response, will depend on how you conduct yourself under interview circumstances. And if you are interviewing for other reasons, to gain information, for a report, to prepare a newscast, to prepare a legal brief for a case in court, or to sell an article, the maturity, skill, and judgment you exercise will bring success or failure. This experience will add to your chances for success, help put money in your pocket, and give the confidence needed to do well.

EXPLANATION OF THE INTERVIEW

An interview is talking with another person or a group for a specific purpose. It is a series of questions and answers. Most are planned. Impromptu interviews, however, occur among business people and others often observed on the street, in a store, even in a home. Unplanned interviews possess characteristics of conversation while more formal interviews tend to proceed in a more structured manner. It is the latter we wish to discuss here since they impose restrictions on the parties involved such as (1) making an appointment; (2) having a limited time period for you to finish the interview; (3) having several separate meetings, all scheduled before you complete your interview purpose.

One common element in an interview is talk; thus, if you can express yourself well things should go smoothly. If you cannot, you may have trouble. Another common element is your physical behavior, your appearance, your walk, your posture, subtle movements of your hands and feet, eye contact, facial expressions. Everything you say and do tells something about you and altogether it tells what you really are. It is your personality. Your thoughts and moods, attitudes and feelings, are all symbolized by your total behavior and you can't hide them. You are kidding yourself if you think you have secretly mastered an art of deceit and won't be discovered. Business executives or sales personnel are quick to detect a phony.

Since the interview situation often places the parties involved close together, perhaps in a small office, the interview permits many personal judgments and subconscious reactions. In effect the interview places all participants in positions of judgment with everyone revealing themselves to other persons present. No one has yet invented a better way to formulate final evaluations of people whether it be a prospective employee or prospective boss.

Occasions for interviews occur in all kinds of employment, inquiries for information, sales situations, personnel work, special reports and surveys, and others.

Remember an interview may be conducted by a group such as when news reporters interview a governor or other official. In contrast to this, a school board may interview a prospective teacher and the teacher may interview the board members. Or a single reporter might interview any executive or administrative group.

HOW TO CHOOSE AN INTERVIEW SITUATION

Select a topic that interests you and one you can complete. Avoid a person or group too distant to reach or who cannot grant the interview within a short time or at a time you can meet. Make your choice and arrangements within twenty-four hours. Why so soon? You may learn that the person you want to interview is on vacation or ill, thus you will be forced to contact someone else.

Since many of the people you might want to interview could have last-minute conflicts, schedule the interview several days ahead of your due date. Thus, if the person must cancel, you still have time to reschedule before the due date. For this assignment, think about a person who has a job you want to hold someday. Use the interview to learn about it. You can also interview someone who makes policies that affect you – school administrators, local and state officials. If you are interested in learning more about a historic or current events topic, interview an expert.

HOW TO PREPARE FOR AN INTERVIEW (THE INTERVIEWER)

1. Since you are the interviewer make an appointment and if it is made in person be prepared to conduct it on the spot should the interviewee suggest you do so. If your appointment is by telephone be pleasant and efficient by using a carefully prepared and rehearsed request constructed as follows: (a) make sure you are talking with the right person, (b) introduce yourself completely, (c) explain why you want the interview, also suggesting the amount of time needed, the date, hour, and place. Do not apologize, (d) leave your name, telephone number, and ask to be called should it be necessary for the interviewee to change the appointment. Sometimes a secretary will take your appointment.

2. Regardless of whether you are interviewing for a job or to acquire information for a report you should acquaint yourself with background data about your interviewee. Ask an assistant to send you information about the interviewee and the business.

Now comes the crux of your interview preparation. What is your purpose and what do you want to know? You will determine the purpose first; second you will prepare a list of about ten lead questions and twenty specific inquiries that will bring out the information you want. Do not read your list of questions verbatim while interviewing. Memorize selected questions from it to be used as needed. You will refer to your list occasionally and originate other questions as the interview proceeds.

3. Dress neatly, carefully and appropriately. Avoid being conspicuous by your appearance. Casual school clothes are not suitable. Dress for an adult's approval who is used to seeing secretaries and other employees attired to meet the business world. You can fail an interview before opening your mouth to speak if appearance suggests carelessness or disregard for the situation. Recently a personnel worker who interviewed job applicants for a large mercantile business told the writers that some applicants appeared for interviews without regard to their appearance and seemingly with an attitude their appearance was a personal matter and none of the interviewer's business. They were not even considered and would have saved everyone's time by not applying.

4.Get the correct address and exact time for the interview. Be sure of this. Allow more time than needed to get there. You might have car trouble or traffic problems. If you are going to a location you haven't had to find before, do a test run before the interview date to make sure you can find it.

5. Study the background information and your list of questions. They should be partially memorized. Be sure you have your questions laid out with adequate space for writing responses to them or provide yourself with an additional notebook for recording the interviewer's answers. Also have a pencil or pen that works. Tape recording is a good idea, but be sure to ask permission to record when you make the appointment.

6. Think of your approaching interview as an enjoyable experience.

HOW TO CONDUCT AN INTERVIEW (TO ACQUIRE INFORMATION)

Arrive ten minutes early at the office of the interviewee. Inquire where to locate Mr./Ms._____, or tell the secretary, if one is present, who you are and that you are there to meet your appointment. When informed that Mr./Ms._____is ready, go into the office, introduce yourself if the secretary fails to do this, shake hands (use a firm grip), politely wait to be seated when invited or seat yourself if your judgment tells you it is appropriate. The host may be busy at a desk and request you to wait a moment. You may stand or sit politely, or look over the office furnishings and arrangements casually, but don't fidget or pace nervously. You might glance over your list of questions to refresh your memory. When your host is ready you may sincerely comment on the office, the view, or something of general interest as an opening remark.

Start your interview by explaining why you are there. State your questions courteously, tactfully, and directly. Initial opening questions may concern (1) history of the business, (2) the nature of the business such as products sold or services performed,

(3) number of employees, labor practices, qualifications of employees, vacations, employee benefits, (4) advantages of this business. Do not press questions on any subject the interviewee obviously doesn't want to discuss. It's your obligation to direct the interview into the desired areas and bring the discussion back if it gets too far off the subject. Remember this is your interview. Bring the interview to a pleasant conclusion (perhaps by saying you have one more question), and do not overstay your time. Should the interviewee offer to show you the place of business, have a cup of coffee, or tour the grounds, accept graciously but don't forget that time may be limited – don't overstay your invitation. Thank the interviewee when it seems appropriate and extend an invitation to visit your school.

While the interview is underway take notes quickly and accurately. (Write clearly so you can read your notes later.) Listen attentively so you won't have to ask to have the information repeated, and should time run out request a later appointment to finish the interview. Thank the interviewee before leaving.

Be courteous at all times. Avoid random, nervous movements, any familiarities, excessive throat clearing, mumbling, and usually it's advisable not to smoke even if invited.

HOW TO INTERVIEW FOR A JOB

Let's suppose you must interview for a job. You will be the interviewee and the interviewer. Questions will be directed to you and you will ask questions about the work. Read again the preceding section on conducting an interview to refresh your thinking. Next, you should have a copy of your resume which includes personal information, honors received, offices held, activities participated in, memberships, a record of your work experience, a list of at least three personal references with complete addresses and telephone numbers (a business person, teacher or other influential person) and/or letters of recommendation. All of these may not be required but they should be available in neatly typed form and correct. Several extra copies of these records should be kept in your files. Before you are interviewed you may be required to fill out an application form and, if so, fill it out completely answering every question fully. Be neat and accurate. Omit nothing and don't assume that a stranger studying the form will be able to read your mind and fill in blank spaces. There are several good books available on resume preparation. Check your school or public library.

When you go into the job interview conduct yourself as you would before any business or professional person. Greet the interviewer cordially, shake hands if appropriate, state your purpose and ask generally what positions are available unless you are applying for a particular one. So you will know what is expected of you ask about the qualifications, responsibilities, duties, and requirements of the offering. Most likely you will be asked questions about your experience, background, training and education. Answer these questions honestly and directly but don't belittle yourself. Suggest that the interviewer might like to examine summaries of your personal history, training, experience and recommendations you have with you. Sit politely while the interviewer reads them. Besides the job you are applying for they may be looking for someone to fill a special position that is not advertised and it's quite possible they would select you, especially if you conduct a superior interview showing alertness and intelligence. Or maybe they will try you out at something less important with the idea of moving you up if you are a superior worker. As the interview progresses you should be ready to talk and give answers or to wait with poise if anything unusual occurs. Sometimes interruptions are planned to test your reactions – the telephone rings, a secretary brings a message, an employee comes in. Or sometimes the interviewer asks a startling or unexpected question. Don't be surprised at anything – just respond intelligently and respectfully.

Before the interview ends, if you haven't been told, inquire about company policy concerning union membership, insurance, advancements, salary or wages, vacations, sick leave, and other important matters. If it appears appropriate you might ask to be shown around the buildings or grounds where you would work. In all instances when you inquire avoid an attitude of distrust or suspicion – just be interested, courteous, alert.

Before the interview concludes ask when you will be notified about the job. If you receive a vague or indefinite answer ask if you may contact them or write them at a future date. It is only fair before you leave that you have their word you will be notified within a reasonable time.

When the interviewer indicates that the interview is ending bring your remarks to a close, extend thanks again, and leave. Sometimes it may be necessary for you to close the interview – you can stay too long.

Here's a hint: If you don't fill out an application form and you want the interviewer to remember you instead of one of a dozen other applicants, hand the interviewer a three-by-five card as the interview ends. On it, neatly typed, include your name, address, telephone number, education, work experience, and type of work you are interested in or qualified to do.

Assignment 1. (Appointment for job interview) The instructor may develop the Interview Assignment as follows:

Two persons at a time sitting back-too-back eight to ten feet apart carry out an imagined telephone conversation. One is a business person, the other a student seeking an appointment for an interview. Other persons, appointed by the instructor, may occasionally answer the telephone instead of the business person. Don't overdo the role-playing – and keep it realistic. The instructor may send the student outside the classroom while the appointment situation is set up. The person seeking the appointment then enters the room, takes a seat, and proceeds to pantomime a phone call to the business person. Be sure to have a specific job description in mind when asking for the interview.

Note: If time permits, students should participate in Assignment 1 before doing Assignments 2 or 3.

Assignment 2. (The job interview)

Two persons role-play the job interview for five to ten minutes. The interviewee should enter the classroom door after the instructor has set up any special circumstances the interviewer will confront. The business person, a secretary, or someone else will admit the student who will take it from there. This should not be rehearsed by the participants since a real interview is not rehearsed; however, the participants should be well prepared to conduct their individual parts and try to make the entire experience true to life.

Assignment 3.

The appointment and interview aspects of this assignment should be role-played success-fully before any student is permitted to actually complete the interview with a business person. Here's the assignment.

1. By telephone make an appointment with a business or professional person whom you do not know personally.

2. Complete an interview to learn about the business, its general operations, policies (labor, products, organization, etc), and future plans. Take notes. Prepare a five to six minute oral report of the interview and what you learned for the class.

The instructor should keep a list of all business persons interviewed in order that future classes will not interview the same ones too often. A letter of appreciation from the interviewer and the instructor to the business person expressing gratitude for the coopera-tion is a good practice.

Assignment 4.

Students wanting work should conduct actual job interviews, then prepare five to six minute oral reports of their experiences for the class.

Chapter **30**

THE BOOK REVIEW

Question: How do you enunciate correctly?
Answer: Sound the letters t, d, p, b, k, g, ch, s, sh, distinctly,
especially those in the middle and at the end of words. Stress
syllables properly.

Time limits: 10-15 minutes.
Speaking notes: Fifty word limit.
Outline your speech: Prepare a 75-100 word complete sentence outline.

PURPOSE OF THE BOOK REVIEW

There are two reasons for this book review assignment. The first reason is that you should have the experience of preparing and presenting a book review so you will know first hand how it is done. While you are doing this, you will gain much valuable information and enjoyment from the book you are reviewing. The second reason is that as a class project you will, as one member of the group, add much to the knowledge of all of the members of the class. Because each member will review a separate book, many different authors' ideas will be presented. This in turn will provide a general fund of information that would otherwise be unattainable.

EXPLANATION OF THE BOOK REVIEW

An oral book review is an orderly talk about a book and its author. This requires that you provide pertinent information about the author as well as what was written. Generally speaking, you should include an evaluation of the work relative to composition and ideas. The ends of your talk will be to inform, to stimulate, to entertain, and, possibly, to convince. The book reviewer is expected to know the material well, to be informed regarding the methods of giving a review, and to be able to present the information in an organized and interesting manner. These requirements demand an unusually thorough preparation.

Occasions for the book review can occur almost anywhere. They arise in scholastic, civic, religious, and other organizations. In practically any kind of club or society, school or church, a book review often forms the basis of a program.

SUGGESTED TYPES OF BOOKS FOR A REVIEW

For this particular experience it is suggested that each student select a different book. It is easier if it is fiction as contrasted to non-fiction or a textbook. You may want to use a book you are reading for another class or a book you have recently read. You probably won't have time to read a new novel before you speak. Whatever the book, it should be approved by the instructor before you start to prepare your speech.

HOW TO CHOOSE A BOOK FOR REVIEW

First of all, follow your instructor's assignment. If you are asked to review a specific type of book, such as science fiction, go to the library and select such a book. If your instructor leaves the assignment open ended, select a book that you enjoyed reading – one you couldn't put down. If you have time to read a book before the assignment is due, check the *New York Times* review of books and the list of best sellers. Finally, go to a bookstore or library and peruse the latest titles.

HOW TO PREPARE A BOOK REVIEW

Every speech must have a purpose. The book review is no exception; for this reason, you should determine your purpose whether it is to inform, to entertain, to convince, to stimulate. Now you ask, "What should go into a book review and how should you go about organizing your material?" Succinctly, your procedure may follow this order if you consider it suitable. Tell about the author – age, family background, education, when the person first published, anecdotes about the author, quotations about the author, home town, prizes won for writing, or why this book was written.

Now, about the book. Why did you choose it? When was it written? Under what circumstances? Why was it written? Is it biographical, historical, fiction, what? What do the reviewers say about it? (Ask your librarian to show you lists of book reviews such as those in *The New York Times, Christian Century, Saturday Review of Literature, New Republic, The Nation,* and others.) What is your opinion? Formulate your own. Do not plagiarize someone else's evaluation of the book. Give examples and comments in answering the following questions: Are the plot and organization well constructed? Is the writer's style interesting? How are situations and characters portrayed? Do the characters seem real and alive? Does the story move forward to a climax? Is the information interesting and useful? Do you recommend the book? Why?

One of the best ways to master the above information is to read the entire book or sections that you are preparing to review several times. First, read it through for enjoyment. The second and third times read for information you plan to use in your review. As for getting your material in mind, use your own method. It is advisable that you should make a careful and detailed outline, after which you rehearse aloud until your sequence of thoughts has been firmly fixed in mind. If you use quotations, limit them to one hundred and fifty words each.

HOW TO PRESENT A BOOK REVIEW

First of all, have the review "in your head." Do not stand before your audience with the book in your hands so that you can use it as a crutch while you give your review by following previously marked pages, or occupy time by reading. This is not reviewing. Use the book only for your quotations. If you use notes, limit yourself to three words or fewer for each minute you speak.

Utilize all of the aspects of good speech – friendliness, animation, vigor, communicative attitude, bodily action and gestures that are appropriate, a voice that is easily heard and well modulated, correct pronunciation, clear articulation, vivid and descriptive language, a neat appearance, poise and confidence. Utilize these and you cannot fail.

SPECIAL HINTS

1. Be sure you have an excellent introduction and conclusion.
2. Be sure your speech is logically organized all the way.
3. Do not fail to evaluate the book.

Chapter *31*

ORAL INTERPRETATION

Question: How can one project to be heard better?
Answer: Use your diaphragm the way singers do rather
than strain your vocal cords. Consult your vocal music
teacher for diaphragm breathing techniques.

Time limits: 4-5 minutes.
Sources for reading aloud: Study bibliography at end of book. Consult school librarian.

PURPOSE OF ORAL INTERPRETATION

Many persons find themselves in a quandary when confronted with a situation that demands oral reading. Too often they seemingly have no idea about the way oral reading should be done. As a result, excellent literary productions go unread or are so poorly read that much of their beauty and thought are lost. No one expects you to master the field of oral interpretation after concluding one appearance before your classmates, but certainly you should have a much clearer understanding of what is involved in reading aloud. This reading experience will help you improve your oral reading from the standpoint of personal enjoyment and ability to read for others.

EXPLANATION AND REQUIREMENTS OF ORAL INTERPRETATION

Oral interpretation, as we use the term here, is reading aloud from the printed page with the purpose of interpreting what is read so that its meaning is conveyed to those who are listening and watching. The purpose may be to inform, to entertain, to arouse, to convince, or to get action. Successful oral reading demands that the speaker must know the material well enough that they can interpret fully and accurately the ideas, meanings, and beauties placed in the composition by the author. To do this capably, a burden of careful, almost meticulous preparation is placed on the reader.

Much attention must be given to understanding what the author is saying; the reader assumes the responsibility of discovering and interpreting the author's meaning through voice and actions.

Occasions for oral reading are practically limitless. Any gathering at which it is appropriate to read aloud is suitable. School, church, and civic gatherings are common scenes of oral reading. Clubs, societies, private groups, private parties, and even commercial organizations, such as the radio, utilize oral reading largely for entertainment. We are not considering the hundreds of news casts and other types of radio and television programs which are read daily in the category of oral reading. One of the most common scenes is in a household with small children.

HOW TO CHOOSE A SELECTION FOR ORAL INTERPRETATION

Choosing a selection is not easy; it is hard work. First of all, be sure to make your choice of a selection for reading early enough that you will have adequate time to prepare it. Your selection should be made on several important bases. Among these are the following: The selection should be suitable to you as its reader. In other words, choose something that you are capable of preparing and later interpreting. For this particular reading experience, it will probably be advisable that you do an interpretation that does not require characterization of several individuals. Of course, if you have had sufficient experience so that you are qualified to portray different characters and make the necessary transitions involved in more difficult interpretations, then go ahead with such a choice of subject. Give close attention to your prospective audience and the occasion. Your choice of a selection must be applicable to both. This means that you need to analyze both your audience and the occasion carefully; otherwise you may read something entirely inappropriate. You must ascertain the kind of environment in which you will be required to read. The size of the building, the seating arrangement in relation to you, the reader, outside noises, building distractions, and other factors will definitely influence your selection. If you observe closely all these bases of choosing a topic, you have a good chance of presenting a credible oral reading.

Sources of material are available in your school library. Check the card catalogue for poetry, prose readings, and interpretations. Your instructor and the librarian will gladly help you.

HOW TO PREPARE AN ORAL INTERPRETATION

Some important steps in preparation are these: Know the meaning of every word, as well as the use of all punctuation. The author wrote a certain way for a reason. Learn all you can about the author so that you may understand why certain words, punctuations, and phrases were used. Try to understand the philosophy and point of view. Acquire a knowledge of the circumstances surrounding the writing of your particular selection. Do the same for the setting of the article so that you may enjoy its perspective more adequately. Try hard to capture its mood.

Adequate preparation may necessitate your paraphrasing and pantomiming the selection to better understand its meaning. This will assist in obtaining a more complete comprehension of what the authors meant and what they might have done had they read their own poetry or prose.

Practice reading aloud until you have the entire selection well enough in mind that you can give most of your attention (eighty to ninety percent) to your audience by maintaining eye contact. This will necessitate a form of memorization that will permit you to use the printed copy as a guide only. Mark your manuscript with suggestions for changes in volume or pace. Use either words or a system of underlining to remind you that you need to slow down or read more rapidly. Highlighting pens can also be used to indicate vocal changes.

HOW TO PRESENT AN ORAL READING INTERPRETATION

Do not forget that the audience is watching you at all times. This includes before and after you read. All this time, they are observing you and forming opinions. Thus it is imperative that you constantly maintain an alert, poised, and friendly appearance. When you rise to read, your confidence and poise should be evident. Do not hurry to your position, but rather take your place easily and politely without hesitation. Pause a few seconds to glance over your audience before beginning to read. Avoid being stiff and cold and unfriendly. Begin your presentation by telling why you made your particular selection; tell something about the author so that the listeners may better understand the writer; provide information concerning the setting of the prose or poetry; and include anything else that will contribute to appreciation and enjoyment of your reading.

Your body should be appropriate to your selection both in posture and action. Any activity and gesture that will add to the interpretation of your reading should be included. Whatever will assist in imparting the mood, emotion, and meaning should be a part of your interpretation. Be careful that you do not make the reading an impersonation.

Naturally, your voice must tell and imply much. Its variety as to pause, rate, pitch, melody, and intensity should be in keeping with what you are interpreting. All of these qualities should have been determined during the periods of rehearsal. If you can feel the emotions and meanings, so much the better.

Your book, or your reading material, should be held in such a way that it does not hide your face nor block the flow of your voice. Your head should not move up and down, as you glance from book to audience. One hand placed palm down inside the book will permit you to mark your place with a forefinger. The other hand held conveniently under the book palm up will act as a support. You need not hold your book in exactly one position, especially while you are looking at your audience. The point to remember is to raise your book in preference to dropping your head in order to read. The audience wants to see your face to catch emotions and meanings portrayed by its changing expressions. For ease in handling your material, type or photocopy the section of the book you are reading and place it in a folder. Use a music stand to hold your manuscript.

If you are reading several selections, treat each one separately. Allow sufficient time between numbers that the audience may applaud and relax slightly and otherwise express enjoyment of what you have done. When concluding a reading, pause a second or two before politely returning to your chair. Avoid quickly closing your book and leaving the stage when you are three words from the end of the last line.

By keeping in mind your audience, the occasion, your material and its meanings, the environment in which you are reading, and your place in the entire picture, you can do an excellent interpretation.

USING A VIDEO
TO IMPROVE YOUR SPEECH PERFORMANCE

1. Set up the camera so that your entire body is in the picture. This allows you to observe your posture, stance, and movement.

2. Have some close-ups of the upper body and face to allow you to observe your gestures and facial expressions.

3. Tape the entire speech. Replay and watch it using a speech evaluation form. Review the strengths and weaknesses of your verbal delivery only.

4. Play the tape again without the audio and evaluate your nonverbal communication.

5. Practice the speech again without taping it. Work on the areas you noted as needing improvement.

6. Tape the speech again. Be sure to keep the first practice session on the tape. Watch the first practice and the second in sequence. Did you make improvements as desired? If not, work more without the tape.

7. Tape a final practice when you feel you have the speech ready for presentation. View it concentrating on what improvements you made.

CHAPTER *32*
PARLIAMENTARY LAW AND STUDENT CONGRESS

Question: Can a person be sure his or her language is in good taste?
Answer: Yes. Simply avoid risque stories, words, and meanings.

Time limits of speakers: Unless otherwise stated in the organization's constitution, five minutes in generally recognized as the maximum amount of time any person may occupy the floor to speak upon a proposal in one speech.
Student motions: Each student will be required to place at least three motions before the assembly and seek their adoption. Motions which are adopted should be reported to the instructor.

PURPOSE OF THIS PARLIAMENTARY LAW EXPERIENCE

A great many persons attempt to lead an assembly in which group discussion is paramount, or they endeavor to participate in a group discussion when they are totally uninformed regarding orderly and proper parliamentary procedure. The results of haphazard procedure are notorious. Ill-will, ruffled feelings, rife confusion, impeded progress, and circuitous thinking are but a few of the byproducts of such incidents.

By mastering the rules of parliamentary procedure, you will be enabled to take your place in any gathering whether you chair or participate. Furthermore, you will be qualified to assist in carrying on all matters of business pertaining to the group's needs.

These experiences are offered in order that you may learn thorough usage of parliamentary law, the proper procedure for conducting or participating in a deliberative assembly.

EXPLANATION OF PARLIAMENTARY LAW

Parliamentary law is a recognized procedure for conducting the business of a group of persons. Its purpose is to expedite the transaction of business in an orderly manner by observing definite procedures. These procedures may and do vary according to the constitutions and by-laws adopted by a group. In the many state legislatures and the national congress, parliamentary procedures are basically the same, but differ in numerous interpretations. The rules of each assembly determine the procedures which prevail for that assembly. There is no one set of rules which applies to all assemblies, despite the fact they may all adopt the same text on parliamentary procedure. The laws followed by a group are their own laws, adopted by themselves, interpreted and enforced by themselves. Kansas and Indiana legislatures might adopt *Roberts Rules of Order* as their rule book for conducting business, yet in actual practice differ widely. In fact, the House and Senate in the same state legislature normally operate under different regulations. This is true of the two houses in the national Congress. One of the obvious divergences here is the Unlimited Debate Ruling in the Senate (this is the reason for the Senate filibusters) and the Limited Debate allowed in the House. There are other dissimilarities which need not be discussed here. The fundamental point is that assemblies do operate under definite laws and regulations.

Occasions for using parlimentary law arise anytime a group meets to transact business. Whether the occasion is a meeting in a church, a school building, a community center, a housing project, a corporation office, or any one of ten thousand other places, the opportunity for practicing parliamentary procedure arises. The formality which governs the extent of the use of parliamentary procedure is dependent upon the group and their knowledge of its rules. Generally, the larger organized groups are more formal and observe their regulations more closely than do small informal gatherings.

CHART OF PRECEDENCE OF MOTIONS AND THEIR RULES

Key to Abbreviations of Their Rules:

No-S – No second required
Und. – Undebatable
Int.   – May interrupt a speaker
2/3   – Requires a 2/3 vote for adoption
Lim. – Limited debate

PRIVILEGED MOTIONS

1. To fix the time to which to adjourn..Lim.
2. To adjourn (unqualified)..Und.
3. To take a recess..Lim.
4. To rise to a question of privilege............................Int., Und., No-S.
5. To call for orders of the day................................Int., Und., No-S.

SUBSIDIARY MOTIONS

6. To lay on the table..Und.
7. To move the previous question (this stops debate)............Und., 2/3
8. To limit or extend the limits of debate................................Lim., 2/3
9. To postpone definitely..Lim.
10. To refer to committee..Lim.
11. To amend..
12. To postpone indefinitely..
13. A Main Motion –
        a. "To reconsider" is a specific main motion.................... ...Int.

INCIDENTAL MOTIONS
(These Have No Precedence Of Order)

To suspend the rules..Und., 2/3

To withdraw a motion...No-S., Und.

To object to a consideration.................... ....Int., No-S., Und., 2/3

To rise to a point of order..Int., No-S., Und.

To rise to a point of information (parliamentary inquiry)...Int., No-S., Und.

To appeal from the decision of the chair...Int., Lim.

To call for a division of the house.....................................Int., No-S., Und.

To call for a division of a question.. Und.

HOW TO USE THE CHART OF PRECEDENCE OF MOTIONS AND THEIR RULES

The best, if not the only, way to prepare for participation in parliamentary law is to be familiar with the precedence of motions and their applications. This can be done with a reasonable amount of study through the use of any standard parliamentary law book. Without this knowledge, you will flounder in any assembly and slow down the entire proceedings. You will find the fundamentals discussed in the following paragraphs; however, it is necessary that you study a parliamentary text in considerable detail if you wish to master many of the technicalities.

Here are fundamentals you should know:

Precedence of motions – This term means that motions are debated in a certain order. To ascertain the meaning of this, study the chart entitled *Chart of Precedence of Motions and Their Rules*. You will notice that number 13 is a main motion. An example of a main motion would be a motion "That the Parliamentary Law Club have a party." This main motion is what the assembly must discuss. It is the *only* main motion that can be under discussion. It must be *disposed* of before any other main motion can legally be entertained by the assembly. If the group, after discussion, votes to have a party, the main motion is disposed of. If it votes not to have a party, the motion is disposed of. But supposing the Club does not want to adopt the motion as it stands. This raises another question.

Amendments – You see, as the motion stand, it simply states that the "Parliamentary Law Club have a party." It does not say *when*. It is obvious that a change will have to be made. Now look at number 11 on the *Chart of Precedence of Motions*. It is "To amend." It is in a position *above* the main motion of the chart. Hence, someone moves "to amend the main motion by adding the words 'Saturday night, June 16.'" This is in order. It is discussed and voted on. If it carries, the group has decided to add the words "Saturday Night, June 16" to the motion. If it fails, the main motion stands as it was originally made and is open to discussion or ready to be voted on. Assuming for a moment that the amendment carried, the business before the house becomes that of disposing of the *main motion as amended*. It is debated and voted on.

If an assembly wished to, it may amend an amendment in the same manner it amends the main motion. It then discusses and votes on the amendment to the amendment. If this does not carry, the amendment remains untouched. If it does carry, the amendment *as amended* is next discussed and voted on. If it, in turn, does not carry, then the main motion remains unchanged and the amendment plus the amendment to it is lost. If it does carry, the main motion as amended is debated and voted on. It is illegal to change an amendment beyond adding one amendment to it.

Other motions – Supposing the group decided to amend the main motion by adding the words "Saturday night, June 16," but still is not ready to decide definitely about having a party. You will note that number 10, the motion directly above number 11, is "to refer to a committee." When a motion is referred to a committee, all amendments automatically go with it. The motion "to refer" will be debated and voted on. If it carries, the main motion is *disposed of* and the house is ready for another main motion. If the motion "to refer to a committee" fails, then the main motion remains before the house as though the motion "to refer to a committee" had never been offered.

Now look at your *Chart of Precedence of Motions* again. You will note many more motions are listed above number 10. The higher you move up this list, the smaller the number of the motion is, but the more important it becomes, until you arrive at the very top of the list, at number 1. This is the most powerful motion of all. The motion on the chart may be placed before the assembly any time during debate on a main motion, provided you always put a motion on the floor that has *precedence*. In other words, John moves a main motion; Susan immediately moved number 9, to postpone the main motion definitely; Adam moves number 6, to lay the main motion on the table; Mary follows by moving number 3, to take a recess. This is all in order. However, when Adam moved number 6, Mary could not move number 8, since Adam's motion, number 6, had precedence.

Actually, the precedence of motions in its simplest form means that a person may place any of the motions on the floor at any time they are in order if it follows the rule of precedence. You have to understand that the numbers appearing before each motion are not put there to count them. Those numbers tell you exactly what motion has precedence over other motions. The most important motion, as far as having power over other motions is concerned, is number 1, to fix the time to which to adjourn. The second most important motion in order of precedence is number 2, to adjourn – unqualified; next is number 3; then number 4; and so on, clear down to number 13, the main motion itself.

Now let us look at the *Chart of Precedence of Motions* once more. You see the thirteen motions divided into three specific groups; namely, *Privileged Motions* from number 1 through number 5, *Subsidiary Motions* from number 6 through number 12, and last you see *Main Motion*, number 13, which can be a motion about anything from abolishing taxes to having a party. Here is the point you should get from studying these thirteen motions. After you have a main motion on the floor, there are seven actions you can take on it. These are the motions numbered 6, 7, 8, 9, 10, 11, 12. They are called subsidiary because they pertain to things you can do to a main motion. At a glance you can see that an assembly can do anything from postponing a motion indefinitely to laying it on the table and taking it off again. These motions do not conflict with the ruling that you can have only one main motion before the house at a time. They are not main motions. They are the ways you change (amend) or dispose of a motion (postpone indefinitely, refer to a committee, lay on the table...). Of course, you can dispose of a motion by adopting or rejecting it. It is obvious that once you have a main motion before the assembly, you have to do something with it, and rules concerning precedence of motions tell you how to do it.

If you will now examine the privileged motions, 1 to 5, inclusive, you will see that they do not do anything to a main motion. They are the actions a group can take while it is disposing of a main motion. For example, if the club were discussing a main motion to have a party, someone could move number 3, to take a recess. If the group wanted to take a recess, they would vote to do so and then recess for five minutes, or whatever time the motion to recess called for. When the recess was over, they would convene again and resume discussing the main motion where they left off when they voted to recess.

The section entitled Incidental Motions is largely self-explanatory. You will note that it concerns those things a person would normally do during debate on a motion. For example, if the assembly were debating the motion "to have a party," you might want to find out whether it was in order to offer an amendment to the main motion at that time, because you were not quite sure of the status of such a move. In this case you would "rise to a point of information," sometimes called "point of parliamentary inquiry." If you observed an infraction of the rules which the chair overlooked, you would immediately "rise to a point of order." You will notice that most incidental motions require "no second" and also permits you to interrupt a speaker. This is true because certain matters must be clarified while debate is in progress. Otherwise too many corrections would have to be made after a motion was adopted or defeated.

IMPORTANT INFORMATION YOU SHOULD KNOW

1. *The chairperson's duties:* To call the meeting to order, to conduct the business of the assembly, to enforce rules, to appoint committees and their chairpersons, to appoint a secretary for each meeting if one is not elected. The chairperson refrains from discussing any motion before the house.

2. *The secretary's duties:* To keep an accurate record of all business transacted by the house. This includes all motions, whether carried or defeated, who seconded the motions and the votes upon them. Also a record of all committees appointed and any other actions of the assembly.

3. *If the chairperson wants to speak on a proposal:* He or she appoints a member to substitute, then assumes the position of a participant in the assembly. The chairperson must gain recognition from the newly appointed chairperson, make remarks on an equal basis with other members of the group, and then resume the chair at any time desired.

4. *To gain recognition from the chairperson:* Rise and address the chairperson by saying "Mr./Madam Chair," depending on the sex of the chairperson. The chair will then address you by name, or may nod to you, point towards you, or give some other sign of recognition. You are not allowed to speak until you get the chair's permission to do so, in other words, recognition.

5. *How to place a motion on the floor:* Gain recognition from the chair; then state your motion by saying, "I move that _____."

6. *How to dispose of a motion:* Either adopt or reject it or apply subsidiary motions to it.

7. *How to second a motion:* Simply call out the word "second." You need not rise or have recognition from the chairperson.

8. *How to change (amend) a motion:* Gain recognition: then say, "I move to amend the motion or amendment by adding the words_____" or "by striking out the words _____" or "by striking out the words _____and inserting the words _____."

9. *How to stop rambling or extended debate:* Move the previous question, number 7, on all motions before the house. This will include the main motion and any subsidiary motions.

10. *How to ask for information:* Rise without gaining recognition, interrupt a speaker if necessary, and say, "Mr./Madam Chair, point of information" or "I rise to a point of parliamentary inquiry." When the chair says, "State your point," you will ask your question.

11. *How to ask a member of the assembly a question:* Gain recognition; then say, "Will the speaker yield to a question?" The chair then asks the person if he or she will yield. If the member says "yes," you may ask one question. If not, you cannot ask your question.

12. *How to exercise personal privilege:* Rise without recognition, interrupt a speaker if necessary, and say, "Mr./Madam Chair, personal privilege!" The chair will say, "State your privilege." You may then ask to have a window closed because a draft is blowing on you, or you may ask whatever happens to be your privilege.

13. *How to call for "division of the house:"* Without rising to gain recognition, simply call out, "Division of the house." This means that you want the voting on a measure to be taken by a show of hands or by asking members to stand to indicate their vote. "Division of the house" is called for when a voice vote has been taken which was so close it was hard to determine what the vote actually was.

14. *What does "question" mean when called out?* This means the person who calls out "question" is ready to vote. It is not compulsory that the chair put the motion to a vote. However, this is generally done if enough persons call out "question." This has nothing to do with the motion for the previous question.

15. *How do you reverse a ruling made by the chair?* Just as soon as the chair makes the ruling, the person who disagrees with it calls out without recognition, "Mr./Madam Chair, I appeal from the decision of the chair." A second is necessary to make the appeal valid. If it is forthcoming the chair asks the person who made the appeal to state the reasons for doing it. This done, discussion follows after which the chair asks for a vote from the assembly by saying, "All those in favor of sustaining the chair raise their hands," then after counting the votes says, "those opposed the same sign." The vote is announced by saying, "The chair is sustained by a vote of seven to three" or "The chair stands corrected by a vote of six to four."

16. *How is a meeting adjourned?* Adjournment may be made by the chair who declares the meeting adjourned, or it may be made after the motion to adjourn is placed on the floor, voted on and carried.

17. *How do you know what order of business to follow?* The assembly agrees upon an order of business. It is the chair's duty to see that it is followed unless rules are suspended by the group, which will permit a change temporarily.

18. *How do you suspend the rules?* A motion is put before the house "that the rules be suspended to consider" certain urgent business. If the motion carries by a two-thirds vote, the rules are suspended.

19. *How do you vote on a motion?* The chair asks for a vote. It may be by voice ("yes" and "no"), roll call, show of hands, by standing, or by ballot.

20. *How does a person object to the consideration of a motion?* Rise without recognition, interrupt a speaker if necessary, and say, "Mr./Madam Chair, I object to the consideration of the motion (or question)." No second is required. The chair immediately asks the assembly to vote "yes" or "no" as to whether they want to consider the question. If two-thirds vote against consideration of the question, it cannot be considered. The objection must be made immediately after the motion to which the member objects is placed before the assembly.

21. *How do you conduct nominations for office?* The chair opens the floor to nominations for a certain office. A member rises and says, "Mr./Madam Chair, I nominate _____." The secretary records nominations. After a reasonable time, the chair rules that all nominations are closed, or someone moves that all nominations to be closed. This is a main motion. It is seconded, debated, and voted on. If it carries, nominations are closed. If not, they remain open. The chair may rule a quick "motion to close nominations" out of

order if it is obviously an attempt to railroad a certain party into office before other nominations can be made.

22. *How does a chair receive a motion and put it before the assembly?* If it requires a second the chair waits a short time to hear the second. If it does not come, the motion is ruled dead for want of a second. If a second is made, the motion is repeated as follows: "It has been moved and seconded that the Parliamentary Law Club have a party Friday night. Is there any discussion?" This officially places the motion in the hands of the assembly.

HOW TO CONDUCT PARLIAMENTARY LAW SESSIONS

Your instructor will advise you in this matter. However, every class member should take a turn acting as chair at one time and secretary another. It is advisable that the chair be appointed by the instructor until the class learns how to nominate and elect a chair. The following steps may then be carried out:

1. The chair should appoint a committee to draw up a proposed constitution and by-laws. (The committee may be elected if the group wishes to do it this way.) If time is limited, the instructor may dispense with drawing up a constitution and by-laws.

2. An order of business should be set up. Normally, it will be something similar to the following:

   A. Call the meeting to order.
   B. Read the minutes from the preceding meeting. Make any necessary changes, then adopt them.
   C. Ask for old business. This may be unfinished business.
   D. Ask for committee reports.
   E. Ask for new business.
   F. Adjourn.

3. In carrying out practice parliamentary law sessions, it is necessary that motions be placed before the assembly. Each student is required to put at least three main motions on the floor and seek their adoption.

   (a) A motion to petition teachers that all written examinations be limited to one hour.

   (b) A motion that tardy students should pay a twenty-five cent fine for each time tardy, the money to be contributed to a school social building fund.

Your instructor will give you a form on which to write your motion.

A STUDENT CONGRESS

A student congress may be composed of a house and senate with different speech classes acting in each capacity or one group may form a unicameral legislature. In either instance the group's purpose is to formulate bills, discuss them, and adopt or reject them by vote. To accomplish these activities the group must know parliamentary law and conduct its business in an orderly manner. This involved (1) determining the scope of legislation to come before the assembly, (2) organizing the legislature by electing officers, forming committees, and assigning seats, (3) holding committee meeting to consider and/or draft bills, and (4) debating and disposing of bills brought before the assembly.

THE FIRST MEETING OF THE GENERAL ASSEMBLY

At the first meeting of the general assembly a temporary chair and a temporary secretary are appointed or elected. Both will take office immediately. The instructor will act as parliamentarian unless one is elected or appointed. The temporary chair will then open the meeting to nominations for a permanent chair (speaker of the house or president of the senate) who will take office as soon as elected. The chair will call for nominations for a permanent secretary who will be elected and take office at once. As next business the presiding officer will appoint standing committees and a chair for each. The assembly may then discuss matters relative to its general objectives and procedures. Adjournment of the first meeting follows.

COMMITTEE MEETINGS

Committee meetings are next in order and, though informal, parliamentary procedure is advisable with an elected or appointed secretary to keep minutes for the group. A committee may originate its own bills and consider bills submitted by members of the assembly which the speaker of the house or president of the senate has referred to them. It will report bills out or "kill them" in committee, according to votes taken after discussion in the committee.

SAMPLE RESOLUTIONS AND BILLS

Keep resolutions and bills short, under 175 words. A resolution is a recommendation of action and does not carry the weight of law as it has no enforcement and penalty clause. A resolution must have a title, and a body. A preamble is optional. The body is composed of sections and each line is numbered.

If a bill or resolution originates in a committee, a member of the committee should be selected to present it to the general assembly. Another member should agree to second the bill. Other members might well prepare to speak for the bill. In case there is a minority report against the bill, their presentation should be similarly organized, even to offering a substitute bill.

A bill has the force of law. It tells what policy is to be adopted, when it is to go into effect, who is to oversee its implementation and enforcement, and what penalties are to be assessed for violations. Lines are numbered. Note the following examples:

A RESOLUTION LIMITING STUDENT DRIVERS AT CENTRAL HIGH SCHOOL

WHEREAS, Space is limited around Central High School, and
WHEREAS, Parking on the street is limited to one hour, and
WHEREAS, Student enrollment is increasing each year, and
WHEREAS, Many students are within walking distance of Central High
School, therefore,

BE IT RESOLVED BY CENTRAL HIGH SCHOOL SPEECH CLASS THAT:

1   SECTION I. The governing officials of Central High School should prohibit
2   all students living within one mile of this school from operating a vehicle to
3   and from school as a means of transportation.

This resolution introduced by _____

A BILL PROVIDING FOR LIMITING STUDENT DRIVERS AT CENTRAL HIGH SCHOOL

BE IT ENACTED BY THE CENTRAL HIGH SCHOOL SPEECH CLASS, THAT:

1   Section I. All students living within one mile of the school shall not operate a
2   vehicle to and from school as a means of transportation.

3   Section II. Any exceptions to Section I must be approved by the school board
4   upon petition.

5   Section III. The policy will take effect at the beginning of the next school year
6   after passage.

7   Section IV. Any student in violation of the policy will serve a three-day in-school
8   suspension.

This bill introduced by _____

THE GENERAL ASSEMBLY IN DELIBERATION

Some student congresses follow the procedures and rules of their state legislatures. Others follow established rules of parliamentary procedure by designating a certain text as their guide. In either case, an agreed upon procedure must be used. To have a successful general assembly, members should know parlimentary procedure and how to use it. Especially important to know are precedence of motions, how to apply the privileged and subsidiary motions. Incidental motions, which have no order of precedence, are of vital importance in the general conduct of the assembly's deliberations and should be thoroughly familiar to all participants.

Under a bicameral student congress the requirement is that each bill must pass the house in which it originates. It is then filed with the secretary of the other house after which the presiding officer of the house refers it to the proper committee. If reported out of this committee and passed by the second house it may be considered as "passed" unless there is a governor who must act on it before it can be considered as "passed." When a governor is used, a lieutenant governor is ordinarily elected and serves as presiding officer in the senate. It thus becomes doubly important that all plans be laid before a student assembly convenes for the first time in order to know what officials to elect, what their duties are, what committees to set up, and what all procedures will be relative to activities of the congress.

A SUGGESTED ORDER OF BUSINESS

The following order of business meets most student congress needs:

1. The meeting is called to order.

2. Minutes of the last meeting are read and adopted as read or corrected.

3. The presiding officer announces the order in which committees will report and the group decides on (a) time limits for individual speakers and (b) the total time allowable on each bill.

4. The spokesperson for the first committee reads the bill, moves its adoption, gives a copy to the secretary. Another members seconds. If the bill belongs to an individual, he or she presents it in a similar manner when granted permission by the chairperson. A friend seconds. Whoever presents a bill then speaks for it. The bill is debated and disposed of according to the rules of the assembly.

5. Each succeeding committee reports and the process of discussing and disposing of each bill is continued until all bills have been acted upon.

6. The secretary announces the bills that were passed and those that were defeated.

7. The assembly conducts any business that is appropriate.

8. Adjournment is in order.

Chapter **33**

THE PANEL DISCUSSION –
SMALL GROUP COMMUNICATION

Question: Does a person who uses good grammar have much advantage?
Answer: Yes. People are judged partially by their grammar.

Participants: Three to six and a chairperson.
Time limits: 30 minutes for most classroom performances. Others vary according to the amount of time available.
Speaking notes: Participants usually find it necessary and convenient to have notes which provide data such as figures, facts, sources, etc., concerning the points of view and information they present. Sources of information: Three or more should be studied.
Outline of discussion: See "How To Prepare For a Panel Discussion" next page.

PURPOSE Of A PANEL DISCUSSION –
SMALL GROUP COMMUNICATION

There is no better method for resolving the world's problems than by "talking them over." The panel discussion, when operating successfully, utilizes this method. It is democracy at work. Every citizen and, certainly, every student should have the experience of deliberately sitting down in the company of other persons to find the answers to problems of mutual concern. This assignment will give this vital experience; hence you should study it carefully.

EXPLANATION OF A PANEL DISCUSSION –
SMALL GROUP COMMUNICATION

A panel discussion occurs when a group of persons sit down together to try to solve a problem or problems by pooling their knowledge and thus arriving at decisions satisfactory to the majority. If they reach these decisions, their purpose is fulfilled. This requires that the panelists enter the panel with open minds and a willingness and desire to hear other viewpoints, opinions, and evidence. Thus by gathering all possible information (facts) and by pooling it, the group can examine a problem bit by bit, point by point, and arrive at a logical solution. No one should consent to join a panel if they do so while harboring preconceived ideas, prejudices, and opinions, which they are unwilling to change in the light of evidence which they do not possess. An attitude of open mindedness is the most valuable asset a panel speaker or anyone else can possess. This does not mean they are vacillating but rather that they will easily and gladly change their minds when confronted by information which perhaps they did not know was in existence.

A panel may vary greatly in the number of members; however, if there are too many participants, progress tends to be slow and laborious. It is, therefore, advisable to limit membership to a maximum of five or six persons besides the chair.

Occasions for a panel discussion are as numerous as the problems that face any group of people. Every club, every society or organization has recourse to the panel as a method of problem solving. Naturally, if an organization has a large membership, its problems will be submitted to committees which will in turn attack them through the discussion method, that is to say, the panel. Today radio and television often feature the panel as a public service. The student should not be led to believe that every panel must have an audience or that certain TV programs dominated by sarcasm, acrimony, and quibbling represent true discussion. Such discussions are not in any sense of the word good panel discussions because they often lack the quality of open mindedness and a sincere desire to solve a problem.

HOW TO CHOOSE A PROBLEM FOR A PANEL DISUCSSION – SMALL GROUP COMMUNICATION

If the problem is not assigned, the panel should meet under the leadership of the chair. At the meeting, various problems should be considered and a selection of a topic for discussion be made by majority vote. Think of school or community problems that affect you directly. The selection should be based on interest to the panelists and the availability of material for research and study. If the discussion will be conducted before a group, then the audience should be considered when the choice is made. In either case the group should select a question they are capable of adequately discussing. Some sample discussion questions are as follows:

1. How may more people be encouraged to vote?
2. How may teacher's salaries be raised?
3. What should be done to improve high school and college curricula?
4. What should be done about cheating at school?
5. What should be the policy relative to paying athletes or granting them special privileges?
6. Should required courses in marriage be taught in high schools?
7. Should all physically and mentally capable students be required to attend school until eighteen years of age, or until graduated from high school?

HOW TO PREPARE FOR A PANEL DISUCSSION – SMALL GROUP COMMUNICATION

Participants should give careful thought to the purpose of a panel discussion, which is to solve a problem. They should prepare their material with this thought uppermost. Their attitude should be that of a farmer who sees a strange plant growing in a field. What should be done about it? Is it harmful? Is it valuable? Should it be dug out by the roots or cut off? Who can tell what kind of a plant it is? In other words, the student should not jump at conclusions immediately after selecting a problem, but, like the farmer, should find out everything possible about the question under discussion and then determine what opinions are most sound.

Let us assume for a moment that the problem has been selected and that the panelists are ready to begin searching for possible solutions. Here are the steps each participant should follow in arriving at possible answers:

The Problem: What should be done to decrease the number of divorces?

Procedure to follow in arriving at possible solutions: (Keep detailed notes on the following data.)

1. Find out all the effects of divorce, both good and bad. Ask your teacher and librarian to help you locate sources of information.

2. Find out what caused these good and bad effects.

3. Now that you know the results of divorces and what causes them, you should decide that anything you suggest as solutions to the problem must meet certain standards. For example,

(a) Any solution must be fair to both the man and woman.
(b) Any solution must be fair to the children of divorced parents.
(c) Any solution must be legal and constitutional.
(d) Any solution must be acceptable to the church.

4. State several tentative (possible) solutions to your problem of divorces. Be sure these answers meet the standards you set up. Under each suggested solution list both the advantages and disadvantages of it. Remember that you are not to be prejudiced for your solutions. You will soon say to the other panelists, "Here are my ideas with their good and bad points. This is what I believe on the basis of the information I could find. However, I'm willing to change my views if your information indicates I should."

5. Now select the one solution which you think is the best from all those you have constructed.

6. Suggest ways and means to put your best solution into action. For example, newspaper publicity, beginning with your school paper.

Note: Outline all of your points, one through six, using complete sentences. State all your sources of information, giving dates, authors, names of books or magazine, pages, volumes. . . Be sure to identify your authorities. Hand this outline to your instructor as evidence of preparation.

Now that you have gathered all of the information on your problem, outlined it, and learned its contents sufficiently well, you are ready to meet with other members of the panel to see what they have discovered. Each one of them has done the same thing you did in trying to find out what should be done to decrease the divorce rate. You will all get together and pool your knowledge. Obviously you will not all have the same information, because you did not all read the same magazines and books and talk to the same people. This means you will not agree with each other because your information is different. Your possible solutions will be different too. Nevertheless, you will pool your knowledge and after thoroughly talking it over and examining all the data carefully, you will decide on possible solutions that are agreed on by a majority of the panel. These solutions will represent the cooperative effort of all of you, rather than only one person.

HOW TO PRESENT A PANEL DISCUSSION –
SMALL GROUP COMMUNICATION

In presenting a panel you merely meet as a group and discuss the information and ideas each one has brought with them. To do this effectively, each participant should approach the panel with an open mind. You must have a desire to find the answers to the mutual problem of the members, not a desire to propound and seek adoption of your personal ideas and solutions. This attitude of open mindedness is probably the most important aspect of discussion.

Now let us assume that the members of the panel have assembled. The chair should have arrived first and previously placed the chairs in a semi-circle so that each person can easily see everyone else during the discussion. The chair will sit near the middle of the group. If an audience attends to hear the panel, the chair should be sure the panelists are all seated in such a manner that they are visible to the listeners. The speakers, in turn, should be just as sure that their remarks are easily heard by everyone present, and they should direct their voices toward the audience as well as the panel.

Before the actual participation begins, each speaker should remind themself not to dominate the occasion, nor withdraw and say little or nothing. Each one should remember further that they will not become angry, impolite, sarcastic, or acrimonious. They will be very earnest and sincere, however, and even persistent if necessary.

The chair, in turn, will insist – gently, but firmly – on a policy of fairness. The chair will encourage the most timid to speak their minds. They will promote harmony and goodwill among the group. They will permit some digression from the main question but direct the discussion in such a way that the main problem is explored. The chair will note the passing of time and make certain that the discussion progresses rapidly enough to be completed within the allotted time.

Now we are ready to begin discussion. The chair will make brief introductory remarks in which they will mention the occasion and reasons for discussing the topic at hand. The chair will introduce members of the panel (if there is an audience) and tell where each is from, their occupation, and anything else appropriate. If there is no audience, the chair should be certain that all members of the panel are acquainted with each other.

The procedure or the actual discussion should be entirely informal throughout. It should be a spontaneous give-and-take affair with free and easy questions, answers, and contributions from everyone without prompting from the chair. This does not mean the chair may not call on a member if they think that it is necessary to do so.

The points to discuss should develop in the following order through informal talk.

1. Define the terms. Be sure you all agree on what you are talking about.
2. Limit your subject if it is too broad. Perhaps you should talk about decreasing divorces in the United States only or in one state, one city, or in one church. (Note: The statement of your question does not limit the discussion in this respect.)
3. Talk about the effects of the high divorce rate.
4. Discuss the causes of the effects of the high divorce rate.
5. Set up standards on which you will base any solutions to your problem.
6. Arrive at several tentative solutions or conclusions to your question. Be sure you discuss advantages and disadvantages of each one.
7. Select one tentative solution as the best one to put into action.
8. Decide on ways and means to go about putting your solution into action.
9. The chair should summarize briefly what the panel has accomplished.
10. If it is desirable, the chair will permit the audience (if there is one) to direct questions to the panel members. They will have to rule on questions that obviously have no bearing on the discussion or other questions that are out of order.
11. The chair will conclude the meeting with a brief summary at the end of the allotted or appropriate time.

Note: To follow through all of these steps will necessitate a constant alertness on the part of all panelists and the chair. Of course, if a number of meetings are scheduled, you may move gradually through the various stages of arriving at a solution. It is not wise, however, to prolong the sessions until the members become tired.

LISTENING TO AND READING THE NEWS

NOTE: By regularly viewing television news, listening to radio news and reading newspapers and magazines, you will be introduced to a wide array of potential speech topics and will observe good writing and speaking practices.

1. Keep a place in a notebook to list ideas for potential speech topics you heard or read about in the news. Record the date you heard or read the news item. This will allow you to locate additional material in a variety of sources on similar dates.

2. Read a wide range of news magazines. Don't overlook specialized "news" publications such as sports magazines.

3. Go to the library and read a magazine you have never read before. If you live in a rural area or a small town, read a newspaper from a major city.

4. As you watch the news on television, observe the way the visuals complement the voice over from the reporters. Think how you can use visuals to add life to your speech.

5. Listen to the news on the radio; a public radio broadcast is preferable. Listen to the way reporters use changes in inflection, volume, and tone to add life to the reports.

6. Read editorials and op-ed pieces (these are the articles appearing on the page opposite the editorial page). Analyze the way the writers build their arguments. Locate articles from two columnists or editorial writers on the same topic with different viewpoints. Analyze how they consider the other side in preparing their columns.

Chapter *34*

THE SYMPOSIUM –
SMALL GROUP COMMUNICATION

Question: Should a person use eloquent phrases when appropriate?
Answer: Yes, if you remember eloquent phrases are usually couched in simple language.

Participants – Three to four speakers and a chair.
Time limits for each speech: 5-6 minutes.
Speaking notes: None for the speakers. The chair may use notes in order to be sure that the order of speakers, topics for discussion, and other information do not become confused.
Sources of information: Three or more should be studied.
Outline of speech: None is required for instructor. Prepare your own to ensure proper organization.

PURPOSE OF THE SYMPOSIUM – SMALL GROUP COMMUNICATION

The symposium, one type of discussion, is being used more and more as a means of informing and enlightening the public. Many persons are unaware of the different types of discussions and the advantages or disadvantages inherent in each of them. Because it will be to your advantage to understand the workings and the technique of the symposium, it is offered here as a new speech experience for you.

EXPLANATION OF THE SYMPOSIUM – SMALL GROUP COMMUNICATION

The symposium is a method of presenting representative aspects of a problem. Usually three or four speakers talk about one general question, with each speaker presenting views on a particular aspect. A chair acts as moderator and leader. They synchronize the different speeches so that unification of ideas rather than a series of unrelated lectures is present. Speakers are charged with the responsibility of fitting their remarks into the main question by making sure that they contribute to the proposition being explored.

The time allotted each speaker is the same, except that the length of the speeches may vary from a few minutes to fifteen or twenty each if time allows. Following the conclusion of the speeches, the participants may form a panel, after which the audience is invited to ask questions of the speakers. Either one of the latter procedures may be omitted – the panel or questioning by the audience.

The whole program may continue as long as an hour and a half if time permits or more if the audience is quite active and the panelists capable.

The purpose of a symposium is to inform and stimulate the listeners. This purpose is accomplished by virtue of the fact that each speaker may support a given point of view. Occasions for the symposium may present themselves any time a group of persons meets. It may be the meeting of a club, a society, a religious, fraternal or business organization, an educational group, any civic gathering or other assemblage. Today radio and television utilize the symposium frequently on certain types of programs.

HOW TO CHOOSE A TOPIC

The members of the symposium should meet with the chair and then by general agreement decide on a proposition. They should choose one that is interesting to everyone, if possible. However, if all of the members of the group do not agree, the one most suitable to the majority should be the choice. It is not to be expected that you can choose a topic on which everyone is well informed. Be sure that your selection is one about which you can secure information by interviews and reading. Consider some of the following topics:

1. What should be done to conserve energy?
2. Should the United States have a program of compulsory national service?
3. What should be done about the nation's homeless?
4. Should scholarships be given to all high school graduates with outstanding records?
5. What should be done to decrease gang violence?

HOW TO PREPARE A SYMPOSIUM – SMALL GROUP COMMUNICATION

First of all, it should be kept in mind that the individual speakers should prepare their speeches according to the suggestions laid down for any speech to inform or stimulate. All the steps of preparation should be included from audience analysis to rehearsal.

The mechanics of overall preparation may be as follows:

I. The members should meet with the chair.

A. The topic to be discussed should then be divided by mutual agreement among the speakers so that each one presents a different aspect of it. For example, if the topic is "What should be done to improve the streets of our city?" The three speakers (if that is the number) could set up these questions:

(1) What should the city administration do to improve the streets?
(2) What should the citizens do to improve the street?
(3) What should be done to improve the efficiency and use of present equipment?

II. Having agreed on the above divisions of the question, each speaker is next obligated to prepare the discussion making sure, of course, that they observe the time limits closely.

The chair should be well prepared on the entire subject, in order to direct discussion on it. A routine responsibility of the chair is to set up the order of speakers.

Having completed this, the chair must prepare brief introductory remarks. These remarks will include these facts: (1) a history and statement of the proposition, (2) reasons for its discussion, (3) relationship and importance of the topic to the audience, (4) definitions of terms of the proposition, (5) names, qualifications, topics, and order of the speakers, and (6) the manner in which the symposium will be conducted. The chair should be familiar with the point of view each speaker will take. The chair should also be aware of the necessity for a brief summary at the conclusion of the performance by the speakers and after the questions are asked by the audience.

Let us assume now that everyone is ready for the symposium. A final check should provide answers to these questions: Does each speaker have sufficient authorities and accurate data to back up their information, ideas, and conclusions? Are these proofs in a form which they can use while they are being questioned by a member of the symposium or the audience? Does each member know how to answer questions from their own group or the audience, to meet objections, to restate arguments, to summarize their point of view? Will the speakers keep their head, their sense of humor, and remain polite when under fire? Does the chair know how to lead the symposium when they form a panel? Does the chair know how to lead the audience and direct questions to the speakers? Do they know what types of questions to permit as legitimate and which to rule out of order? If the answers to these questions are not known to the participants, they are obligated to discover them.

HOW TO PRESENT A SYMPOSIUM – SMALL GROUP COMMUNICATION

Throughout the entire symposium, good speech practices should be followed. Aside from keeping these in mind, the procedure may be as follows:

1. The symposium members may be seated side by side with the chair at one end.

2. The chair will make introductory remarks, will introduce members of the symposium, and then will present the first speaker and the topic.

3. The first speaker will deliver their speech after which the chair will present the other speakers in a similar manner.

4. At the conclusion of the speeches the chair will briefly summarize the ideas of the speakers.

5. Following the chair's summary, the symposium will be continued according to one of the alternatives listed below:

(a) The speakers will form a panel for a limited time and discuss the ideas that were presented after which the chair will summarize briefly, then adjourn the meeting.

(b) The speakers will form a panel as indicated in (a) above, after which the audience will be permitted to question the speakers for a limited or unlimited time by directing questions through the chair. The chair will conclude the symposium with a brief summary followed by adjournment.

(c) Following the speeches and the chair's brief summary, the audience will be permitted to question the speakers a definite or indefinite time by directing questions through the chair. At the conclusion of audience participation, the chair will summarize the matter of the individual speakers, and then adjourn the meeting. In this case there is no panel by the speakers.

Chapter *35*

THE LECTURE FORUM

Question: Do gestures make a speech better?
Answer: If they are appropriate to all elements of the
speech situation, yes.

Time limits: 7-8 minute speech. Questioning period 5 minutes.
Speaking notes: 15-word maximum limit.
Sources of information: Three are required, preferably four. For each source give the specific magazine or book it was taken from, title of the article, author's full name, date of publication, and the chapter or pages telling where the material was found. If a source is a person, identify the source completely by title, position, occupation, etc.
Outline your speech: Prepare a 75-150 word complete sentence outline.

PURPOSE OF THE LECTURE FORUM

Persons who give speeches often do so without knowing how many unanswered questions they leave in the minds of their listeners. These questions are unanswered because the audience have no chance to voice their questions. It is becoming evident daily that speakers can be more helpful to their listeners if the speakers remain on stage following their lectures to answer questions which have arisen in the minds of their audience.

Most students do not receive training in answering questions about the material they present in speeches; thus, when they are confronted with a forum (question period) following a speech they are in danger of awkwardly handling themselves and their audience. This lecture forum type of speech is designed to provide experience in speaking as well as answering questions. It should be both enlightening and challenging to the student speaker.

EXPLANATION OF THE LECTURE FORUM

The lecture forum is a speech followed by a period in which members of the audience are permitted to direct questions to the speaker. The purpose of the lecturer generally is to inform the listeners on a worthwhile subject. The speaker could present a speech intended to motivate or one to persuade; however, the speech to convince would probably not suit the lecture forum atmosphere so well as the speech to inform. We cannot preclude the speeches to motivate and to persuade, because they can well be followed by periods of questioning and often should be; but we can and do suggest that for most lecture forums the speaker should utilize the time by discussing an informative subject. The reason for this is that usually an expert or someone else equally informed is asked to speak for a group to analyze a subject. If, during the lecture the expert does arrive at a decision regarding a policy that they believe should be carried out; it's done so scientifically, in the presence of the audience. Having reached a solution does not change the purpose to inform to that of attempting to convince the audience that they should adopt the solution. The speaker stops when they reaching the solution, although suggestions may be given for carrying it out. If the audience wants to follow the advice, that is their privilege. The speaker should not urge it on them.

The lecture forum demands that the speaker be well informed, better informed than any member of the audience. It demands further that the speaker be capable of receiving and answering questions from an audience. In short, the speaker should be something of an expert and an excellent speaker.

Occasions for the lecture forum occur whenever an informative speech is in order. These speeches may be given before committees, business groups, church organizations, civic audiences, educational meetings, fraternal orders, and the like. There is scarcely a limit to the occasions for lecture forums.

HOW TO CHOOSE A TOPIC FOR A LECTURE FORUM

You will be expected to know your subject unusually well, since you will appear before your audience to inform them and be present to open the meeting to questions centered around your remarks. Thus, it is advisable to choose a topic of interest to you and your listeners, as well as a subject about which you can secure plenty of information. Do not select a subject for which there are only limited sources. An apology to an audience for ignorance on your subject is not conducive to confidence in you as a speaker. Base your choice then, on interest, appropriateness, and the availability of source materials. Examine the list of informative or persuasive topics in the appendix for ideas.

HOW TO PREPARE FOR A LECTURE FORUM

Since this is an informative speech, you should read the chapter in this text entitled "The Speech To Inform." Here you will find complete information relative to preparing this type of speech. Follow it closely.

HOW TO PRESENT A LECTURE FORUM

You should read the chapter in this text entitled "The Speech to Inform." It will tell you how to present your speech but not how to conduct the period of questioning from your audience. A discussion of this point follows:

Immediately after the conclusion of your lecture the audience will be advised by the chair or yourself that they may question you. In making this announcement several points should be explained politely but thoroughly, such as:

1. Tell the audience to please confine their questions to the material presented in the lecture, because you are not prepared to answer questions outside this scope.

2. Request your audience to ask questions only, unless you wish to permit short speeches on the topic from the audience. Whatever policy you intend to follow – strictly a

questioning period or a question and short speech period – must be specifically announced and understood, or you will run into trouble with those persons who want to make short speeches. If you allow short speeches, announce a definite time limit on them. For the classroom one minute is enough. In large public gatherings, two minutes is adequate.

3. If the audience is small and informal, permit the speakers to remain seated during the forum period; that is, do not ask them to stand while participating. If the gathering is large, require them to stand. Conduct yourself in a like manner, that is, by standing, or seating yourself.

4. Announce the exact amount of time which will be given to the period of questioning. Do not make this questioning period too long. You can always extend the time if the questions are coming briskly at the moment you are scheduled to close. On the other hand, do not continue to hold an audience for the announced time if it becomes obvious that they no longer care to ask questions. It is better to have them go away wanting more than having had too much.

5. Once your announcements are made, open the question and answer period by telling the audience to direct their questions to you. Also explain that you will answer the questions in the order in which they are asked. Thus, if two persons speak at once you will designate which one may ask his question first. The speaker should be urged to speak out rather than to raise their hands, and then wait to be called on.

Having made the above explanations to your audience, tell them you will be glad to answer their questions as best you can. Do not promise to answer all questions, since it is likely that no one could do that. If a question is raised that you do not feel qualified to answer, tell your interrogator you do not have the information necessary to give a reliable answer. However, if you do not know the answer because you are poorly prepared, you will quickly lose the confidence and respect of your audience – and you should.

If questions are asked which do not pertain to the subject under discussion, politely tell the interrogator that the question is beyond the scope of your talk and you are not prepared to answer it. Should you by chance possess information which will enable you to answer it, state briefly that the question is somewhat afield but you know that _____; then make a very brief reply. Do not let this take you off your subject more than a moment. Should hecklers trouble you, handle them politely but firmly. Do nothing drastic.

If some questions are obscure and long drawn out, it may be necessary for you to rephrase them. If you do this, inquire of the person who gave the question as to whether or not your rephrasing asks what they want to know. At other times it may be necessary for you to ask for a restatement of an inquiry. Do this anytime that you do not hear or understand the question clearly.

Observe acceptable speaking practices throughout your lecture and the period following. Retain an alert and friendly attitude. Do not become ruffled when you meet obvious disagreement or criticism. Simply explain your position firmly but politely. Do not engage in a debate or an exchange of unfriendly remarks and accusations. Dismiss the matter and move on to the next question. If some of the questions are "hot" and they will be, keep your head, add a touch of humor to cool them off if it seems advisable; then reply as capably as you can. If any person asks a question that cannot be heard by the entire audience, repeat it to the audience then give your answer. When you are ready to turn the meeting back to the chair, conclude with appropriate remarks in which you sincerely express your pleasure for having been with the audience. Also compliment them for their interest in the subject.

Chapter **36**

DEBATE

Question: Should a person slap or pound a speaker's stand?
Answer: Generally no, unless it is done lightly.

Time limits:	1st Affirmative Constructive	– 8 minutes
	cross-x of 1st Affirmative	
	by Negative	– 3 minutes
	1st Negative Constructive	– 8 minutes
	cross-x of 1st Negative	
	by Affirmative	– 3 minutes
	2nd Affirmative Constructive	– 8 minutes
	cross-x of 2nd Affirmative	
	by Negative	– 3 minutes
	2nd Negative Constructive	– 8 minutes
	cross-x of 2nd Negative	
	by Affirmative	– 3 minutes
	1st Negative Rebuttal	– 4 minutes
	1st Affirmative Rebuttal	– 4 minutes
	2nd Negative Rebuttal	– 4 minutes
	2nd Affirmative Rebuttal	– 4 minutes

These time limits are standard for competitive debate. They may be shortened proportionately for class debates.

Speaking notes: Use notes sparingly, but efficiently. They are necessary in good debating.

Sources of information: You will need many. In your debate you will be required to state your sources of information to prove the validity of your statements.

Outline of speech: Prepare a 75-150 word complete sentence outline to be handed to your instructor before the debate starts.

Number of speakers on a team: Two speakers on a team is the conventional number.

PURPOSE OF THE DEBATE

This assignment is proposed because many persons want the experience of debating. It is proposed also because debating can be done in speech classes without the long periods of training undergone by competitive debaters. This does not mean that long periods of practice are not desirable. They are. Such training produces truly superior speakers. But debating can be done effectively and with good results in speech classes. It provides excellent experience in communicating, since it pits two or more speakers with opposing ideas against each other. It tests your ability to express these ideas and to defend them under direct challenge. This teaches tact, resourcefulness, ability to think on one's feet, and it teaches that ideas must be backed by evidence, not by mere conjecture and opinion. Experience of this kind is beneficial and should be a part of every speech student's life.

EXPLANATION OF A DEBATE

A debate is a speaking situation in which two opposing ideas are presented and argued. The ideas represent solutions to a problem. The proponents of each solution attempt to convince the audience that their idea should be adopted in preference to all others. Actually, a debate, in the sense used here, consists of two opposing speeches to convince.

A debate team may be composed of one or two persons depending on the debate format. Two-person teams are the most common for topics that deal with a policy change and this exercise is structured for that type of format.

Debates are divided into constructive speeches and rebuttals. Constructive speeches introduce the arguments and position of each speaker while the rebuttals review and extend the constructive issues. Refer to the time limits above for the order of speeches. It is at once apparent that the affirmative team leads off and closes the debate. While this may seem like an unbeatable advantage, both teams have the same amount of time allotted to them, and the second negative constructive followed by the first negative rebuttal is a powerful advantage for the negative.

After each of the constructive speeches a member of the opposite team will be given 3 minutes to cross-examine or question the speaker. Each team member will take turns asking questions. One negative team member will cross-examine the first affirmative speaker and the other negative team member will cross-examine the second affirmative after the constructive speech. The same is true when the affirmative cross-examines the negative. The purpose of cross-examination is to gain additional information from the speaker or to clarify what the speaker said. Cross-examination is not a time to argue; it is a time for questions to be asked and answered.

Occasions for debates occur in practically all academic classes, although regularly organized debate groups and speech classes enjoy them most frequently. Inter-school debates among high schools are nationwide, as are intercollege contests. Debates provide excellent program material in schools, over TV, radio, before civic organizations, churches, business groups, or clubs. Any group of persons willing to listen to a sound discussion of opposing ideas always welcomes good debate. For sheer enjoyment with, perhaps, some thought thrown in, humorous debates are a fine type of entertainment. Even though they are light in treatment of subject matter and their purpose is to entertain, they require the same skillful preparation that the regular debate does.

TOPICS FOR DEBATE

Topics for debates are worded in a statement of resolve that asks for a change to be made in the way we currently do something. The affirmative team supports the topic. The negative team defends the present way of doing things. The topic is also called a resolution. You may want to ask your instructor what the current national high school or college topic is for debate. Each year one topic is chosen for interscholastic high school competition and one for college. You may want to debate those topics or some part of them.

HOW TO CHOOSE A TOPIC FOR DEBATE

Since two teams will be concerned with the choice of topic, consult your opponents, to reach agreement on a subject for debate. Remember that one team will uphold the proposition under debate, while the other will argue against it. So, in choosing a topic, it should also be decided which team will debate affirmative (for the topic) and which will debate negative (against it).

In arriving at an agreement on the subject, be sure that all of you have an interest in the subject and that you can find information about it. If you are in doubt about the availability of source materials, check with your school and city librarians before making a final decision. One answer to the problem of what to debate is to ask your instructor to assign the subject and the side you will argue. The following are sample topics. Notice their structure: they all use the term "should be" and they all suggest a policy change:

1. Resolved: That the federal government should significantly increase social services to homeless individuals in the United States.
2. Resolved: That the federal government should initiate and enforce safety guarantees on consumer goods.
3. Resolved: That the federal government should guarantee comprehensive medical care for all citizens in the United States.
4. Resolved: That smoking should be prohibited by law.
5. Resolved: That students caught cheating should be expelled from school.
6. Resolved: That capital punishment should be abolished.

HOW TO PREPARE A DEBATE

The following outline briefly states what each speaker should do in each speech.

First Affirmative Constructive
1. State the resolution.
2. Define terms of resolution.
3. Present affirmative reasons for change.
4. Present proof for reasons for change.
5. Present affirmative plan.

First Negative Constructive
1. Explain basic negative approach.
2. Present negative position.
3. Argue affirmative definition of terms (optional).
4. Prove affirmative reasons for change are not significant.
5. Prove status quo can achieve affirmative reason for change without affirmative plan (inherency).

Second Affirmative Constructive
1. Attack negative position.
2. Rebuild affirmative reasons for change.
3. Answer all first negative attacks.
4. Present added advantages.

Second Negative Constructive
1. Extend (develop in light of opponent's attacks) negative position.
2. Attack affirmative plan as unworkable and undesirable.

First Negative Rebuttal
1. Extend on first negative constructive arguments in light of second affirmative responses.
2. Review reasons for change and why they are insufficient.

First Affirmative Rebuttal
1. Answer second negative attacks on plan.
2. Return to affirmative case to rebuild affirmative reason for change.

Second Negative Rebuttal
1. Review first negative attacks on reasons for change.
2. Return to plan attacks – show how plan is still unworkable and undesirable in light of first affirmative rebuttal.

Second Affirmative Rebuttal
1. Answer attacks on affirmative plan by proving it workable and desirable.
2. Return to case and emphasize reason for change.

As stated earlier in this chapter, a debate is really two or more opposing speeches to convince. Your purpose, then is to convince your audience that you are correct in your point of view. To refresh your memory about the speech to persuade, reread Chapter 9.

Because a debate is an activity in which two colleagues team against two other colleagues, it is necessary that preparation for the contest be made jointly by each pair of debaters. This can best be done if the following suggestions are carried out:

1. Decide who will be the first speaker.

2. Make a mutual agreement that both colleagues will search for materials to prove your side of the question. Later these materials can be exchanged to help each of you to strengthen your arguments.

3. Begin your hunt for information on your subject. Whenever you find something pertinent, take notes on it. Be sure to be able to give the exact reference for the information. Record the following items: The author's name and qualifications, the name

of the article, the name of the magazine, newspaper, or book in which you found the item, and the exact date of publication. Take your notes on four inch by six inch cards; then at the top of each card write briefly what the notes on that card concern. For instance, on a health care topic, labels might be: cost of care, uninsured, Canadian system.

4. Take only complete and exact quotes. It is very important in a debate to have accurate information. Therefore, when quoting sources copy the information exactly as it appears in the publication. Don't leave anything out or add anything. You could set yourself up for an attack by the opposition if you do not take the quotation exactly as it is written.

I. Divide your entire case into four parts. Theses parts are called stock issues. An affirmative must prove all issues; a negative can win by disproving any one of the issues.

A. **HARM**—This shows a need for the specific proposal you are offering by showing some harm is currently happening that needs to be solved.

B. **INHERENCY**—This shows that there is something that currently exists in our present system that prevents us from solving the harm. You must show the harm is inherent. For example in a topic that would ask for the elimination of a retirement age we have a law that is in the present system that stipulates mandatory retirement at a certain age for certain occupations. Therefore, the law prevents the present system from solving the problem.

C. **PLAN**—You have to come up with a plan of action to solve the harm you identify. In other words, you need a solution to the problem, and you need to show that solution works.

D. **DISADVANTAGES**—You need to show that there will not be problems that happen (disadvantages) if we accept your solution.

II. Your finished affirmative case should be set up as follows:

A. Introduce the topic's importance and state resolution.

B. Define your terms. If you are arguing that compulsory military training should be established in the United States, you must tell what you mean by "compulsory." Will anyone be excepted? What does "military training" mean? Does it refer to the infantry, the air force, or a technical school for nuclear specialists? In other words, state exactly what you are talking about.

C. Show that your proposal is needed (stock issue of harm).
1. To prove the need give examples, illustrations, opinions of authorities, facts, and analogies which all point to the need for your proposition. Give enough of these proofs to establish your point.

D. Show that we cannot solve the problem in the present system.

E. Show that your proposition is practical (it will work).
   1. Give proofs as you did to establish your need in point C, above.

F. Show that your proposal is desirable (its results will be beneficial). That there will be no disadvantages to it.
   1. Give proofs as you did in point C, above.

G. Summarize your speech, then close it by stating your belief in your proposal.

III. Negative colleagues should set up their case as follows:

   A. Prepare material that denies that there is a problem

   B. Prepare to defend the fact that the present system can take care of any problem on its own, assuming one exists.

   C. Find reasons the affirmative solution will not work.

   D. Prepare material that shows problems or disadvantages that would occur if the affirmative plan is adopted.

Note: All your arguments need to be presented in constructive speeches. The rebuttal speeches are used to provide further support for your arguments, to deny the opposition's arguments, and to summarize why you are winning.

 IV. Rebuttal is easy if you follow a plan.

   A. In refuting points, try to run the debate. Take the offensive. This is easy but you must follow a plan. The plan is to take your main speech point by point. Reiterate the first point you made, tell what the opposition did to disprove it; then give more evidence to re-establish it. Now take you second point, do exactly the same thing over again. Continue this strategy throughout your rebuttal and close with a summary, followed by astatement of your belief in the soundness of your proposal.

   Do not talk about points brought up by your opponents, except as you refer to them while you re-emphasize your own points. You must carry out this plan of advancing your own case or you will be likely to confuse yourself and your audience. Refuse to be budged from the consideration of your plan for advancing your own case.

   B. The final speech by each side in the debate should be the strongest. Each side needs to prove why they should win the debate. Concentrate on those points you are winning. Remember, the affirmative needs to win all the stock issues and the negative need win only one.

V. The points (stock issues) listed above apply to both affirmative and negative speakers. When each team tries to run the debate, that is, take the offensive, there is a real argument. Because each plays upon their own case, the two proposals and their arguments are easily followed.

VI. Colleagues should plan their cases together and rehearse them together. They should have their material so well in mind that they make little reference to their notes, except when bringing up objections raised by the opposition. Practice should be continued until a student feels complete mastery of the material. They should not memorize a debate speech word for word. A speaker should know the sequence of points and the evidence to prove the point. Besides this, they need a well-planned introduction and conclusion.

HOW TO PRESENT A DEBATE

A debater's attitude should be one of confidence but not "cockiness." Debaters should be friendly, firm, polite and very eager to be understood. A sense of humor is helpful if well applied.

Movement, gestures, and use of notes should be done without awkwardness. Posture should be one of ease and alertness.The voice should be conversational in quality, earnest, and sincere. Everyone should hear it easily.

When debaters rise to speak they should address the audience and opponents. No more is needed. Many debaters utter trite, stereotyped phrases which would be better left unsaid. The debater should make a few introductory remarks about the occasion, the audience, and pleasure of debating a timely question. They should move into the debate by defining the terms. This should all be done informally and sincerely in a communicative manner. There is no reason why a debate should be a formal, cold, stilted, unfriendly affair.

After a debate is concluded, it is customary and advisable for the teams to rise, walk to the center of the room, and shake hands.

HOW A DEBATE IS CONDUCTED

1. The two teams sit at tables on opposite sides of the room facing the audience.

2. A timekeeper sits on the front row in the audience. The timekeeper signals the debaters by raising time cards. If the two card is up, this means that the speaker has two minutes left. When time is "up," the stop card will be raised. The speaker should stop speaking within ten seconds after the final signal.

3. One, three, or five judges may be used. They are provided with ballots which carry spaces in which to write their decisions. After a debate is concluded, the judges, without consultation, immediately write their decision.

4. Debaters may refer to their teammates by name, or as "my colleague." Opponents may be referred to by name or as "my opponent" or "the first negative speaker" or "the second affirmative speaker " or "the negative" if that is their side of the debate. Debaters may refer to themselves as "we," or "my colleague and I."

QUESTIONS TO HELP YOU IN EVALUATING OTHERS' SPEECHES

1. Did the speech achieve its intended result? Did it inform, persuade, entertain, etc. as the speaker intended?

2. Was the speech clearly and effectively organized.

3. Did the introduction catch your attention?

4. Did the speaker give you a reason why the speech was important to you personally?

5. Was the speech delivered well with good posture, appropriate gestures, eye contact, and rate and volume of speech.

6. Did the speech contain sufficient and appropriate supporting materials?

7. Was the conclusion effective? Remember: When critiquing a speech, be positive, take time to comment on good points as well as areas for improvement.

Chapter 37

RADIO AND TELEVISION SPEAKING

Question: Should "beginners" use gestures?
Answer: Yes, from the start. Use what comes naturally
and follow your instructor's advice.

Time limits: See your instructor for the exact time.
Speaking notes: Unless your instructor directs otherwise, you will write out your speech word for word. A copy of your speech should be in your instructor's hands at least one day before you are scheduled to speak.
Sources of information: Two or more. List them at end of your written speech.
Outline of speech: None is required for instructor.

PURPOSE OF RADIO AND TELEVISION SPEAKING

If one understands preparation and presentation of radio and television speech through first-hand knowledge and experience, they are much freer to evaluate and appreciate it as well as actually to participate in it. Real experience in studios provides at least an acquaintance. Such experience should enlighten and interest all speech students. It will pose real problems while answering many questions for all who take part.

EXPLANATION OF RADIO AND TELEVISION SPEAKING

Radio and television speech is that which is broadcast either live or through tape. It may be dramatization, debate, discussion, or any of the many different types of speech. Its chief characteristics are its strict adherence to definite time limits and language usage suitable to an audience of average people. Generally such speeches are read, which permits a person to meet these requisites of time and diction. The requirements of these public speaking media are: a pleasing voice, proper speech construction, good English, correct pronunciation, clear enunciation, desirable appearance, stage presence, and cooperation of all who make the broadcast. Willingness to rehearse and promptness at the studio are of major importance. The person who is tardy or who arrives only five minutes before time to go on the air has no business near a studio.

HOW TO CHOOSE A TOPIC FOR RADIO OR TELEVISION

Follow all of the principles set up for selecting any subject but keep in mind that a radio or television audience is the most diverse and varied in the world. Hence, unless you deliberately intend your speech for a limited group of persons, you will select a topic that can be presented to cross sections of listeners. Examine the appropriate lists in the appendix for topic ideas.

HOW TO PREPARE A RADIO OR TELEVISION SPEECH

All principles involving the preparation of the type of speech you intend to present apply here. It is wise to do review work regarding your speech, whether it be informative, a eulogy, a goodwill speech, or any other kind of speech. After deciding what kind of speech you will present, prepare it by giving special attention to details and correctness. No excuses can be offered for errors when you have a written copy lying before you. It should be typed double-space for easy reading.

The final preparation should be the submission of your speech to the instructor for approval. After the preparation is completed, numerous rehearsals will be required before you are ready to step before the microphone. If possible you should practice with a microphone while a friend listens critically and offers suggestions for improvement. The use of a recording machine for practice will add greatly to the quality of your speech. If desirable, after several rehearsals, you may write time signals in the margins of your paper to tell you where you should be at the end of two, three, or four minutes, etc. These may be checked with the studio clock while you present your speech.

HOW TO PRESENT A RADIO OR TELEVISION SPEECH

Ordinarily, these speeches are presented with the thought that the audience will be scattered far and wide throughout the nation, possibly the world. They may be congregated in groups of two, three, four, or there may be only one person in a home. Your presentation should be so tempered that it meets all situations. If you ask yourself how you would speak were you to step before these small groups of people in person, your type of presentation becomes quite clear. It should be remembered that, if this is radio only your voice will be heard. This means that enough animation, clarity, force, and emphasis are needed to give interest. If you utilize television, then of course you are in full view for all to see and hear. This calls attention to posture, gestures, movement, and appearance.

In presenting your speech avoid rustling your paper in any way. Do not cough, sneeze, clear your throat, or shout into the mike. In radio speaking keep a uniform distance from the mike all the time. This will prevent fading or sudden increase in volume. If you feel like gesturing, go ahead. It will add life to your speech. Just be sure to talk into the microphone, with or without gestures. If you stand about ten inches from it you will be close enough provided the mechanism is sensitive. The best plan is to rehearse with a live microphone and thus be fully prepared. (If it is desirable each speaker may be assigned to another person who will introduce them. This will add realism to the project.)

In television speech various kinds of mechanical devices are used to give the impression speakers are looking directly at the viewer although in reality they may be reading the speech. Microphones are kept out of camera range or may be in full view depending on the program. Should you be scheduled to speak on television, inquire ahead of time at the studio regarding the clothes that will look best, facial make-up, use of jewelry, what signals the manager will give, how to identify and respond to the "live" camera, and numerous other details, especially those concerning the stage crew. A visit to a television station will reveal many methods utilized to make speeches more effective when telecast. Become acquainted with them.

Chapter *38*

THE RADIO PLAY

Question: What should you do if you run out of breath?
Answer: Pause and take a breath. Slow down and breathe
more deeply.

Place of production: See your instructor.
Time limits: See your instructor for exact time limits. Fifteen minutes should be adequate. Whatever it is, the variance should not be more than thirty seconds.

PURPOSE OF THE RADIO PLAY

A radio play will provide great enjoyment and add much to a person's background and experience. It will acquaint students with numerous problems relative to this type of production. It will build confidence in those who participate and give them improved stage poise. It offers an opportunity for self-expression not presented before. Sometimes students show a marked personality improvement after participation in dramatic productions. It is for these reasons that this experience is suggested.

EXPLANATION OF A RADIO PLAY

A radio play is a dramatic production for radio broadcast. It is characterized by musical backgrounds, involved sound effects, time limits, and lack of stage action by the players. The various parts are read, rather than memorized. An announcer is used to narrate or describe, according to the requirements of the drama. The purpose of radio drama is largely that of entertainment, although the purpose may be altered to suit any type of occasion and audience. Requirements for a radio play are these: a cast, a director, a play, and an announcer, music and sound effects. The coordination of all these constitutes the play.

SUGGESTIONS FOR SELECTING RADIO PLAYS

Under your instructor's supervision, visit your school library and/or your dramatics department. Secure copies of different plays, read a number of them, and assist in selecting one or more for radio production.

It is probable that the selected play will have to be edited, cut considerably, or rewritten for radio adaptation. It might be helpful to ask your English or dramatics teachers for assistance. If not, you should write to any of the large dramatic publishing companies for help.

HOW TO PREPARE A RADIO PLAY

It should be kept in mind that you are not expected to be professional in this production. However, you are expected to do your best. The following things must be done:

1. Be sure that a radio studio or an appropriate room is available.

2. The instructor will appoint a student director or chair for each play.

3. Casts must be chosen. They should not be too large (four or five persons as a maximum) or difficulty in broadcasting may be encountered. In casting the players, it is desirable to select persons who have definite contrasts in voice so that listeners may identify them easily.

4. Narrators or announcers must be designated. They should prepare their own scripts in conjunction with those of the players.

5. Sound effects technicians must be designated and their equipment assembled. Considerable experimentation should be conducted until the desired effects are attained. Practice in timing sounds is extremely important. A door may slam too soon, or other sounds happen too late, if care is not exercised.

6. Scripts for the players may be secured by copying the various parts from the play books. This should be done only if a play is being produced for the class audience; otherwise, copyrights may be violated. If desirable, each group may write and produce its own play.

7. All players must follow the director's instructions willingly, regardless of any personal differences in interpretations.

8. Many rehearsals must be scheduled and held. For all practical purposes they should be conducted with live microphone when possible.

HOW TO PRESENT A RADIO PLAY

The entire presentation must be a coordination of all the characters, sound effects, music, announcing, and timing so that they become a unit. Every detail should be so well-planned and worked out that there are no weak spots, breaks, or embarrassing silences.

Successful presentation demands close attention to scripts and cues, and absolute quiet from all players not engaged in speaking or producing sound effects. Special attention should be given to the mechanics of production, such as distance from the microphone and turning from it to create an illusion of distance. Rustling papers, careless whispers, clearing the throat, coughing, and incorrect reading must be avoided.

Players must read their parts in such a way that they impart the naturalness and ease of everyday, normal speaking individuals. Characters must be made to live each time a player reads, and the reading must seem to be a particular character caught on life's stage for a few moments.

The timing should be executed to the point of perfection. This can be done successfully by using scripts which are marked to show just how far the play should have progressed at the end of three, five, ten minutes.

The director should use prearranged signals to indicate to the actors how the performance is progressing. These signals are well established among radio personnel and should be used. The more basic ones are listed in the following order:

1. *Get ready or stand by* – This is a warning signal which may be used to precede other cues. Its most general use is to warn the performers of the first cue which will place the program on the air. This stand-by cue consists of raising the arm vertically above the head.

2. *Cue* – This cue is the green light or go ahead signal which tells any member of the cast to execute whatever should be done at a particular moment. Actors will know what to do because the script will tell them. The cue consists of pointing to the actor who is to execute it. It should be made from the stand-by position by lowering the arm to horizontal and pointing to the person who is to execute the cue.

3. *Speed up* – If the director wished the cast or any person in it to pick up the tempo, they indicate this by rotating an index finger clockwise. The speed of the rotating finger will indicate whether to speed up just a little or a great deal.

4. *Slow down* – The signal to stretch the time or slow the tempo is indicated by a movement which appears as though the director were stretching a rubber band between two hands. The amount and manner of stretching will show how much slowing down is needed.

5. *On the nose* – When the director touches the tip of the nose with an index finger it means the program is running on time.

6. *To move closer to the microphone* – To indicate this action the hand is placed in front of the face, palm inward.

7. *To move away from the microphone* – To indicate this action the hand is placed before the face, palm outward.

8. *To give more volume* – The signal for more volume is made by extending the arm, palm upward, then raising the hand slowly or quickly to indicate how much volume is wanted.

9. *To give less volume* – The signal for less volume is made by extending the arm, palm down, and lowering the hand quickly or gently, depending on how much the volume should be decreased.

10. *Everything is okay* – This signal is a circle made with the index finger and thumb while extending the hand toward the performers. Whenever given it means that as of that moment all is going well.

11. *Cut* –The cut signal is given by drawing the index finger across the throat. It means that the director wants somebody or something to stop. It may pertain to sound effects, crowd noises, or something else.

APPENDIX A

ADDITIONAL TOPICS

Most of the following topics can be adapted for speeches having a variety of purposes. For example, a speech on recycling could be informative about different recycling techniques. A persuasive recycling speech could be developed to encourage all citizens to do their fair share to protect the environment. A recycling motivating speech could be developed to inspire the audience to write Congress on behalf of legislation aimed at mandatory, nation-wide recycling. Likewise, a speech on the subject of swimming could be informative (a discussion of the different strokes), persuasive (the importance of teaching all children how to swim), a body language speech (illustrating the different strokes), a personal experience speech (my experience as a lifeguard), etc.

Study the following list of suggested speech topics with the idea that many of the subjects can be adapted for a variety of purposes.

PERSONAL EXPERIENCES

Moving
Flying
Sports
Summertime Activities
Parental Divorce
Friends
Crime
An Embarrassing Experience
Family
Accidents
Movies
Travel

PET PEEVE/OPINION

Bad Drivers
Too Much Homework
Curfew
School Regulations
Politicians
Waiting in Line
Grades
Racial or other types of discrimination

BODY LANGUAGE

Sign Language
Self-defense
Physical Therapy
Hang Glide
Referee Signals
Sporting Techniques (golf, swim, bowl, football)
CPR
Playing a Musical Instrument
Dancing

SPEECH TO INFORM

Health Care Costs
Space Exploration
AIDS
Costs of College Education
Recycling
Ozone Depletion
Baseball Card Collecting
Teenage Gangs
Homelessness
Best Vacation Spots in the World
Living Wills

SPEECH TO PERSUADE

Trauma of Child Abuse
Rally for a Political Candidate or Cause
Save the Rain Forests
Stop Gang Violence
End Sex Discrimination
Drug Education
Pep Rally for Sports Team
Care about the National Debt
End Political Corruption
Save our Inner Cities
TV and Movie Violence
Population Control
AIDS Education
Multilingual Education
Change Names of Sports Teams Referring to Native Americans

SPEECH TO MOTIVATE

Term Limits for Elected Officials
Wetlands Protected with Taxpayer Money
Sex Education for all Public Schools
Change Your Eating Habits
Candidates Should Not Be Allowed to Accept Political Action
    Committee Money
Telephone Solicitation Should Be Regulated
National Health Care Insurance
Federal Programs to Assist Homeless
Exercise to be Healthy
Lowering Teen Pregnancy Rates
Learn a Foreign Language

SPEECH TO ENTERTAIN

Eavesdropping
Embarrassing Moment
School
Learning to Cook
Getting a Pet to the Vet
Finding an Old Diary
Parents
I Predict . . .

AFTER DINNER SPEECHES

Best Friends
Gender Communication
A Success Story
Of all the Sad Words
Ten Years from Now
A Better World for All
Raising Parents

EULOGY

A Well Known Person in your Community
A Past President
A Leader for Minority or Women's Rights
A Grandparent or Other Relative
Classmate
A Religious Leader
A Teacher

TOPICS FOR A LECTURE FORUM

How May Our Government be Improved?
Drug Abuse Today
TV and Movie Violence
Teen Pregnancy
Population Control
AIDS Education
Multilingual Education
Saving the Family Farm
The Right to Die
Best Vacation Spots in the U. S.

APPENDIX B

SPEECHES FROM HISTORY

HOUSE DIVIDED AGAINST ITSELF
Abraham Lincoln
(1858)

If we could first know where we are, and whither we are tending, we could better judge what to do, and how to do it. We are now far into the fifth year since a policy was initiated with the avowed object, and confident promise, of putting an end to slavery agitation. Under the operation of that policy, that agitation not only has not ceased, but has constantly augmented. In my opinion, it will not cease until a crises shall have been reached and passed. "A house divided against itself cannot stand."

I believe this government can not endure permanently half slave and half free. I do not expect the Union to be dissolved; I do not expect the house to fall; but I do expect that it will cease to be divided. It will become all one thing, or all the other.

Either the opponents of slavery will arrest the further spread of it, and place it where the public mind shall rest in the belief that it is in the course of ultimate extinction; or its advocates will push it forward till it shall become alike lawful in all States, old as well as new, North as well as South. Have we no tendency to the latter condition? Let any one who doubts carefully contemplate that now almost complete legal combination - piece of machinery, so to speak - compounded of the Nebraska doctrine and the Dred Scott decision.

Put this and that together, and we have another nice little niche, which we may, ere long, see filled with another Supreme Court decision, declaring that the Constitution of the United States does not permit a State to exclude slavery from its limits. And this may especially be expected if the doctrine of "care not whether slavery be voted down or voted up," shall gain upon the public mind sufficiently to give promise that such a decision can be maintained when made.

Such a decision is all that slavery now lacks of being alike lawful in all the States. Welcome or unwelcome, such decision is probably coming, and will soon be upon us, unless the power of the present political dynasty shall be met and overthrown. We shall awake to the reality, instead, that the Supreme Court has made Illinois a slave State. To meet and overthrow that dynasty is the work before all those who would prevent that consummation. That is what we have to do. How can we best do it?

There are those who denounce us openly to their own friends, and yet whisper to us softly that Senator Douglas is the aptest instrument there is with which to effect that object. They wish us to infer all, from the fact that he now has a little quarrel with the present head of the dynasty; and that he has regularly voted with us on a single point, upon which he and we have never differed. They remind us that he is a great man and that the largest of us are very small ones. Let this be granted. "But a living dog is better than a dead lion." Judge Douglas, if not a dead lion, for this work, is at least a caged and toothless one.

How can he oppose the advance of slavery? He does not care anything about it. His avowed mission is impressing the "public heart" to care nothing about it. A leading Douglas Democratic newspaper thinks Douglas's superior talent will be needed to resist the revival of the African slave-trade. Does Douglas believe an effort to revive that trade is approaching? He has not said so. Does he really think so? But if it, how can he resist it? For years he has labored to prove it a sacred right of white men to take negro slaves into the new Territories. Can he possibly show that it is less s sacred right to buy them where they can be bought cheapest? And unquestionably they can be bought cheaper in Africa than in Virginia.

He has done all in his power to reduce the whole question of slavery to one of a mere right of property; and as such, how can he oppose the foreign slave-trade? How can he refuse that trade in that "property" shall be "perfectly free," unless he does it as a protection to the home production? And as the home producers will probably ask the protection, he will be wholly without a ground of opposition.

Senator Douglas holds, we know, that a man may rightfully be wiser today than he was yesterday - that he may rightfully change when he finds himself wrong. But can we, for that reason run ahead, and infer that he will make any particular change, of which he himself has given no imitation? Can we safely base our action upon any such vague inference?

Now, as ever, I wish not to misrepresent Judge Douglas' position, question his motives, or do aught that can be personally offensive to him. Whenever, if ever, he and we can come together on principle, so that our cause may have assistance from his great ability, I hope to have interposed no adventitious obstacle. But clearly, he is not now with us - he does not pretend to be, he does not promise ever to be.

Our cause, then, must be entrusted to, and conducted by, its own undoubted friends - those whose hands are free, whose hearts are in the work - who do care for the result. Two years ago the Republicans of the nation mustered over thirteen hundred thousand strong. We did this under the single impulse of resistance to a common danger.

With every external circumstance against us, of strange, discordant, and even hostile elements, we gathered from the four winds, and brave all then, to falter now? - now, when that same enemy is wavering, dissevered, and belligerent! The result is not doubtful. We shall not fail - if we stand firm, we shall not fail. Wise counsels may accelerate, or mistakes delay it; but, sooner or later, the victory is sure to come.

GIVE ME LIBERTY OR GIVE ME DEATH
Patrick Henry

No man thinks more highly than I do of the patriotism, as well as abilities, of the very worthy gentlemen who have just addressed the House. But different men often see the same subject in different lights; and, therefore, I hope it will not be thought disrespectful to those gentlemen, if, entertaining as I do opinions of a character very opposite to theirs, I shall speak forth my sentiments freely and without reserve. This is not time for ceremony.

The question before the House is one of awful moment to this country. For my own part, I consider it as nothing less than a question of freedom or slavery; and in proportion to the magnitude of the subject ought to be the freedom of the debate. It is only in this way that we can hope to arrive at truth, and fulfill the great responsibility which we hold to God and our Country. Should I keep back my opinions at such a time, through fear of giving offense, I should consider myself as guilty of treason toward my country, and of act of disloyalty toward the Majesty of Heaven, which I revere above all earthly kings.

Mr. President, it is natural to man to indulge in the illusions of hope. We are apt to shut our eyes against a painful truth, and listen to the song of that siren, till she transforms us into beasts. Is this the part of wise men, engaged in a great and arduous struggle for liberty? Are we disposed to be of the number of those, who having eyes, see not, and having ears, hear not, the things which so nearly concern their temporal salvation? For my part, whatever anguish of spirit it may cost, I am willing to know the whole truth; to know the worst, and to provide for it.

I have but one lamp by which my feet are guided, and that is the lamp of experience. I know of no way of judging of the future but by the past. And judging by the past, I wish to know what there has been in the conduct of the British ministry for the last ten years to justify those hopes with which gentlemen have been pleased to solace themselves and the House. Is it that insidious smile with which our petition has been lately received? Trust it not, sir; it will prove a snare to your feet. Suffer not yourselves to be betrayed with a kiss. Ask yourselves how this gracious reception of our petition comports with those warlike preparations which cover our water and darken our land. Are fleets and armies necessary to a work of love and reconciliation? Have we shown ourselves so unwilling to be reconciled that force must be called in to win back our love? Let us not deceive ourselves, sir. These are the implements of war and subjugation; the last arguments to which kings resort.

I ask gentlemen, sir, what means this martial array, if its purpose be not to force us to submission? Can gentlemen assign any other possible motive for it? Has Great Britain any enemy in this quarter of the world to call for all this accumulation of navies and armies? No, sir, she has none. They are meant for us: they can be meant for no other. They are sent over to bind and rivet upon us those chains which the British ministry have been so long forging. And what have we to oppose to them? Shall we try argument? Sir, we have been trying that for the last ten years. Have we anything new to offer upon the subject? Nothing. We have held the subject up in every light of which it is capable; but it has been all in vain.

Shall we resort to entreaty and humble supplication? What terms shall we find which have not been already exhausted? Let us not, I beseech you, sir deceive ourselves longer. Sir, we have done everything that could be done, to avert the storm which is now coming on. We have petitioned; we have remonstrated; we have supplicated; we have prostrated ourselves before the throne, and have implored its interposition to arrest the tyrannical hands of the ministry and Parliament. Our petitions have been slighted; our remonstrances have produced additional violence and insult; our supplications have been disregarded, and we have been spurned, with contempt, from the foot of the throne!

In vain, after these things, may we indulge the fond hope of peace and reconcili- ation. There is no longer any room for hope. If we wish to be free - if we mean to preserve inviolate those inestimable privileges for which we have been so long contending - if we mean not basely to abandon the noble struggle in which we have been so long engaged, and which we have pledged ourselves never to abandon, until the glorious object of our contest shall be obtained - we must fight! I repeat it, sir, we must fight! An appeal to arms to the God of Hosts is all that is left us!

They tell us, sir, that we are weak –unable to cope with so formidable an adversary. But when shall we be stronger? Will it be the next week, or the next year? Will it be when we are totally disarmed, and when a British guard shall be stationed in every house? Shall we gather strength by irresolution and inaction? Shall we acquire the means of effectual resistance by lying supinely on our backs and hugging the delusive phantom of hope, until our enemies shall have bound us hand and foot?

Sir, we are not weak if we make a proper use of those means which the God of nature has placed in our power. Three millions of people armed in the holy cause of liberty, and in such a country as that which we possess, are invincible by any force which our enemy can send against us. Besides, sir, we shall not fight our battles alone. There is a just God who presides over the vigilant, the active, the brave. Besides, sir, we have no election. If we were base enough to desire it, it is now too late to retire from the contest. There is no retreat but in submission and slavery! Our chains are forged! Their clanking may be heard on the plains of Boston! The war is inevitable – and let it come! I repeat it, sir, let it come!

It is in vain, sir, to extenuate the matter. Gentlemen may cry, Peace, Peace – but there is no peace. The war is actually begun! The next gale that sweeps from the north will bring to our ears the clash of resounding arms! Is life so dear, or peace so sweet, as to be purchased at the price of chains and slavery? Forbid it, Almighty God! I know not what course others may take, but as for me, give me liberty or give me death!

Delivered on March 23, 1775, before the Second Revolutionary Convention of Virginia, in the old church in Richmond.

ON THE FEDERAL CONSTITUTION
Benjamin Franklin
From a speech in Philadelphia before the Constitutional Convention of 1787.

(The Constitution was adopted only after much debate. In the following speech one well-known individual expressed his feelings about signing the document.)

I CONFESS that I do not entirely approve of this Constitution at present; but, sir, I am not sure I shall never approve of it, for, having lived long, I have experienced many instances of being obliged, by better information or fuller consideration, to change opinions even on important subjects, which I once thought right, but found to be otherwise. It is therefore that, the older I grow, the more apt I am to doubt my own judgment of others. Most men, indeed, as well as most sects in religion, think themselves in possession of all truth, and that wherever others differ from them, it is so far error. Steele, a Protestant, in a dedication, tells the pope that the only difference between our two churches in their opinion of the certainty of their doctrine is, the Romish Church is infallible, and the Church of England is never in the wrong. But, tho many private persons think almost as highly of their own infallibility as of that of their sect, few express it so naturally as a certain French lady, who, in a little dispute with her sister said: "But I meet nobody but myself that is always in the right."

In these sentiments, sir, I agree to this Constitution with all its faults - if they are such - because I think a general government necessary for us, and there is no form of government but what may be a blessing to the people if well administered; and I believe, further, that this is likely to be well administered for a course of years, and can only end in despotism, as other forms have done before it, when the people shall become so corrupted as to need despotic government, being incapable of any other. I doubt, too, whether any other convention we can obtain may be able to make a better Constitution; for, when you assemble a number of men, to have the advantage of their joint wisdom, you inevitably assemble with those men all their prejudices, their passions, their errors of opinion, their local interests, and their selfish views. From such an assembly can a perfect production be expected?

It therefore astonishes me, sir, to find this system approaching so near to perfection as it does; and I think it will astonish our enemies, who are waiting with confidence to hear that our counsels are confounded like those of the builders of Babel, and that our States are on the point of separation, only to meet hereafter for the purpose of cutting one another's throats. Thus I consent, sir, to this Constitution, because I expect no better, and because I am not sure that it is not the best. The opinions I have had of its errors I sacrifice to the public good. I have never whispered a syllable of them abroad. Within these walls they were born, and here they shall die. If every one of us, in returning to our constituents, were to report the objections he has had to it, and endeavor to gain partizans in support of them, we might prevent its being generally received, and thereby lose all the salutary effects and great advantages resulting naturally in our favor among foreign nations, as well as among ourselves, from our real or apparent unanimity. Much of the strength and efficiency of any government, as well as of the wisdom and integrity of its governors. I hope, therefore, for our own sakes, as a part of the people, and for the sake of our posterity, that we shall act heartily and unanimously in recommending this Constitution wherever our influence may extend, and turn our future thoughts and endeavors to the means of having it well administered.

On the whole, sir, I can not help expressing a wish that every member of the convention who may still have objections to it, would, with me, on this occasion, doubt a little of his own infallibility, and, to make manifest our unanimity, put his name to this instrument.

THEIR FINEST HOUR
Winston Churchill

The Battle of France is over. I expect that the Battle of Britain is about to begin. Upon this battle depends the survival of Christian civilization. Upon it depends our own British life, and the long continuity of our institutions and our Empire. The whole fury and might of the enemy must very soon be turned on us. Hitler knows that he will have to break us in this Island or lose the war. If we can stand up to him, all Europe may be free and the life of the world may move forward into broad, sunlit uplands. But if we fall, then the whole world, including the United States, including all that we have known and cared for, will sink into the abyss of a new Dark Age made more sinister, and perhaps more protracted, by the lights of perverted science. Let us therefore brace ourselves to our duties, and so bear ourselves that, if the British Empire and its Commonwealth last for a thousand years, men will still say, "This was their finest hour."

(The excerpt contains the conclusion only. The speech was delivered to the House of Commons, London, England, then broadcast June 18, 1940, in the early stages of World War II.)

INAUGURAL ADDRESS
John F. Kennedy, January 20, 1961

Vice President Johnson, Mr. Speaker, Mr. Chief Justice, President Eisenhower, Vice President Nixon, President Truman, Reverend Clergy, Fellow Citizens: We observe today not a victory of party but a celebration of freedom – symbolizing an end as well as a beginning – signifying renewal as well as change. For I have sworn before you and Almighty God the same solemn oath our forebears prescribed nearly a century and three quarters ago.

The world is very different now. For man holds in his mortal hands the power to abolish all forms of human poverty and all forms of human life. And yet the same revolutionary beliefs for which our forebears fought are still at issue around the globe – the belief that the rights of man come not from the generosity of the state but from the hand of God.

We dare not forget today that we are the heirs of that first revolution. Let the word go forth from this time and place, to friend and foe alike, that the torch has been passed to a new generation of Americans – born in this century, tempered by war, disciplined by a hard and bitter peace, proud of our ancient heritage – and unwilling to witness or permit the slow undoing of those human rights to which this nation has always been committed, and to which we are committed today, at home and around the world.

Let every nation know, whether it wishes us well or ill, that we shall pay any price, bear any burden, meet any hardship, support any friend or oppose any foe to assure the survival and the success of liberty. This much we pledge – and more.

To those old allies whose cultural and spiritual origins we share, we pledge the loyalty of faithful friends. United, there is little we cannot do in a host of cooperative ventures. Divided, there is little we can do – for we dare not meet a powerful challenge at odds and split asunder. To those new states whom we welcome to the ranks of the free, we pledge our word that one form of colonial control shall not have passed away merely to be replaced by a far more iron tyranny. We shall not always expect to find them supporting our view. But we shall always hope to find them strongly supporting their own freedom – and to remember that, in the past, those who foolishly sought power by riding the back of the tiger ended up inside.

To those people in the huts and villages of half the globe struggling to break the bonds of mass misery, we pledge our best efforts to help them help themselves, for whatever period is required – not because the Communists may be doing it, not because we seek their votes, but because it is right. If a free society cannot help the many who are poor, it cannot save the few who are rich.

To our sister republics south of our border, we offer a special pledge – to convert our good words into good deeds – in a new alliance for progress – to assist free men and free governments in casting off the chains of poverty. But this peaceful revolution of hope cannot become the prey of hostile powers. Let all our neighbors know that we shall join with them to oppose aggression or subversion anywhere in the Americas. And let every other power know that this hemisphere intends to remain the master of its own house.

To that world assembly of sovereign states, the United Nations, our last best hope in an age where the instruments of war have far outpaced the instruments of peace, we renew our pledge of support – to prevent it from becoming merely a forum for invective – to strengthen its shield of the new and the weak – and to enlarge the area in which its writ may run.

Finally, to those nations who would make themselves our adversary, we offer not a pledge but a request: That both sides begin anew the quest for peace, before the dark powers of destruction unleashed by science engulf all humanity in planned or accidental self-destruction.

We dare not tempt them with weakness. For only when our arms are sufficient beyond doubt can we be certain beyond doubt that they will never be employed. But neither can two great and powerful groups of nations take comfort from our present course – both sides overburdened by the cost of modern weapons, both rightly alarmed by the steady spread of the deadly atom, yet both racing to alter that uncertain balance of terror that stays the hand of mankind's final war.

So let us begin anew – remembering on both sides that civility is not a sign of weakness, and sincerity is always subject to proof. Let us never negotiate out of fear. But let us never fear to negotiate. Let both sides explore what problems unite us instead of belaboring those problems which divide us. Let both sides, for the first time, formulate serious and precise proposals for the inspection and control of arms – and bring the absolute power to destroy other nations under the absolute control of all nations. Let both sides seek to invoke the wonders of science instead of its terrors.

Together let us explore the stars, conquer the deserts, eradicate disease, tap the ocean depths and encourage the arts and commerce. Let both sides unite to heed in all corners of the earth the command of Isaiah – to "undo the heavy burdens. . . [and] let the oppressed go free." And if a beachhead of cooperation may push back the jungle of suspicion, let both sides join in creating a new endeavor: not a new balance of power, but a new world of law, where the strong are just and the weak secure and the peace preserved.

All this will not be finished in the first one hundred days. Nor will it be finished in the first one thousand days, not in the life of this administration, nor even perhaps in our lifetime on the planet. But let us begin.

In your hands, my fellow citizens, more than mine, will rest the final success or failure of our course. Since this country was founded, each generation of Americans has been summoned to give testimony to its national loyalty. The graves of young Americans who answered the call to service surround the globe.

Now the trumpet summons us again – not as a call to bear arms, though arms we need – not as a call to battle, though embattled we are – but a call to bear the burden of a long twilight struggle, year in and year out, "rejoicing in hope, patient in tribulation" – a struggle against the common enemies of man: Tyranny, poverty, disease and war itself.

Can we forge against these enemies a grand and global alliance, North and South, East and West, that can assure a more fruitful life for all mankind? Will you join in that historic effort?

In the long history of the world, only a few generations have been granted the role of defending freedom in its hour of maximum danger.

I do not shrink from this responsibility – I welcome it. I do not believe that any of us would exchange places with any other people or any other generation. The energy, the faith, the devotion which we bring to this endeavor will light our country and all who serve it – and the glow from that fire can truly light the world.

And so, my fellow Americans: Ask not what your country can do for you – ask what you can do for your country.

My fellow citizens of the world: Ask not what America will do for you, but what together we can do for the freedom of man.

Finally, whether you are citizens of America or citizens of the world, ask of us here the same high standards of strength and sacrifice which we ask of you. With a good conscience our only sure reward, with history the final judge of our deeds, let us go forth to lead the land we love, asking His blessing and His help, but knowing that here on earth God's work must truly be our own.

DEMOCRATIC CONVENTION KEYNOTE ADDRESS
Barbara Jordan
Delivered July 12, 1976 in New York City

One hundred and forty-four years ago, members of the Democratic Party first met in convention to select a Presidential candidate. Since that time, Democrats have continued to convene once every four years and draft a party platform and nominate a Presidential candidate. And our meeting this week is a continuation of that tradition.

But there is something different about tonight. There is something special about tonight. What is different? What is special? I, Barbara Jordan, am a keynote speaker.

A lot of years passed since 1832, and during that time it would have been most unusual for any national political party to ask that a Barbara Jordan deliver a keynote address . . . but tonight here I am. And I feel that notwithstanding the past that my presence here is one additional bit of evidence that the American Dream need not forever be deferred.

Now that I have this grand distinction what in the world am I supposed to say? I could easily spend this time praising the accomplishments of this party and attacking the Republicans, but I don't choose to do that. I could list the many problems which Americans have.

I could list the problems which cause people to feel cynical, angry, frustrated: problems which include lack of integrity in government; the feeling that the individual no longer counts; the reality of materials and spiritual poverty; the feeling that the grand American experiment is failing or has failed. I could recite these problems, and then I could sit down and offer no solutions. But I don't choose to do that either.

The citizens of America expect more. They deserve and they want more than a recital of problems.

We are a people in a quandary about the present. We are a people in search of our future. We are a people in search of a national community. We are a people trying not only to solve the problems of the present – unemployment, inflation – but we are attempting on a larger scale to fulfill the promise of America. We are attempting to fulfill our national purpose; to create and sustain a society in which all of us are equal.

Throughout our history, when people have looked for new ways to solve their problems, and to uphold the principles of this nation, many times they have turned to political parties. They have often turned to the Democratic Party.

What is it, what is it about the Democratic Party that makes it the instrument that people use when they search for ways to shape their future? Well I believe the answer to that question lies in our concept of governing. Our concept of governing is derived from our view of people. It is a concept deeply rooted in a set of beliefs firmly etched in the national conscience of all of us. Now what are these beliefs?

First, we believe in equality for all and privileges for none. This is a belief that each American regardless of background has equal standing in the public forum, all of us. Because we believe this idea so firmly, we are an inclusive rather than an exclusive party. Let everybody come.

I think it no accident that most of those emigrating to American in the 19th century identified with the Democratic Party. We are a heterogeneous party made up of Americans of diverse backgrounds.

We believe that the people are the source of all governmental power; that the authority of the people is to be extended, not restricted. This can be accomplished only by providing each citizen with every opportunity to participate in the management of the government. They must have that.

We believe that the government which represents the authority of all the people, not just one interest group, but all the people, has an obligation to actively, underscore actively, seek to remove those obstacles which would block individual achievement . . . obstacles emanating from race, sex, economic condition. The government must seek to remove them.

We are a party of innovation. We do not reject our traditions, but we are willing to adapt to changing circumstances, when change we must. We are willing to suffer the discomfort of change in order to achieve a better future. We have a positive vision of the future founded on the belief that the gap between the promise and reality of America can one day be finally closed. We believe that.

This my friends, is the bedrock of our concept of governing. This is a part of the reason why Americans have turned to the Democratic Party. These are the foundations upon which a national community can be built.

Let's all understand that these guiding principles cannot be discarded for short-term political gains. They represent what this country is all about. They are indigenous to the American idea. And these are principles which are not negotiable.

In other times, I could stand here and give this kind of exposition on the beliefs of the Democratic Party and that would be enough. But today that is not enough. People want more. That is not sufficient reason for the majority of the people of this country to vote Democratic. We have made mistakes. In our haste to do all things for all people, we did not foresee the full consequences of our actions. And when the people raised their voices, we didn't hear. But our deafness was only a temporary condition, and not an irreversible condition.

Even as I stand here and admit that we have made mistakes I still believe that as the people of America sit in judgment on each party, they will recognize that our mistakes were mistakes of the heart. They'll recognize that.

And now we must look to the future. Let us heed the voice of the people and recognize their common sense. If we do not, we not only blaspheme our political heritage, we ignore the common ties that bind all Americans.

Many fear the future. Many are distrustful of their leaders, and believe that their voices are never heard. Many seek only to satisfy their private work wants. To satisfy private interests.

But this is the great danger America faces. That we will cease to be one nation and become instead a collection of interest groups: city against suburb, region against region, individual against individual. Each seeking to satisfy private wants.

If that happens, who then will speak for America? Who then will speak for the common good? This is the question which must be answered in 1976. Are we to be one people bound together by common spirit sharing in a common endeavor or will we become a divided nation?

For all of its uncertainty, we cannot flee the future. We must not become the new puritans and reject our society. We must address and master the future together. It can be done if we restore the belief that we share a sense of national community, that we share a common national endeavor. It can be done.

There is no executive order; there is no law that can require the American people to form a national community. This we must do as individuals and if we do it as individuals, there is no President of the United States who can veto that decision.

As a first step, we must restore our belief in ourselves. We are a generous people so why can't we be generous with each other? We need to take to heart the words spoken by Thomas Jefferson: "Let us restore to social intercourse that harmony and that affection without which liberty and even life are but dreary things."

A nation is formed by the willingness of each of us to share in the responsibility for upholding the common good. A government is invigorated when each of us is willing to participate in shaping the future of this nation.

In this election year we must define the common good and begin again to shape a common future. Let each person do his or her part. If one citizen is unwilling to participate, all of us are going to suffer. For the American idea, though it is shared by all of us, is realized in each one of us.

And now, what are those of us who are elected public officials supposed to do? We call ourselves public servants but I'll tell you this: we as public servants must set an example for the rest of the nation. It is hypocritical for the public official to admonish and exhort the people to uphold the common good if we are derelict in upholding the common good. More is required of public officials than slogans and handshakes and press releases. More is required. We must hold ourselves strictly accountable. We must provide the people with a vision of the future.

If we promise as public officials, we must deliver. If we as public officials propose, we must produce. If we say to the American people it is time for you to be sacrificial; sacrifice. If the public official says that we (public officials) must be the first to give. We must be. And again, if we make mistakes, we must be willing to admit them. We have to do that. What we have to do is strike a balance between the idea that government should do everything and the idea, the belief, that government ought to do nothing. Strike a balance.

Let there be no illusions about the difficulty of forming this kind of a national community. It's tough, difficult, not easy. But a spirit of harmony will survive in America only if each of us remembers that we share a common destiny. If each of us remembers, when self-interest and bitterness seem to prevail, that we share a common destiny.

I have confidence that we can form this kind of national community. I have confidence that the Democratic Party can lead the way. I have that confidence. We cannot improve on the system of government handed down to us by the founders of the Republic, there is no way to improve upon that. But what we can do is to find new ways to implement that system and realize our destiny.

Now, I began this speech by commenting to you on the uniqueness of a Barbara Jordan making the keynote address. Well I am going to close my speech by quoting a Republican President and I ask you that as you listen to these words of Abraham Lincoln, relate them to the concept of a national community in which every last one of us participates: "As I would not be a slave, so I would not be a master. This expresses my idea of Democracy. Whatever differs from this, to the extent of the difference is no Democracy."

(Reprinted with permission from *Vital Speeches of the Day*, Vol. 42, No. 21, August 21, 1976.)

SPEECH
Heinmot Tooyalaket (Chief Joseph) of the Nez Percés

The earth was created by the assistance of the sun, and it should be left as it was . . . the country was made without lines of demarcation, and it is no man's business to divide it . . . I see the whites all over the country gaining wealth, and see their desire to give us lands which are worthless. . . The earth and myself are of one mind. The measure of the land and the measure of our bodies are the same. Say to us if you can say it, that you were sent by the Creative Power to talk to us. Perhaps you think the creator sent you here to dispose of us as you see fit. If I thought you were sent by the Creator I might be induced to think you had a right to dispose of me. Do not misunderstand me, but understand me fully with reference to my affection for the land. I never said the land was mine to do with as I chose. The one who has the right to dispose of it is the one who has created it. I claim a right to live on my land, and accord you the privilege to live on yours.

GLOSSARY

Affirmative – The team or speaker in a debate who supports the topic under discussion.

Amendment – A change in a bill or motion which adds to or deletes information.

Analogy – A comparison between two things. A literal analogy compares similar things, such as two boats. A figurative analogy compares things that function similarly but are not actually the same such as comparing a computer to the human brain.

Anecdote – A short story or recalling of an incident, usually humorous.

Body language – A type of nonverbal communication that involves use of the body such as gestures, posture, or movement.

Communication – Intentional or unintentional words, actions, or symbols which others interpret.

Conclusion – The part of a speech which summaries and emphasizes the speaker's main ideas.

Constructive speech – The first speech given by a speaker in a debate which presents or builds a case for acceptance or rejection of a topic.

Debate – A contest in which the affirmative and negative sides of a proposition are advocated by opposing speakers.

Decoding – The process of interpreting a message.

Encoding – The process of constructing a message.

Eulogy – A speech of praise that is delivered in honor or commemoration of someone living or dead.

Extemporaneous – A speech given with an outline or a few notes.

Impromptu – A speech given with little or no advance preparation.

Inform – To instruct, provide information.

Introduction – The beginning of a speech which should get the audience's attention, give them a reason to listen, and introduce the topic.

Lecture forum – A speech followed by a period of questions from the audience.

Manuscript – A complete text of a speech that is used as speaking notes.

Motion – A formal proposal.

Negative – The team or person in a debate who opposes or disagrees with the topic under discussion.

Nonverbal communication – Any message not involving words such as gestures, tone of voice, facial expressions, or symbols.

Outline – The main features of a speech usually presented in sentences, phrases, or single words.

Panel discussion – A group of people trying to solve a problem through discussion.

Pantomime – A performance involving only body language to tell a story.

Persuasion – The process of influencing another to change, modify, or adopt an attitude or behavior.

Pet peeve – Something that upsets or disturbs you or causes you to react negatively.

Plagiarize – To take another's work and represent it as your own.

Rebuttal speech – The second speech given by a debater which responds to the opponent's arguments.

Recapitulation – Restating a point or points.

Self-disclosure – The act of revealing personal information about yourself.

Simile – When two unlike things are compared such as to say he is a bright light in my life.

Stage fright (speech anxiety) – The natural nervousness that occurs when being faced with giving a speech or some othertypeofperformance

Stock issues – The major requirements or issues an affirmative must include in a constructive speech..

Succinct – Using few words; concise.

Symposium – A presentation involving several speakers each of whom discusses a different aspect of a problem.

Thesis – The major idea being made in a speech.

Toastmaster – The person who presides at a dinner and who is responsible for introducing guests, speakers, and programs.

Verbal communication – A message which relies on the use of words, either spoken or written.